The Project and Programme Support Office Handbook

Volume 2 Advanced

The Project and Programme Support Office Handbook

Volume 2 Advanced

David E Marsh
MBA, DMS, FMS, MBCS

Project Manager Today
PUBLICATIONS

Project Manager Today
PUBLICATIONS

First published 2001, revised 2002
Project Manager Today,
Unit 12 Moor Place Farm, Plough Lane, Bramshill, Hants, RG27 0RF UK www.pmtoday.co.uk

ISBN for complete set of 2 volumes: 1-900391-07-4
ISBN for this volume: 1-900391-06-6

British Library CIP data
Marsh, David, 1947-
The project and programme support office handbook
Vol. 2: Advanced David E Marsh
1. Industrial project management - handbooks, manuals, etc
2. Office management - handbooks, manuals, etc
I. Title
658.4'04
ISBN 1-900391-06-6

Printed and bound in Great Britain by Intype London Limited

To my wife, Gerry

Foreword

I am delighted that David Marsh has brought together his wealth of experience in these two volumes so that organisations have a ready source of reference to all aspects of creating, implementing or using a Project or Programme Office.

As businesses and organisations increasingly adopt project based structures, they realise that effective project management needs an infrastructure to support it. We have seen the rapid growth and adoption of PRINCE2 and with it the development of qualifications in that method. There has also been an explosion in the provision for training and qualifications in project management. However, while many people have implemented project and programme offices successfully, there is little guidance readily available to steer them towards success.

With the launch of an ISEB qualification in Project and Programme Support and the publication of these two volumes which mirror the syllabus, anyone thinking of starting a PSO or looking for help will find it here.

David Marsh comes from an engineering and IT background. Although many of the examples given in these two volumes come from the world of IT, their application is universal. David has seen at first hand the problems and solutions adopted by many different organisations developing both 'virtual' and 'real' PSOs.

Now anyone can share his experiences and the world of projects will be all the richer for his contribution.

Ken Lane
Editor
Project Manager Today

Contents

Chapter One

The Advanced Project and Programme Support Office

1. Introduction

If your organisation has a Project or Programme Support Office (PPSO), I will be surprised if anyone can remember how or why it was created. In many organisations there seems to have been a process of 'Immaculate Conception'; not only has it no recognised mother or father, but no one can remember who created it, or why.

As a consequence it is often the poor relation of the organisation's support functions. Until fairly recently I have heard the PPSO described as the 'Island of no hope' – the place where failed project managers go!

The purpose of writing the two volumes of the Handbook (Foundation and Advanced) is my attempt to make organisations realise that the PPSO can offer so much more – indeed I believe that if they are designed and implemented correctly, they become a major repository of the organisation's knowledge. Not only are they the keepers of the Epistemology, but they can, and must, contribute both added and higher added value to the organisation; otherwise why should they exist?

In the first volume of the Handbook I describe the basic skills and knowledge required in the Office. The second volume concentrates on the ways in which the radical transformation can take place to convert the existing PSO (or PPSO) into a new and dynamic support function for programmes or projects. This chapter sets out the reasons for this approach. From here on we will use the abbreviation PSO to refer to both project and programme support offices, except where the context indicates that I am dealing solely with one or other type of office.

The secret of this radical and drastic transformation is to:

- **Design the PSO to meet the organisation's requirements;**
- **Define what it is to do in terms of reference and performance criteria;**

- Train and equip it with staff who have the required skills, knowledge and experience;
- Provide those staff with appropriate tools;
- Monitor the value and benefits they provide;
- Keep the PPSO up to date.

2. So why does the dysfunctional PSO exist?

There are many reasons why an organisation's PSO does not fulfil its true role. One of the most important relates to the way it was implemented in the first place. A lot of existing PSOs were set up as a follow-on from a project. Typically someone on the project team displayed an expertise with the project planning software. Then it was recognised that these skills would be useful to other projects and so the PSO was born, based around one person's skills and a hope that the skills acquired on one project driving a software package would be useful to others.

From such humble beginnings the embryonic PSO tries to grow. It faces difficulty in growing, so it either offers other services or is tasked with providing administrative support. Throughout this process, however, the service provided is primarily for the Programme or Project Manager, not the organisation. Gradually it gets bigger. However, it finds difficulty attracting staff and, although it offers useful advice on how to do things, this is not often acted upon. The services provided by this typical PSO are programme and project-centric; they do not work with, or interface with, other business support functions.

Typically there is no interface with finance and accounts, purchasing, or HR. As a consequence the systems developed internally in the PSO to capture valuable data – about who does what and how much is spent on what – is not available for the rest of the organisation. It can be described as a clock where all the cogs don't mesh. As a consequence all the cogs work very hard to make up for this lack of efficient interfaces. Why does it happen? It's because no one designed it as a whole – no one looked wide and hard enough to find the links and build them into the PSO processes. It's because, after all, the PSO is just a 'bit of an idea' that someone had many years ago.

The same sad story can be found in a many guises either in whole or part in most organisations – only a precious few have built their PSO to a design and even fewer have developed and installed that PSO as a project – controlled and directed by the management of the organisation.

3. Starting the transformation process

As with all great undertakings, you need to create a vision for the end point and then get the plans in place. The first step, therefore, is to audit what you have now. What does the PSO supply? When was it built? Who actually uses what?

This audit must be conducted with honesty. You can fool others but never fool yourself! The audit will provide the basis of a position paper to the most senior managers whom you can involve.

In order to reassess the requirements, you will need to discuss them, not only with the immediate programme and project managers, but also with finance and accounts, procurement and HR. This is not an exclusive list. In one organisation I found that the most enthusiastic supporters of the reorganisation of the PSO were the sales people. They needed to know what was going on in projects so they could give better estimates to potential clients.

When you have identified the requirements you can then produce a high-level design for the new functions and identify the costs and benefits. The resulting terms of reference and business case must then be submitted, together with a request to senior management to start a formal project to put the new PSO in place.

Numerous additional activities will be needed alongside this approach, not the least of which is winning the confidence and support of the business departments. Failure to capitalise on this valuable source of support and influence can severely reduce your chances of success.

The need to create a vision of what can be done is perhaps the most important part of the process. When creating the vision ensure that the expectations of the keepers of this vision are managed, in that they understand this is the final vision, but there will be many partial steps on the way.

The voyage of redevelopment can then begin. Ensure you follow two basic rules:

- **Minimise the pain – maximise the gain**
- **80/20 rule OK!**

'Minimise the pain' refers to the effort or cost of getting benefits. Design the project approach so that it provides some benefits as quickly as possible and minimises the costs to obtain them. Early wins will help ensure continued support.

'80/20 Rule OK!' refers to the solutions or infrastructures that are developed during the project. It is far better to get all the people doing 80% of what's required now rather than 100% never!

All too often the PSO redevelopment becomes more of a crusade with the PSO team becoming zealots, seeking to convert everyone to the new approach. Remember, this is a business function that is being developed, not a religious experience. Finish off the redevelopment with defined and agreed terms of reference for the PSO and also the performance or service levels it is to provide.

Sounds simple, doesn't it? However, realistically it will take at least a year to accomplish – even more for most organisations. There are many things to be faced including the re-skilling of the members of the PSO and also changing its old and new customers' attitudes, so that they use the new business function as it should be used, not as it was.

4. Keeping the PSO up to date

Having completed the PSO, the next major hurdle is keeping it up to date. The one certainty about an organisation is that changes will occur. The PSO must be regularly audited – once every eighteen months – to ensure that it is still meeting its Terms of Reference and also continuing to meet the needs of the organisation. This audit must be conducted under the same regime of honesty that was used to re-establish it in the first place. The audit may reveal the need for further mini-projects to enhance or update the PSO.

Dealing with today is one thing – the real secret of success for the PSO is getting ready to deal with tomorrow. This means that the management of the PSO must be looking ahead to what the PSO will be handling in those over-the-horizon programmes and projects, and gathering information in advance so that when the programme or project manager asks : 'Have you got anything to help me on this new programme or project?' – the answer is not – 'Well, we have some templates etc from previous projects – you could see if they fit.' The value-added PSO will have answers already developed for new initiatives and ways of working. That's the future – the forward-thinking PSO, ready for tomorrow's programmes and projects today!

5. Summary

All this will seem a tall order if your PSO just does the plans or provides minute takers for project meetings. Is it worth it? Well, without an effective and efficient programme and project support function, not only do the programmes and projects suffer, so does the whole organisation. The PSO must transform itself so that it can provide added value and higher added value to the organisation. If it doesn't, it can only (and perhaps it should) wither and die.

Chapter Two

The Role of a PSO in Supporting Programmes

1. What is a Programme?

The CCTA* published one of the first definitions of a programme in 1994. It described a programme as:

> 'a portfolio of projects selected and planned in a co-ordinated way so as to achieve a set of defined business objectives, giving effect to various (and often overlapping) initiatives and/or implementing a strategy.
>
> 'Alternatively, a single, large or very complex project, or a set of otherwise unrelated projects bounded by the business cycle. The programme includes the controlled environment of management responsibilities, activities, documentation and monitoring arrangements by which the portfolio of projects achieve their goals and the broader goals of the programme.'

A Guide to Programme Management CCTA 1994*

This definition has been further refined through a research project carried out by members of the Association for Project Management/British Computer Society Specialist Interest Group on Programme Management[†] to include other forms of programmes.

1.1 What is Programme Management?

Similarly, CCTA defined programme management as:

> 'the selection and co-ordinated planning of a set of projects so as to achieve a set of business objectives and the efficient execution of these projects within a controlled environment such that they realise maximum benefit for the resulting business operations.'

---

*CCTA is the Central Computer and Telecommunications Agency – part of the Office of Government Commerce. It aims to improve the delivery of public services by the best use of Information Technology.

[†]See Appendix 1 – List of contacts

In 1999 the updated guide, now called *Managing Successful Programmes,* had as the definition:

> 'the co-ordinated management of a portfolio of projects that change organisations to achieve benefits that are of strategic importance.'

In the wider environment of the private sector, however, an almost universally accepted definition is:

> 'a Board-led initiative – managed as a programme of interdependent or independent projects and other activities in order to obtain major sustainable benefits for the organisation'.

1.3 How does a Programme differ from a Project?

Projects are usually focused primarily on products and their delivery. These products enable business objectives to be met. A programme focuses on the achievement of business objectives and the realisation of business benefits through the utilisation of project products and their assimilation into the operational environment. The management of change and transition is therefore a key aspect of programme management.

Programme management begins before there are any projects and continues beyond the conclusion of projects within the programme, until change is implemented, or the transition is complete. It is not simply multi-project management or a higher level of project management.

1.4 The Programme Management Framework or Method

A programme management framework, or method, provides the organisation with a coherent set of activities designed to deliver the programme's objectives. It supports the senior management who have to plan and control the activities, set priorities, and allocate resources for the implementation of the group of related projects or a single, large complex project. It ensures that the impact of changes in business operations is co-ordinated and that the transition to new ways of working is explicitly managed. It also focuses management attention on clearly defined benefits, understood at the outset of the programme and managed throughout implementation, delivery and completion.

Diagram 1 Schematic view of a programme and its constituent projects

Resource Code	B R M A I Q A T D T T T D						B R M A I Q A T D T T T D						B R M A I QT A T D T T D						B R M A I Q A T D T T T D						TOTAL
DETAILED PLAN (Man days per week)	Month 1					Total	Month 2					Total	Month 3					Total	Month 4					Total	TOTAL
New Services Programme																									
On-line stoplist	3		5					3			4			23			34			3		4			79
Support Banknet 98.1		3		4			3			4			3		5				5			6	6		39
Electronic Commerce Transaction certificate	2		22	2				2		3	4			4 56						66		67			228
Euro Transaction processing							4	5	6										4	5	6				30
Timeframe edits for debit products		2		3	4		2		3	4				2		3		4							27
Chip support			4							4				4							4				16
Euro Transaction processing (output)	2			4			5		6 55					34					12		99				217
Support CVC results													2	3	4	5	6								20
Authorisation 98.2· System edits for 98.1 release data elements		2		3	4		2		3	4				3		4									25
Chip new network format			5										3		4				2	3	4	5	6		32
Authorisation 98.2· Updating AMCC for euro compliance		3				4	3		4				2		3	4			3		4				30
ECC format out / Suppression limitation amount field			22			2		4						4					3		4				35
Addendum changes (INET)							3		4				3			4			2		3	4			23
Chargeback reason Code consolidation (INET)		3				4																			7
Chip new network format													6 55												61
SuperCom release 98.2· Hub-site automation		2		4																					6
Super Com Programme																									
Superflash	1 2	3	4	5	6		1 2	3	4	5	6		1 2	3	4	5	6		5 6						74
ISDN for SuperCom	3		5										23			34									65
SuperCom release 98.1Internal stats (phase 1)		3		4			3		4				3		5				4						26
SuperCom item research	2		22	2				2		3	4			4 56					2						97
SuperCom table management							3		4											2	3	4	5	6	21
Hub-site automation		3		4				4					3		4						3			4	21
Superfax			4											4						3		4			15
Superflow	2		4				5		6 55					34					4		2	3		4	115
SuperCom Debit							3		4				3		4				3		4				21
Migration AS400 Stand-in								4						4						4					12
Porting of scoring tools			4					4																	8
Infrastrucure Programme																									
Clearing reengineering - new editing module		4	5	6																4	5	6			30
Consolidated Settlement								4	5	6				4	5	6									30
Corporate card interchange			5				1 2	3	4	5	6		1 2	3	4	5	6		1 2	3	4	5	6		68
Master agreement		3		4			3		5					3		4				23		34			79
Euro Internal Systems			22	2				3			4		3			4			3		5				46
Update Intranet	3		4				2		22	2				2		3	4			4 56					102
Debit Fraud reporting		4						3		4			3		4										18
Corporate database									4						4										8
Authorisation round robin	2		4					3	4	5	6		3	4	5	6									42
Inter-application table mngt	3						2		4				5		6 55						34				109
Audit trail replacement	22																								22
Migration Stoplist AS400																					23				23
SAFE migration from AS400	3																								3
	34	30	101	62	40	16	21 22	52	183	59	44	4	13 32	101	333	50	106	4	18 41	122	249	107	72	14	1930

1.5 Concepts of Programme Management

The key concepts of programme management are:

- **a strategic context;**
- **senior management direction and control;**
- **business benefits orientation;**
- **optimisation of resources and assets.**

In addition, programme management uses a specific set of terms:

- **Blueprint –** *a vision of the future business operations;*
- **Tranches –** *consecutive periods of time within a programme during which some of its constituent projects will be undertaken and completed;*
- **Islands of stability –** *review points at the end of a tranche of work;*
- **Programme management phases –** *identification, definition, execution, benefits realisation, closure;*
- **Transition –** *managing the assimilation into the working environment of the products of projects within a programme.*

1.6 Components and Functions in Programme Management

The main components and functions typically used are:

- **an organisation structure with defined roles and responsibilities;**
- **a framework for running the programme.**
- **Phase One –** *identifying the programme;*
- **Phase Two –** *defining the programme;*
- **Phase Three –** *running the programme(s);*
- **Phase Four –** *closing the programme(s) completing, realising and putting in place arrangements for sustaining the business benefits.*

1.6.1 The Organisation Structure

As with all management tasks, programme management must be carried out within a defined and agreed organization structure. To be successful this structure must contain the following key elements:

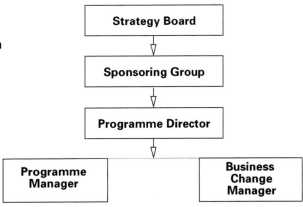

Diagram 2
Programme Organisation Structure

Strategy Board

Sponsoring Group

Programme Director

Programme Manager

Business Change Manager

Sponsoring group

This is the team or board which commissions the programme on behalf of the organisation and:

- **supports the programme director;**
- **defines the business priorities;**
- **defines the business change required.**

Programme director

Provides strategic direction and guidance and makes decisions on the control actions needed to be exercised on the programme.

Programme manager

Manages the programme day-to-day on behalf of the programme director. This entails:

- **efficient multiple project management;**
- **co-ordination and monitoring programme progress;**
- **managing interfaces and dependent project plans;**
- **ensuring resources are utilised effectively.**

Business change manager

This role exists to maximise the improvement to the business operation(s) through benefits management, undertaking transition planning, change management, and management of risk. In particular, he or she has specific responsibilities for:

- the blueprint;
- transition management;
- business operations risk management;
- benefits management: clarifying business operations
  benefits, managing benefits delivery, and maximising
  future benefits realisation.

Design authority (optional role)

This role takes the responsibility of managing the design of processes and business information systems that are affected or created by the programme. This ensures consistency within the portfolio of projects and with the supporting services, infrastructure plans and policies and standards. In particular, there is specific responsibility for:

- co-ordination of technical assurance;
- maintenance of technical design integrity;
- quality management;
- policies and standards;
- infrastructure interfaces.

1.6.2 Identifying the programme

The first phase of the framework supporting a programme is the identification and definition of the aims and objectives of the programme. This phase starts with a programme mandate and ends with the completion of the programme brief. The programme brief:

- provides the agreed basis on which the programme definition will be prepared (as in 1.6.3 below);
- describes the programme
- documents Terms of References, both for the programme and the programme director.

It also contains a benefits framework – an outline description of expected benefits, the business operations affected, and the current and target performance measures.

*See example document **4**: An example of a programme brief.*

1.6.3 Defining the programme

In the second phase the programme brief is used to develop an investment appraisal for the programme, the blueprint, its required benefits profile, execution options and the initial programme plan. This information is collated into the programme definition.

The programme definition formalises the agreed objectives and plans agreed between the programme director and the senior management group to whom the director reports and is accountable. In addition it provides a basis for funding the programme. This is the key monitoring and control document.

See example documents **5**: *An example of a programme definition.*

1.6.4 Running the programme
This phase of the framework consists of processes, standards and documents which are used to monitor and control the implementation of the programme.
The documents recommended for this are:

A benefits management plan
Specifies who is responsible for achieving the benefits, and how they should be managed, measured, and monitored (the benefits management regime).

The benefits profile
Describes the planned benefits to be realised, when, where, and how. This is agreed between the target business area, the programme director and service providers where applicable.

The blueprint
Is the vision for the programme, with business models, operational performance measures, culture and other change plans, organisation structures, information systems and services requirements, etc.

The transition plan
Describing how the transition from the current business operation to the envisaged blueprint operation will be managed and achieved.

The business case
This justifies the commitment of resources to the programme. It;
- demonstrates that the most cost-effective combination of projects has been selected when compared with costed alternatives
- provides the wider context and justification for any infrastructure investment and the costs of implementing particular policies and standards.

The design management plan
Helps to preserve the overall integrity of the programme and its coherence with plans for infrastructure and support services. It includes the technical architecture design (where appropriate), the configuration management plan, the policies and standards to be applied, and the technical transition and quality plans.

The programme (work) plan
Sets out the schedule of work, the timing, the resourcing and control arrangements for the constituent projects.

The quality plan
Describes quality objectives for the programme's design and execution for the future view of the business, as expressed in the blueprint, and for managing any third-party services that may be required.

The resourcing plan
Shows how the programme will be resourced and specifies the support, infrastructure, and third-party services when required.

The risk management plan
Contains the record of all risks identified that threaten the business environment and the programme itself. It assesses possible impacts, what should be done and when, in order to avoid, remove and control risk. It also details processes for managing risk.

A communication plan
Lays out how the objectives, plans and progress of the programme are to be communicated in order to promote common ownership, facilitate knowledge transfer and training. It ensures that those involved and affected by the programme have relevant and consistent information about the programme and its progress.

See example documents **6-16** *: Examples of these documents.*

1.6.5 Closing the programme, realising and sustaining the business benefits
This consists of processes which support the orderly closing down of the programme and a review of what has been achieved. These processes are documented in the programme closure report. The report describes the closure of the programme and its constituent projects and the lessons learnt at both programme and project level.

One of the key factors in achieving a successful programme is ensuring that the organisation adopts a benefits achievement regime. There is no standard approach to achieving this culture shift – what is important is that the design and development of the plan for this must take into account both the specific needs of the organisation and the areas affected by the programme.

Therefore, this phase includes the execution or completion of the transition plan, the benefits management plan and the delivery of benefits. In most programmes, the benefits start to be realised during the execution phase.

The success, or otherwise, of these plans is documented in the programme benefits review report. This is prepared at the end of the programme (or tranche) and describes the findings, conclusions and recommendations of the programme benefits review.

2. The Role of the Programme Support Office

The Programme Support Office typically provides the following support activities:

- **assistance/support to the programme director and the programme manager;**
- **the focus for programme/project reporting/control activities;**
- **advice/support to programme and project managers on the programme management methods and standards;**
- **a repository for master copies of programme documentation;**
- **preparation of programme status reports;**
- **analysis of the programme's constituent project interfaces/dependencies;**
- **procedures and systems to help the organisation to measure and sustain the business benefits achieved during, and on completion of, the programme.**

3. Summary

Programme management is substantially different from project management. The use of a framework or method to operate programme management is vital for the successful management of multiple and interrelated projects. Programme management provides the following functions for the organisation:

- **Integration of business strategy implementation and individual projects;**
- **Control of programme and project definition, initiation and authorisation in terms of:**
  the scope, objectives, constraints and their impact on the organisation;
  the products or deliverables required and the resources to be used.
- **The processes to manage the following issues:**
  prioritisation;
  monitoring of progress made;
  control of the programme and individual projects.

These functions and processes are supported by information from a range of sources including the organisation's business, financial and resource asset utilisation plans, the individual project plans and their progress reports.

Effective programme management and support systems ensure that the programme:

- **meets the business requirements;**
- **is delivered within the agreed budget and timescale;**
- **provides resilient end products of the quality required;**
- **optimises its use of the resources available;**
- **is implemented under an appropriate risk management strategy;**
- **has considered and employed an appropriate and effective communication strategy.**

The programme support office plays a vital role in all these areas.

Chapter Three

PSOs within the Organisation

1. Introduction

This chapter focuses on the factors which affect how many PSOs are required and where they should be located.

2. A Programme or Project Support Office – or both?

In deciding whether to maintain two separate entities the organisation must first assemble all the relevant facts. This same information-gathering process applies to both the establishment of a PSO or a review of existing arrangements.

Use the following steps in deciding how many PSOs are required:

2.1 Step One: The reason for the PSOs' establishment

To decide if the Project and Programme Support Offices should be one entity, the organisation must understand why the PSOs were implemented and their current role and portfolio of services. This can be achieved by obtaining a copy of the PSOs' terms of reference. With an existing PSO, all too often these will either be 'lost', or so out of date that they have to be re-established.

2.2 Step Two: What does the Programme and/or Project Support Office provide?

This review involves producing a list of each of the services or standards. Each of these must be assessed in respect of the following questions:

- **What is the service or standard?**
- **When were they developed?**
- **Who developed them?**
- **What are they designed to achieve?**
- **Are they complete?**
- **Are they actually in use?**
- **When were they last reviewed and updated?**
- **Do the users like to use them – if not, why not?**

- Are they vital/essential/useful to the organisation?
- Do they meet future requirements?

These are standard questions but it may be necessary to add others to meet specific requirements, or local working arrangements.

2.3 Step Three: The Information Systems used by PSOs

The third part of this assessment involves the information systems that are used to support the operation of the PSOs. As with step two, the organisation must make a list and assess their completeness in respect of:

- What are these information systems?
- When were they developed?
- Who developed them?
- What are they designed to achieve?
- Are they complete?
- Are they actually in use?
- When were they last reviewed and updated?
- Do the users like to use them – if not why not?
- Are they vital/essential/useful to the organisation?
- Do they meet future requirements?

2.4 Step Four: Staffing of the PSO

The final information-gathering step is to assess the staffing of the existing or proposed programme and/or project support office.

2.4.1 The Staffing of the Programme Support Office

The staffing of the programme support office may be logical rather than physical. Therefore the staffing may be part-time and the members of the 'office' located in a number of places in the organisation. If the organisation has established a physical programme support office the organisation may have allocated staff to this function on a full or part-time basis.

The typical members of the PSO are:

- programme support professionals
- business/financial analysts;
- information, process other technology specialists;

- **planning and control specialists;**
- **strategic and business risk analysis and management specialists;**
- **programme managers;**
- **information administration and management staff.**

2.4.2 The Staffing of the Project Support Office

The staffing of the project support office can also be logical rather than physical. Typical staff of a project support office are:

- **project support professionals**
- **project managers;**
- **quality management specialists;**
- **configuration management specialists.**
- **planning and control specialists;**
- **risk analysis specialists;**
- **consultancy support staff;**
- **information administration and management specialists.**

2.5 Deciding how many offices

Having gathered all the relevant information the organisation can now decide how many separate PSOs are required. The deciding factors vary between organisations. The following section looks at those factors typically used.

2.5.1 Volume of Programmes or Projects

If the organisation is only running a very small number of programmes it tends to have a combined PSO. If the organisation has a large volume of both programmes or projects it can have two or even three separate offices. However, the number of programmes and projects is not the only deciding factor.

2.5.2 Types of Programmes or Projects

Added to the consideration of volume is the type of programmes or projects being carried out. There are four main types of programmes:

- **business change;**
- **mega projects;**
- **multi-projects linked or directed to a single goal;**
- **disparate projects collected together.**

The first two types of programme typically have their own programme support office. The third can be supported by a separate programme office but tends to be supported by a combined PSO. The fourth nearly always has a combined PSO.

Projects can also be grouped into types:

- **single function;**
- **technology-driven projects;**
- **multi-function technology driven;**
- **soft or people driven;**
- **business systems;**
- **infrastructure;**
- **special events.**

A predominance of multi-function, business systems and soft or people-driven projects usually requires the organisation to adopt a separate programme support office. A predominance of the others results in a combined programme and project support office.

2.5.3 Services provided or required

The types of services provided or required from the PSOs also influence the decision. Those organisations whose requirements are for high-level (executive management) support services for their programmes often prefer a separate programme support office. This is also the case when the programme support function directs which projects should be included in the organisation's portfolio. The converse occurs when there is little difference between the nature and level of the support required or provided. For example the more up-to-date project support offices which provide a consultancy type approach and operate through a regime of constructive audit, usually also provide the programme support function.

2.5.4 Information systems required or used

Of all the factors relating to how many offices are needed, this is the strongest indicator of the outcome of this decision process. If the organisation has, or will, be designing information systems that support both programmes and projects as a single entity then the tendency is for the offices to be a single entity. Those organisations where they are, or will be, designed to use separate information systems typically have two separate PSOs.

2.5.5 Staffing

Those organisations which see the programme and project support offices working for different levels of management, staff them accordingly. A combination or separation of PSOs follows suit. However, this is not the case where the programme support office is staffed in a logical way. The project support office can manage the co-ordination and allocation of staff who perform the programme support function and in such cases there is usually only one office.

2.5.6 Affordability

The costs of sustaining two separate offices must also be taken into account. The typical oncosts of any employee can add approximately 40 per cent to their salary costs. In addition there is also the cost of providing accommodation and working equipment. This again can run into several thousands of pounds per employee. As in all business decisions the cost and benefits must be carefully considered.

2.5.7 The Decision Grid

The weightings between the elements described above will vary from organisation to organisation – what is important is that these relativities are discussed, agreed and then applied to the decision grid. (Diagram 3)

3. How many PSOs

Having decided on separate offices the next decision is how many. The typical options or configurations are:

- **the three-level PSO;**
- **the two-level PSO.**

3.1 The Three-Level PSO

In this option the PSO is located at three levels in the organisation.

The top level is that of business strategy or programme identification and definition. Here the PSO supports the corporate planning process by ensuring that the organisation commissions a portfolio of programmes, projects, business activities and other initiatives which enable it to achieve its business targets and strategies.

Diagram 3 The Decision Grid: Do you require both a Programme and Project Support Office?

	CONSIDER		
	Separate	Combined	Suggested Importance Weighting
Volume of programmes or projects			
Large numbers of each	✓		H
Small number of programmes		✓	H
Types of programmes or projects			
Business Change, Mega , Multi-project single goal programmes	✓		M
*Multi disparate project programmes	? Consider	✓	M
Multi function, business system, soft or people projects	✓		M
Single function, special events projects		✓	M
Services provided			
Programme Office support executive level only	✓		H
Programme Office directs portfolio	✓	? Consider	H
Little or no difference in reporting levels and types of support		✓	H
Information Systems required or used			
Combined Information Systems		✓	M
Separate Information Systems	✓		M
Staffing			
Separate staff	✓		M
Programme staff controlled by Project Office		✓	M
Affordability			
High staff on-costs		✓	L
High infrastructure costs		✓	L

Top-level PSOs also co-ordinate the plans and progress reports from the portfolio of programmes, projects, business as usual and other initiatives for executive-level management. This top-level PSO may also support individual programmes – however, it is more likely that the support of individual programmes and projects will be dealt with at the second- and third-level PSO.

The second level is that of individual or collective support to the programmes. Here the PSO provides support services to both the programme managers and the programmes themselves. This PSO will either be located in the department that executes the programmes or in an independent department such as management services or finance.

The third level of PSO is usually concerned with individual projects. This level of PSO provides support to both the project managers and the projects. This PSO will also either be located in the department that executes the projects, or in an independent department.

Diagram 4 **Example of an Organisation Structure for a three-level PSO**

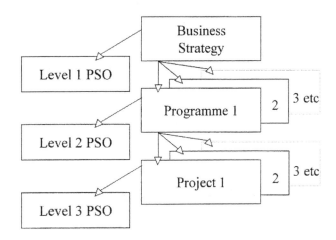

3.2 The Two-Level PSO

The two-level PSO either eliminates the top level, or combines the first and second, or the second and third levels. If the top-level PSO is eliminated, this functionality is performed as part of the strategic planning process by that department, supported by information from the PSO.

If the top two levels are combined, the PSO is located in the strategic planning department, the department that executes the programme, or an independent department. The location depends on the activities of the PSO, i.e. whichever department the PSO supports is most likely to be its 'home'. The third-level PSO is usually located within the department with which it is most involved.

If the lower levels are combined, the PSO is located as part of the department that executes the programmes and projects, or in an independent department. As before, the location depends on the role of the PSO – does it have an audit role reporting to senior management, or does it predominately help the programme and project managers?

Diagram 5 **Example of an Organisation Structure for a two-level PSO**

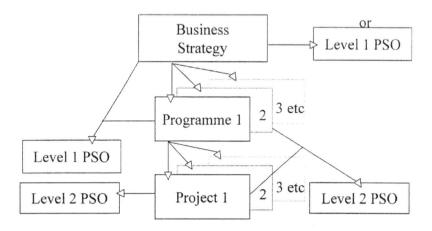

4. The Position of the PSOs in the Organisation

Who should 'own' the PSO(s) and where does it fit in the hierarchy of the organisation? Of course, it depends on the organisation and how it intends to use the PSOs. There are a number of factors affecting 'ownership' that need to be considered:

- **Why was the PSO(s) established;**
- **What role and services are provided by the PSO(s)?**
- **Who uses the PSO(s) services?**

The first two factors are the most important. For example, if the PSO(s) were established to provide support to the strategic planning process, and its role and services were designed to ensure that the programmes and projects are managed and controlled to prescribed standards, it is likely to be owned by a department independent from that responsible for the programme's execution.

The position of the PSO(s) in the organisation's hierarchy is similarly influenced by the above factors. For example, if the PSO(s) is supporting executive or senior level managers than it is very likely to be located at that level. If, however, it supports the programme or project managers then it is likely to be located at that level. If the PSO(s) supports both groups and operates at both levels, then either:

- **the position and level of the PSO(s) can be located at the higher of the two points;**
- **the PSO(s) can be split into two, with the respective parts located at the relevant levels.**

If the PSO is split, appropriate management arrangements must ensure that the two (or more) PSO(s) continue to work in harmony and mutual support. This requires retaining them as one logical unit in the organisation structure, although they are divided into two or more physical locations.

5. Summary

The decision to have separate programme and project support offices is based on a wide range of factors. It is vital that the assessment is performed as impartially as possible and that internal politics are minimised. What is important is that a clear and considered choice is made, because the structure will affect both the efficiency of the office(s) and the perception of its effectiveness from within the organisation.

Chapter Four

Designing and Installing a PSO

1. Introduction

Having identified the need for a PSO, or PSOs, and its fit within the organisation, the activities to design and install it must be managed as a project. This chapter describes how to approach such a project.

2. The Project Management Team

In all projects the design of the project management team is one of the most critical factors. In a project to design and implement a PSO, selecting the senior management to form the project steering committee or management board can be a difficult decision. This is due largely to the potentially large number of managers affected by the project and who, therefore, should be considered for inclusion on the project's management board.

It is important to select managers for the project management board to be responsible for three key functions:

- **Sponsorship –** *the sponsor is responsible for providing the strategic direction that the project must follow and any executive-level decisions that are needed,*
- **The design authority –** *charged with overseeing and verifying that the design aspects of the project are acceptable/correct,*
- **Resource management –** *resource managers who are to provide the resources used to develop the deliverables or products during the project.*

It can be advantageous to appoint more than one person to each of these areas, but ensure the project management board is compact. If it is too large, it will soon become a discussion rather than a decision-making committee.

3. The 'Self-Help' Development Approach

One of the most successful development approaches is one based on the strategy of a 'self-help project'. This means that the development of any new procedures, systems or services is undertaken by staff under the direction of the 'owner of the vision' – the manager who controls the project objectives.

The 'owner of the vision' could be the project manager or a member of the project management board. Sometimes it is advisable to employ an external consultant for this role if the organisation's members lack the knowledge of what the project is trying to achieve. If such a consultant is employed, use him or her as an advisor rather than as the person who does the work. This self-help approach reduces the need for activities to 'sell the ideas' that are normally required to make the project a success.

In addition, by using this approach, the project management board which controls the project is at the sharp end. Board members are often the resource or line managers of the staff allocated to developing the new services, so there is strong pressure on the staff to complete the work.

This approach also helps manage the expectations of senior management and ensures the benefits realised are obtained with as little pain as possible.

When designing the method of approach, it is important to include activities to manage the following:

- **the introduction of any new or redesigned procedures and other services;**
- **any personnel issues that arise;**
- **the impact of the consequential changes in operational procedures and processes that affect other departments.**

The use of a project management method such as PRINCE, that can handle such a wide-ranging project, is essential. When designing the approach to provide the new services there are two important tips which are worth following. The first of these is adopt the maxim 'Gain first; pain later'. All too often the development of the new Project Support Office services takes a long time to provide anything tangible. It is better to give some form of output from the development process as soon as possible and to show that as the services grow, even more benefits will be realised. The danger of waiting until a new service is finished completely before rolling it out is that it postpones the point at which the organisation sees any benefit. Of course it is important to manage the expectations of the recipients of the services and to explain that, at the start, accuracy or reliability cannot be guaranteed. There is normally a ready acceptance of this honest approach – providing it is delivered as planned and agreed.

The second important tip is to provide 80% of everything rather than 100% of some things and nothing of others. This is a 'difficult pill to swallow' for most PSOs. Why is it that people become perfectionists when they become a member of a PSO! If you build only 80% of the structure within 20% of the specified time there is often no need to develop the other 20%!

4. The Communication Strategy
The plans for the project (the PSO) and its progress must be communicated to all relevant members of the organisation. All too often this critical aspect of a project's management is left entirely to chance, or only considered when things have gone wrong. A communication strategy must be prepared as part of the official start-up of any project.

The communication strategy should describe what should be communicated to whom, and when. It must be reviewed and agreed by the project management board.

5. Project Initiation Document
All projects, no matter how small, should have a project initiation document. This defines the project's aims and objectives and provides the terms of reference for the project manager and project team. The design or re-engineering of a PSO is no exception to this requirement.

See example documents **17**: *A project initiation document for setting up a PSO.*

6. Problems faced by the Project Team – The Stoppers!
In all projects the project manager and the project team face problems and sometimes resistance to the changes they try to achieve. In trying to introduce a PSO you are likely to face the following 'stoppers' which come from organisations after analysing why they have not had a PSO before.

6.1 Cost
One of the most common reasons given for not having the services already is the cost

of developing them. The following figures give some idea of the relative costs of the in-house and out-sourced approach.

- **Life cycles**
  - *In-house* £10,000
  - *Bought* £1-5,000

- **Project Management Framework**
  - *In-house* £10,000
  - *Bought* £1-5,000

- **Library of Deliverables**
  - *In-house* £20,000
  - *Bought* £X,000

It is critical when deciding how to build or provide the new service that the 80/20 rule is taken into account. Is the gain of having a 100% 'own generated' development life cycle worth the cost when compared to buying one from outside and then adjusting it for use? Only the senior management of the organisation can answer that question, but, remember, it is vital to consider the costs and benefits in terms of the various users and customers of the service.

6.2 Time

As with cost the same consideration must be made in respect of the time to create the PSO. The examples below are based on experience of the time taken by in-house teams. Putting the job out to a team of contractors can reduce the time considerably – but the cost will also rise considerably!

- **Life Cycle Development** 6 months
- **Programme or Project Management Method** 6-18 months
- **Library of Deliverables** 6-12 months

6.3 Information

The lack of suitable information is often quoted as the reason why a service is not in place. However, often the real reason is that the owners of the information do not feel secure enough, or trust a PSO enough, to release information. Even if the PSO has the information, there is still a lot of clerical work needed to make it available to others. When carrying out any conversion and cleaning of data it is vital to check that the information/example deliverables is still current and useful. Start by checking its usefulness and then clean it – not the other way round! Also, get the information on to paper to begin with. Sort it, check if required and only then clean it up and do any conversion needed.

6.4 How to

Another common reason – but seldom admitted to – is a lack of know-how. The PSO and the services it provides often start off by accident, rather than by design, and staff are assigned to its development who have little or no experience of building a PSO or a new service.

They work from what they believe is necessary rather than carrying out the analysis previously described. Setting up, designing, or re-engineering a PSO and its services is an investment – it's a project and should be treated just like any other major new system or change project. If the organisation does not have the required skill, not just for building the service but also in managing such a project, then it is vital to get specialist advice.

Look for specialists in setting up such environments – not just general consultants who have done a bit of time in a programme or project support office.

6.5 Politics

Political considerations provide some of the greatest hurdles to the success of such projects. The first of these political issues will concern who owns the PSO and services. This can cause the design or re-engineering of the PSO to stall before it starts. The most successful approach is to sell the concept of the PSO and its new services to the top of the organisation or, as near the top as possible. If this succeeds, the PSO development team will have the degree of authority that is vital for the project to succeed. If it fails to do this, the team will have to paddle around in the 'treacle' of middle management politics – the worst and stickiest sort, as no one will make any decision, they just add more treacle!

6.6 Interfaces with other departments

Potential problems can also arise when the changes, or new services, affect other departments in the organisation. Ensure that any potential interfaces are identified and ensure that the systems used by these departments work with, and are supported by, those used by the PSO.

The departments most commonly affected are:

- **Accounts;**
- **Personnel;**
- **Purchasing;**
- **Sales.**

6.7 New departmental procedures and standards
A wide range of existing departmental procedures may need to be amended including:

- **personnel procedures (grading and names);**
- **programme and project commissioning procedures;**
- **programme and project planning procedures;**
- **progress and expenditure reporting procedures;**
- **programme and project managers' and team leaders' skills profiles;**
- **purchase requisition procedures.**

6.8 The Technical Environment
IT and other technically-based systems are required to support PSOs efficiently and effectively. If these systems are not available, the PSO's progress can be hindered.

A recent example occurred on a consultancy assignment where the logical solution demanded that all project managers and team leaders had access to the planning and tracking software. But, until the software was available and people were trained in its use, it was impossible to implement the revised planning and monitoring processes.

The requirement to integrate planning and progress tracking information with an accounts department system can also prove difficult. It is often possible to reformat the planning and progress tracking information so that the accounts department systems can handle it by automatic transfer.

6.9 Changes in Working Practices
The changes in working practices required to support the implementation of the PSO are substantial and should not be underestimated. New procedures and documents will be required to support the new services. This occurred in the example described earlier. All the project managers and team leaders needed to be trained in the use of the planning and control software and how the new system of planning and tracking progress was to operate.

Dealing with changes in working practices usually reveals further requirements and interfaces that need to be established. A 'strong hand on the tiller' is required to ensure that the project does not grow and become out of control.

6.10 Managing the Change

The changes to working practices are important but it is the management of change that must be given the most attention.

It is interesting that in order to manage the change successfully you must *decrease* the level of expectation of certain members of the organisation while motivating others. Those who usually need their expectations slowed down are the senior management. Their requirements are usually simpler, so they believe that they should be implemented first and with little effort. This is the expectation, but the reverse is often true. Explanations of the plan for the development of the service, and the progress made, are needed to convince them that in reality their service cannot be delivered until some of the lower-level services are in place.

At the other end of the scale, you must motivate change at the 'sharp end'. Such new services, functions and procedures will demand change in roles and responsibilities. Overcoming the natural resistance to change is the challenge. All of this work needs to be carefully planned and controlled.

You will also have to tackle a lack of vision of what a value-added PSO can deliver. Part of the purpose of this handbook is to address that shortcoming and to help the reader to acquire such a vision.

7. Summary

Are there any general rules to follow? Yes!

First: **The implementation process is more about the business issues than the technical ones.**

Second: **Expectations, change of culture and implementation of revised procedures need to be managed and controlled.**

Third: **You will always want the PSO to do more – but keep it simple – remember the 80/20 rule.**

The design and implementation of an appropriate PSO and supporting services is never easy to accomplish – but the benefits make it really worthwhile.

Chapter Five

Staffing the PSO

1. Introduction

You have designed the PSO; now the next major action is to staff it. This chapter looks at how to decide how many staff, with what experience, skills or training are needed. This decision must be based on the agreed role and terms of reference for the PSO and whether the organisation has a logical or physical PSO.

Having decided what the PSO and its staff are expected to provide the organisation is then faced with a further problem – where to find such staff.

This decision is further complicated because in essence two sets of staff/skills are required. The first set of staff/skills needed are those to develop and implement the PSO. The second are those needed to operate the PSO once it is installed. If the wrong set is selected then there is obviously a substantial chance that the PSO's implementation or operation will not be a success.

In addition there is also a problem in identifying suitable training for the members of the PSO. There is a plethora of training available at all levels for programme and project managers. However, apart from the internationally recognised ISEB Certificate in Programme and Project Support, there is very little other specific training available for PSO staff.

2. PSO Roles

The most significant factor which decides the required staffing is the role of the PSO. The classification of the roles shown below reflect those typically experienced in organisations. For ease of description they are treated as separate entities, although in practice they are often combined. The PSO implemented by most organisations performs more than one of these roles:

- **audit;**
- **assistance;**
- **support;**
- **services.**

The activities described below for each of these roles are also merely typical, they may well be performed in other roles than those allocated in this chapter. You will also have to consider whether the PSO is to be implemented as a logical or physical entity.

2.1 Audit

Not only does this category cover a wide range of activities, but these activities can be performed in various ways. The two main types of audit are:

- **conformance (policing),**
  or
- **constructive.**

Both of these forms of audit deal with the following aspects of the programme or project:

- **what it is delivering – the whole programme or project;**
- **how it is being delivered and managed – the programme or project management;**
- **the adherence to agreed quality standards – the programme or project management and the outputs, deliverables or products.**

2.1.1 Conformance (policing) audit

This phrase is often used to describe those PSOs whose role is regarded as checking that the programme or project is conforming to defined processes and standards. There are, however, very few organisations that have processes and standards which are fully comprehensive. Therefore, the auditor has to interpret or assess what these processes and standards would have been if they had been in place.

The staff/skills required to perform this role must be extremely strong in character, and have sufficient knowledge and experience to deal with the auditing of those activities that relate to the missing processes and standards.

Those appointed must be able to deal with the potential confrontation and politics inherent when performing this type of audit. There are various training courses available for these types of audits, including courses which lead to certificates in assessment or quality management systems audit.

2.1.2 Constructive audit

This form of audit works on the basis that the processes and standards provided for the programme and project manager are not 'tablets of stone', but guidance and advice. In this form of audit an assessment is made not only of the conformance to the agreed processes and standards but also the use and applicability of those processes to the programmes and projects that are using them. It is less confrontational and more consultative. As with the conformance audit there is a need to deal with the missing components. However, in this case the auditor identifies how the programme or project manager has dealt with these gaps and decides if this local infilling should be passed on to others.

In a similar vein, any non-conformance to the established processes and standards is assessed to see if the programme or project manager has changed them to reflect the current working arrangements.

The staff/skills required in this role are strength of character, personal skills (tact and diplomacy) and sufficient knowledge and experience to deal with the auditing and assessment of those activities that relate to the missing processes and standards. The staff appointed to this role must deal with both the assessment and the analysis.

These staff also need more experience and knowledge of programme and project management support than those for the conformance audit. There are few training courses specifically designed for these types of audits, so the organisation must design its own training programme. This programme should typically consist of conventional auditing training (as in the previous section), supplemented by management consultancy, with coaching and mentoring in the actual role.

2.2 Assistance

The assistance role covers those PSOs who provide direct assistance to the programme and project managers.

This assistance is a personal service to those managers in respect of:

- **consultancy;**
- **coaching and mentoring;**
- **training;**
- **advice – what to do, where to get it, etc.**

2.2.1 Consultancy assistance

Consultancy assistance is usually needed for the programme or project support infrastructure, the operation of the programme or project management processes, or the use of the supporting standards. The consultancy can either be advice or work on particular activities for the programme or project manager.

The staff/skills required in this role are personal skills (tact and diplomacy) and sufficient knowledge and experience to assure the programme or project manager that the advice is both relevant and reliable.

These staff also need at least as much experience and knowledge, both of programme and project management and the support activities, as the staff they help.

Training for this role includes both programme and project management, as well as management consultancy. To ensure the staff have the relevant training it is necessary for the organisation to design individual training programmes, supplemented with coaching and mentoring.

CASE STUDY

A branch of the MoD used its PSO in the role of support and conformance audit of their project managers' use of PRINCE. After many years of providing this role the organisation commissioned an independent review of the PSO to ensure it was providing what the organisation wanted.

The review identified that the PSO had become regarded as the 'method police' and did not provide value added services. The review also recommended a change to a constructive audit role and the provision of a comprehensive supporting infrastructure including:

- **template plans;**
- **estimating guidelines;**
- **standard templates;**
- **a deliverable library.**

To implement a new PSO the MoD commissioned a project to develop this new infrastructure and retrained the existing staff in the new role.

2.2.2 Coaching and mentoring

The coaching and mentoring role is more than advice. It integrates the support activities with personal coaching or mentoring of the programme and project managers in how they perform the role.

The coaching and mentoring role is particularly important in organisations which have recently introduced the concepts of formal programme and project managers, or whose existing programme and project managers need to have their skills widened. This situation is increasingly common as organisations now recognise and use programmes and projects to deliver their strategic targets and goals.

The staff/skills required for this role are excellent personal skills (tact and diplomacy), an extensive knowledge and experience of both programme and project management, and the ability to coach and mentor senior staff. The training for this role centres around the coaching and mentoring skills.

CASE STUDY

A major financial institution, providing services for major European banks, carried out a review of the management of its programmes and projects. This review identified that the organisation needed to implement a common programme and project management method and a supporting infrastructure including:

- **project or system development methods;**
- **template plans and deliverables;**
- **estimating guidelines.**

A PSO was established to support this change by providing one-to-one help to the programme and project managers to implement the new way of working.

The organisation recognised that they did not have sufficient skills to perform this role, so they employed three consultants who were experienced in developing both the infrastructure, and the training and coaching programme for project managers.

The use of this approach meant that the new infrastructure was operational within two weeks, without major disruption to the programmes and projects and also with the full cooperation of the staff.

Once the conversion work was completed, the organisation then trained its own staff to provide the continuing support.

2.2.3 Training

In some organisations the role of the PSO is directed towards the provision of training for the programme and project management teams. This training can be provided by the PSO staff or facilitated by them – they can identify what training is required and who should provide it, and commission it.

The training provided can cover:

- **programme and project management skills and techniques;**
- **the programme and project life cycle operated by the organisation;**
- **the programme and project management methods used by the organisation;**
- **the project or system development methods used by the organisation;**
- **the use of the programme and project support infrastructure – the processes and techniques etc.**

The staff required for this role need knowledge of programme and project management and experience of training of programme or project managers. The training for this role must include programme and project management, management consultancy and training. The organisation can design individual training programmes, supplemented with coaching and mentoring.

2.2.4 Advice

The PSO can also advise, but not in an audit or consultancy role. Instead it offers advice to the programme or project managers. This is not necessarily a weak role. PSO advice is commonly found in organisations whose programme and project managers' skills and experience do not need to be directed or supported; the PSO simply provides information. This information includes advice about the processes and standards that apply to the programme or project and where to get resources.

The staff who perform this advisory role must have experience both of the organisation's agreed processes and standards, and of programme and project management. Also they must be able to influence and convince programme and project managers. Furthermore, they need to communicate effectively with, and influence, the senior management who have the line management authority over the programme and/or project managers.

The training for this role includes programme and project management, management consultancy and influencing skills. The organisation can design individual training programmes, supplemented with coaching and mentoring.

2.3 Support
The most common role of the PSO is that of support to the programmes and projects, with responsibility for:

- **programme and/or project life cycle;**
- **programme and project management methods;**
- **project or system development methods;**
- **standards;**
- **templates;**
- **example deliverables.**

This list is what the PSO supplies to the programme and/or project managers. The activities performed directly for the programme and/or project managers are included in the services role described later in this chapter.

2.3.1 Programme and/or project life cycle
The support of the programme and/or project life cycle contains:

- **support of the business strategy development and review process;**
- **the quantification of the organisation's existing workload and commitments (portfolio);**
- **the quantification of the commitments required for any new programmes and projects;**
- **the monitoring of actual and projected resources and progress in executing the portfolio;**
- **support to the executive-level in making decisions**

concerning the contents of the portfolio;
- **support of the programme and project idea process;**
- **support of the programme and project feasibility study process;**
- **custodianship of the records relating to the portfolio.**

In addition, the PSO may also develop, install and maintain the processes on behalf of the organisation.

The range of staff and skills needed by the PSO to support these activities is very wide. Therefore it is essential that the PSO's role is clearly defined so that the appropriate skills can be selected.

Training for this type of role must be designed for each individual. Experience has shown that it is usually better to select good managers and provide them with the training in the programme and project support role, rather than the other way round.

Whatever training programme is selected, it will need to be supplemented with coaching and mentoring.

2.3.2 Programme and project management methods
The role of the PSO in supporting the programme and project management methods can include their development, installation and maintenance and advice to the programme and project managers on their use. This support role can be extended to the production of publications on these methods as well as providing training in their use.

The staff required for this role need experience of programme and project management and knowledge of how to tailor programme and project management methods.

The training for this role must include programme and project management and method consultancy. The organisation must design individual training programmes, supplemented with coaching and mentoring.

2.3.3 Project or system development methods
The support of the project or system development methods is similar to that of the programme and project management methods. The only difference is that these methods can span many departments, and therefore their maintenance or updating

requires the involvement of several departments. This type of support can also include support for the accompanying estimating guidelines, and any tools provided for the project or system development team.

The staff performing this role must have experience of project or system development and of their development and tailoring. They must also have the ability to work with and co-ordinate other departments, and knowledge of the implications involved in maintaining or updating methods.

The organisation must design individual training programmes, including method consultancy, supplemented with coaching and mentoring.

2.3.4 Standards
The support of the organisation's standards includes their development, maintenance, application and use. These standards include:

- **programme and project life cycle documents;**
- **programme and project management methods documents;**
- **project or system development methods documents;**
- **planning and progress reporting documents.**

The staff for this role need a detailed understanding of the processes or methods that use the standards and why the standards are required.

The training for this role must include technical training in the various methods and management consultancy skills. The organisation must design individual training programmes, supplemented with coaching and mentoring.

2.3.5 Templates
The support of the templates provided for the programme and project managers includes their development, implementation, maintenance, updating and use.

The skills required to support this role must include a detailed understanding of the processes or methods that use the templates and why the templates are required.
The training for this role includes technical training in the various methods that use the templates, and management consultancy skills. The organisation must design individual training programmes, supplemented with coaching and mentoring.

2.3.6 Example deliverables

The support of the example deliverables includes:

- **the identification of candidate deliverables in the programmes and projects to be included in the deliverable library;**
- **the development of the directory or dictionary which indexes the deliverables in the library;**
- **updating the directory or dictionary to ensure it reflects changes in other parts of the PSO infrastructure;**
- **updating the deliverables to reflect changes in the organisation's standards or operating processes.**

The skills required for this role are predominately that of administration, together with a general understanding of the use of the deliverables.

2.4 Services

The range of services that can be provided by the PSO include:

- **programme and project management tools support;**
- **planning;**
- **progress monitoring and reporting;**
- **procurement of resources and materials;**
- **risk, issue, change and configuration management support;**
- **hints and tips;**
- **administration.**

2.4.1 Programme and project management tools support

The support given to the organisation's programme and project management tools by the PSO can vary from supplying the tools to providing training and a full help desk. In some organisations the PSO selects and implements the tools.

The skills required to provide this support include a detailed knowledge of the tools and an understanding of how they are used by the programme and project managers. Therefore the training for this role must include a good understanding of the programme and project management functions as well as the specific requirements of the organisation's relevant processes and standards, tailored to the individual and supported by on the job coaching and mentoring.

2.4.2 Planning

The planning service can be a one-off or continuing service throughout the programme or project. The planning service can be, at its simplest, the translation of the programme or project manager's instructions into a plan or development of the complete plan. If the PSO develops the complete plan, it is normal for the programme or project managers to review it and tailor it to their specific requirements. This service can also include the monitoring of progress.

The staff required to perform this role will depend on which end of the range of planning services they operate. If it is simply the translation role, then the PSO staff will need skills in developing and updating plans, and in the use of the organisation's planning software.

If the role is at the other end of the range, then the PSO staff will also need experience of the planning process and the organisation's project or system development methods. This must be supplemented with a good understanding of the organisation's programme and project management methods.

The training required for this role, therefore, needs to include generic training in programme and project planning, as well as specific training in the organisation's project or systems development methods. An appreciation of the programme and project management methods, processes and standards adopted is also needed.

Such training programmes will need to be specifically designed.

2.4.3 Progress monitoring and reporting

The role of progress monitoring and reporting can be performed by the PSO as part of the planning service or on a stand-alone basis. The range of services includes:

- **being a mailbox for the receipt of time sheets, delivery notes and subcontractors' invoices, etc;**
- **receiving progress reports from the programmes or projects;**
- **the collection or measurement of the progress at source;**
- **being responsible for updating the plans to reflect the progress made;**
- **authorising payments to subcontractors.**

The information will need to be collated and then incorporated into a report which can include a comparison of the actual progress or expenditure to that planned. An analysis of the reasons for any variations can also be included.

The skills required for this role will, therefore, vary according to the type of support provided. At its simplest, it is an administrative or clerical role, at the other extreme a quantity surveyor or estimator with substantial planning skills is required. The training reflects this and must be specifically designed.

2.4.4 Procurement of resources and materials
The procurement of resources and materials by the PSO is a very common role, particularly in engineering programmes and projects. The procurement role can vary considerably and includes:

- **the identification and specification of what needs to be procured;**
- **the identification of sources of the required goods;**
- **the organisation and operation of procurement competitions;**
- **the management of the procurement;**
- **the administration and progress chasing of the procurement;**
- **checking the quality and quantity of the items procured.**

As in previous sections, the staff required for this role will depend on which of the previously described range of activities they are to provide or support. In planning the training programme, it is important to include generic procurement methods and techniques, and a complete understanding of the organisation's interfacing processes. In particular, any processes, standards or rules that the organisation uses in such procurements must be understood.

2.4.5 Risk, issue, change and configuration management support
Support to the risk, issue, change and configuration management processes used by the programme and project managers is another of the most common services provided by the PSO. The range of services provided includes:

- **administration support to the processes;**
- **organisation of the processes;**

- **provision and updating of the support infrastructure;**
- **operation of the risk, issue and change logs and other record systems;**
- **management and operation of the processes.**

To supply risk management services successfully, the PSO will need to ensure that their staff are trained in the current methods used by the organisation and the supporting software tools, and have a good understanding of the general principles of risk management and the various techniques that are available.

The other services of issue, change and configuration management do not demand such a wide understanding of their logic ,and can be supported by PSO staff who have received in-house training in the organisation's procedures.

All staff operating these support services need a general appreciation of all the functions of programme and project support, and of the programme and project management methods operated by the organisation. Staff can largely be trained in house and external training is only needed for risk management.

2.4.6 Hints and tips
The provision of hints and tips to the programme and project managers can involve any of the components of the programme and project support infrastructure.

The PSO must therefore ensure that it has an effective mechanism to collect the information, and store and retrieve it, so it can be disseminated efficiently.

The hints and tips to be provided can be extensive. Some of the less common ones worth considering are:

- **advice about the use of support tools provided for the programme and project managers;**
- **sources of specialist help about the programme and project support tools, either internal or external;**
- **sources of other specialist help or services – internal or external;**
- **sources of information in the organisation about processes that may interface with the programme or project management process.**

There is little specific training that can be identified to support this type of service. What is important is that the information provided is both up to date and accurate.

The skills needed to operate this service are those of a good administrator. The members of the PSO providing this service only need an appreciation of the programme and project management support processes.

2.4.7 Administration
The administration services role includes:

- **administrative support to the programme and/or project boards;**
- **secretarial and administrative support for the programme and project managers;**
- **meeting arrangements and administration;**
- **filing, travelling and accommodation services;**
- **circulation of reports.**

As with the previous section, the skills required for this role are those of a good administrator. Also, as before, it is desirable for the administration staff to have an appreciation of the programme and project support process and the programme and project management methods used by the organisation.

3.   The Logical or Physical PSO
The PSO can take two forms. The physical PSO has staff permanently allocated to the role, while a logical PSO operates largely without permanent staff. The organisation must decide, as part of the design process for the PSO, which to adopt. Although the physical PSO is more common, the organisation should, in the interest of economy, look to move as much of the support infrastructure as possible to a logical implementation.

3.1 The Logical PSO
The logical PSO is where the processes and procedures of the PSO have been designed and implemented to become part of the normal day-to-day operations of the organisation. The PSO functions are generally executed by the systems, procedures and processes rather than designated people.

However, logical implementations do require a custodian and must be supervised. It is essential therefore to establish a process, or a person, to ensure that monitoring and control takes place and to be the focus for the definition and implementation of any updating.

The logical PSO typically uses seconded staff from elsewhere in the organisation to fulfil specific functions at predefined times. For example, a PSO implemented to support the strategic planning process can use business analysts to assist in defining the portfolio of programmes and projects. Once this is completed, staff return to their previous duties.

3.2 The Physical PSO

A physical PSO has permanent staff who perform the majority of services. This PSO is often found in organisations where the role of the PSO involves audit, consultancy or other 'personal service' activities. This type of PSO can also have a logical element, when permanent staff are supplemented by others to meet special demands.

CASE STUDY

The Automobile Association's programme and project managers, as part of the annual job planning process, provided the PSO with a defined number of their hours, to be used as required. The PSO manager acted as a clearing house for requests of assistance and the availability of the programme and project managers.

Their time was generally used for providing consultancy, audits or coaching and mentoring to other programmes and projects. The scheme proved to be extremely successful as the programme and project managers felt that these 'community service' hours assisted not only the recipient, but also improved their own skills.

4. Summary

The PSO's role and responsibilities dictate the staff and skills it requires. It is important that the PSO staff members match the requirements of these roles and responsibilities. When selecting a suitable training programme for the PSO, it is vital that the needs of the staff are individually assessed and training designed to meet their needs. The experience, skills and training needs are summarised in Diagram 6 overleaf.

Diagram 6 Experience, skills and training required by PSO Staff

PSO Role	Experience		Skills			Training		
Audit – Conformance	PgM,PM		SC	AT		ISEB	QMS	
Constructive	PgM,PM	MC	SC	PS		ISEB	QMS?	MC
Assistance – Consultancy	PgM, PM	MC		PS	T/C/M	ISEB	T/C/M	MC
Coaching/Mentoring	PgM, PM	MC		PS	T/C/M	ISEB	T/C/M	MC
Training	PgM, PM	MC		PS	T/C/M	ISEB	T/C/M	MC
Advice	PgM, PM	MC		PS		ISEB		MC
Support – Prog & Project Lifecycle		MC		PS	T/C/M	ISEB		MC
Prog & Project Management Methods	PgM, PM	MC		PS	T/C/M	ISEB		MC
Project or System Development Method/s		MC		PS	T/C/M	ISEB	(PgM, PM)	MC
Standards				PS		ISEB	(PgM, PM)	MC
Templates				PS	AM	ISEB	(PgM, PM)	MC
Example Deliverables				PS	AM	ISEB	(PgM, PM)	MC
Services – Prog & Project Management Tools							(PgM, PM)	
Planning						ISEB	(PgM, PM)	PST
Progress Monitoring & Reporting					AM	ISEB	(PgM, PM)	PST?
Procurement					AM		(PgM, PM)	PCM
Risk, Issue, Change & Configuration Management					AM		(PgM, PM)	RM
Hints and Tips					AM		(PgM, PM)	
Administration					AM		(PgM, PM)	

Key

AM – administration skills. AT – auditing. C – management consultancy. ISEB – ISEB certificate in programme and project support. M – mentoring. PCM – procurement methods. PGM, PM – programme and project management. (PGM, PM) – experience of programme and project management. PS – interpersonal skills. QMS – quality management and other audits. RM – risk management. SC – strong character. T – training.

Chapter Six

Selling the PSO to the Organisation

1. Introduction

The PSO is just like any other business function or department except that it exists to help others do their job. As a consequence it is often seen as an overhead, providing something that could be done by the people it helps. Therefore the need for, and the benefits of, a PSO must be sold to the organisation throughout its design, implementation and probably for its entire lifetime!

The selling campaigns should be based on the PSO providing quick wins and early deliverables to the organisation. The following sections describe an approach that has worked very effectively in a number of organisations. It is not supplied as a formula or checklist, but is designed to help identify a strategy that will be appropriate. One very important thing to remember is that a successful selling campaign is directed at people, not at an organisation.

2. Who should the PSO be sold to?

The first step in designing the selling strategy is to decide on the target audience. The instant answer is everyone in the organisation, because everyone in the organisation has a view and input. Therefore, for the strategy to succeed, you must identify all the potential targets – if any are excluded they will cause problems. So ensure everyone is listened to, but design the strategy to address the sources of power in the organisation.

Who to include in this list of sources of power will be specific to each organisation. However, experience has shown that the following groups nearly always appear on the list:

- **executive and senior management;**
- **programme managers and project managers;**
- **team leaders;**

- **programme and project team members;**
- **wannabes;**
- **support staff.**

2.1. Selling to Executive and Senior Management

The PSO should be sold to the management of the organisation on the real (tangible) benefits that it will provide for the organisation and, in particular, the benefits and information services it will provide for executive and senior managers.

This group of managers will require considerable amounts of information, but it must be collated and condensed into readable, comprehensible statements. These statements must provide the relevant managers with a view of the portfolio of programmes and projects. They must also describe where the individual programmes and projects are, where they should be: are they on schedule, within budget, under-resourced or over-allocated. These statements are very useful, but the added-value reports that executive and senior management require are those which contain an analysis and predictions of the remainder of the programme or project. Therefore the selling strategy should concentrate on what information a PSO can provide. However, do not oversell the services that can be provided.

2.2 Selling to the Programme, Project Managers and Team Leaders

When selling to this group, it is important to remember that they want the PSO to allow them to get on with their role without too much 'interference'. Indeed it is often clear that many of them do not want the spotlight on their programme or project and most do not want a PSO that provides reports that conflict with their progress reports.

However most are 100% behind what the PSO is doing. Regrettably though, don't bank on any tangible support when you need it. This group wants help, therefore sell the PSO to them on the basis of the help and support it can provide.

2.3 Selling to Programme or Project Team Members

This group also wants to get on with the job without 'interference'. It often seems that this group would rather do the work they like to do or the work that was planned for someone else, rather than the work that was planned for them. Initially the selling strategy will need to overcome an attitude of 'why should we supply the PSO with information on what we have done, no one has ever asked for it before!' Selling to team members after the PSO has been implemented must also address their concerns of who is using the information they provide and for what purpose.

This group wants the PSO to tell them what to do, when to do it and how. Beware, they are very unforgiving and often complain about how often the PSO gets it wrong, particularly if processes have to be changed to correct problems. It is important therefore to make sure that the PSO gets it right first time. However this group is fully supportive once the process becomes part of business-as-usual.

2.4 Selling to Wannabes

This phrase describes the many programme or project managers or team leaders who view a job in the PSO, or the manager of the PSO, as a tempting proposition. They see a number of perceived advantages:

- **power to report on other programmes or projects;**
- **exemption from being reported on;**
- **no more project boards or users to deal with;**
- **a role which seems ill-defined enough to be easy;**
- **they read an article on it once and it seems very easy;**
- **they worked in one once so it will be easy.**

This group is both an asset and a liability. They are a liability because they think that they can do the job better than anyone else and criticise any perceived errors. To counter this the selling strategy needs to include the same sort of approach as the previous group. The wannabes can be an asset if you utilise their enthusiasm to help sell the concepts and benefits of the PSO to others in the organisation.

2.5 Selling to the PSO staff

One group often forgotten is the existing or proposed staff of the PSO. Most of the staff of the PSO should be there because they either want to make a career in programme and/or project support, or see it as a stepping stone to being a programme or project manager. It is vital that before the PSO is implemented and during its operation, they are sold the reason for the PSO.

The PSO gives many opportunities for its staff to be involved in new things, particularly new tools and techniques. The thought of being the first in the organisation to use a new tool, or of being the expert in that tool, can be extremely motivating.

3. What is to be sold

Having decided who these groups are and what sorts of things will appeal to them, the next step in designing the selling strategy is to decide on what is going to be sold.

3.1 Hard Deliverables not Soft Deliverables

Quite often organisations follow a tendency to go for soft deliverables based around the use of the word 'better' – 'better control', 'better information'. A selling strategy based on this approach nearly always runs into problems because it is difficult to prove the changes have occurred. It is always preferable to start by selling hard deliverables, quantified and based around proven processes and technology.

In selling these deliverables do not fall into the trap of ignoring the possible use of software and other tools. While it is the processes that must be right, making them really work effectively may mean selecting suitable tools.

3.2 No Hot Air

This is perhaps one of the greatest dangers – ensure what is being sold can be delivered. It is better to deliver more than promised rather than fail to deliver what was promised by .005 per cent. When deciding what to sell, ensure that it will, and can be, provided.

3.3 Use of proven procedures technology/tools

The selling campaign must be based on what can be delivered. To make sure that it can be achieved, visit other organisations that already have a PSO. Look, listen and ask questions; build the selling strategy on what can be delivered and ensure that what is proposed is tried and tested.

3.4 Not a Test Bed

The cycle times of new products or updated existing products in the arena of programme and project support tools seems to get shorter each year. As a result it is very easy to think that the latest release of an existing product will be tried and tested. Regrettably that is not always the case. It is therefore recommended that the selling strategy is not based on being the first with a new software product. Don't be a test bed for new software.

4. Why should the organisation buy into the PSO?

The following section describes some of the points which should appear in the selling strategy.

4.1 ... Because it makes the business more profitable

The recommended start point is to emphasise that the PSO is designed to make the organisation more profitable. Then to follow that statement with a list of those major benefits which will be provided.

4.1.1 Only valid, approved programmes or projects take place

This is one of the major benefits, which is of interest to all levels of management. The implementation of and support from the PSO to the processes which ensure that only approved programmes or projects are commissioned, meet the following requirements:

1) Senior management – to ensure that they know how the organisation decides what programmes and projects are commissioned and that they are aligned to the strategic goals of the organisation.

2) The programme and project managers – are aware of the processes used to authorise the start up, monitoring and strategic direction of their programmes and projects.

3) For the programme and project team leaders – it provides a level of assurance that the programme or project is likely to continue.

4.1.2 All resources are utilised efficiently and perform valid work

The PSO and its associated processes will provide the mechanism for ensuring that the line or resource managers are able to plan all the work that their staff perform. In addition, any programme or project managers who request resources do so for programmes and projects that are authorised and approved.

4.1.3 Confidence in planned delivery dates and costs is improved

Another major point to emphasise is the improvement in confidence in delivery dates that the PSO and its processes will provide.

4.1.4 Clients are invoiced easily and efficiently

The PSO infrastructure can be designed to provide this functionality, although this particular advantage may not be relevant in all cases. Where this is relevant however, it is a major advantage because it ensures that there is a direct link from the invoice to the working documents, thus eliminating much paperwork and potential inaccuracy.

4.1.5 New work can be estimated

Another major point to sell is the ability to estimate any new or proposed work. This is important for sales or customer satisfaction and helps the organisation to predict and manage the use of its resources.

4.1.6 Summary reports are prepared and compared quickly

This benefit is only of interest to the organisation if it knows it is currently experiencing pain, either in generating such reports, or because of the lack of such reports. This point is very important, because organisations only really value what is seen to be required.

4.1.7 Risks can be managed

One of the major problems experienced by programme and project managers is ensuring that executive and senior management are aware of the risks that have been identified, and that they receive updates on the actions planned and executed to manage these risks.

A well designed PSO infrastructure will be able to provide this information for the individual programmes and projects and also collectively across the various portfolios.

4.1.8 Issues can be identified and resolved

As with the risks, programme and project managers experience problems in ensuring that senior management are aware of the issues that have been identified and that they receive updates on the actions planned and executed to manage these issues.

The reasons for buying into the PSO should be because it makes the business more profitable through timely and accurate information. For the organisation to set-up the PSO, it is vital that it sells itself and shows sufficient justification, based on the above, to all levels of management in the organisation.

5.   Things not to sell to the organisation

This section looks at those areas which experience has shown should not be included.

5.1 Because it is fashionable

Possibly the worst reason to present to an organisation is that you should have a PSO because it is fashionable.

5.2 Because the Organisation 'has not got one'

Another selling strategy that must be avoided is 'because we haven't got one'. This diverts the organisation away from determining what it really needs the PSO to provide.

5.3 Because Programmes and Projects want more clerical support

This selling strategy is doubly flawed. First it sets the PSO as a low grade support unit rather than the real added value business support function that it should be. Secondly, it makes the assumption that providing centralised administrative support services for programmes and projects is more economical. This is a dangerous assumption – what the organisation needs is management support and that is the real added value area that should be sold.

6. Summary

The key to a successful selling strategy is to realise that the PSO must be sold to everyone. Therefore plan the campaign to ensure that they all receive something from the selling process. The key to make them appreciate the PSO at its start-up, and its continued operation, is to go for quick wins – provide something that is needed, understood and agreed by the management.

Do not delay support while working for the perfect solution. Deliver a little at a time, making sure it is as right as possible, or ensure that users understand it is a temporary solution and a permanent solution will replace it.

Finally, if the manager who has been given the role of implementing the PSO has no experience of this sort of project, get some experienced help. It is not possible to learn and be successful at the same time.

Chapter Seven

Programme and Project Life Cycle

1. Introduction

To ensure that an organisation's investments in programmes and projects are successfully managed by executive-level management, the organisation will need a number of interlinked processes to commission, maintain and control them. This chapter provides an overview of these linked processes (referred to as a life cycle); the individual constituent processes, the documents which support them, and the role of the PSO in supporting them.

Experience has shown that unless all the components described in this chapter are implemented in some form, the organisation will not have an effective management and control system for its programmes and projects. Also, each organisation must define all these functions and processes as separate from the programme and project management processes.

2. Programme and Project Life cycle – Purpose and Benefits

The programme and project life cycle gives executive-level management control over which programmes and projects are commissioned and their execution. This ensures that investments made in programmes and projects are directed towards the attainment of the organisation's business goals. The control is exercised through a system of three formal review processes:

- **Start-up process:** *The two-stage approval process which is used before work commences on the programme or project.*
- **Execution monitoring process:** *Those reviews and approvals which are carried out during the programme and/or project.*
- **Programme and project closure process:** *Two reviews which are undertaken at the end of the programme and/or*

project, which assess the effectiveness of their management and the benefits that have been achieved.

The programme and project life cycle also provides the interfaces with processes used for programme and project management and for progress monitoring and control. Thus the programme and project life cycle provides the basis to enable executive-level management to effectively and efficiently manage each programme or project.

3. The roles within the life cycle

The operation of the life cycle will involve a large number of different members of the organisation in one or more of the following roles:

Diagram 8 **The roles involved in programme and project life cycle**

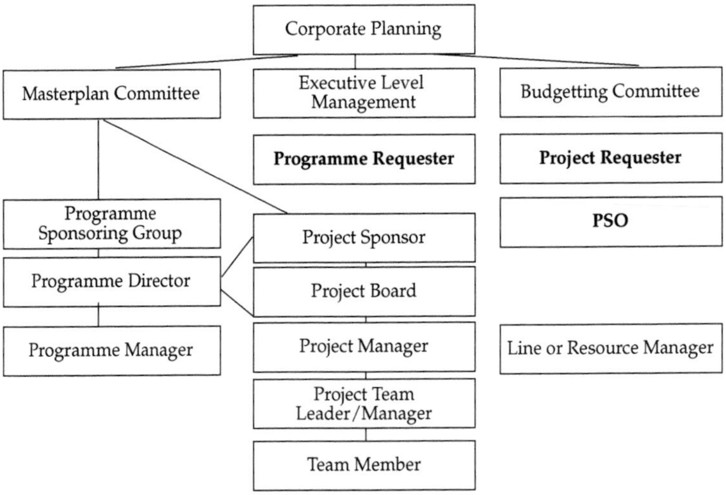

Note: The roles described here may be performed by different groups or given different names – what is important is the functionality. The functionality described in this chapter may need to be supplemented or amended to reflect the specific needs of the organisation.

Corporate planning (the board)

The organisation's ultimate decision-making body responsible for which strategic aims and objectives, business goals and targets should be adopted by the organisation.

Executive-level management

The managers responsible for developing the organisation's strategic plan and the supporting definition of the business goals and targets.

Budgeting committee

The group of executive and senior management collectively responsible for the collation and completion of the organisation's budgeting process. They also ensure sufficient budget allocation for programmes and projects so that the organisation can finance its agreed portfolio of programmes and projects.

Masterplan committee

Members of executive and senior management who are responsible for examining and recommending, to the board, which new, and continuing, programmes and projects should be included in the masterplan portfolio. Such a committee also reviews the progress made in the delivery of the portfolio and makes recommendations on any required control action.

*See example document **18**: The terms of reference for a masterplan committee.*

Programme director and project boards

The members of management who oversee the execution of the programmes and projects contained in the masterplan portfolio. They are responsible for the tactical deployment of resources and for ensuring that products or deliverables meet the required quality standards.

Programme and/or project sponsor

The members of the organisation who are the sponsors of a programme or project. This role is normally undertaken by a senior manager who acts as the customer for the programme or project, ensuring that the programme or project delivers the requirements of the programme or project requester.

Programme or project requester

The member of the organisation who requests a programme or project. Their first responsibility is to ask an executive-level manager to be the sponsor of the programme or project. They may also act as the customer for the programme or project, by accepting the deliverables from the execution of the programme or project, and may be the ultimate authority on the programme's or project's requirements.

Programme and project managers

The members of the organisation who have overall responsibility for the management of a programme or project in respect of:

- the planning of effort, schedule and budget required to realise the programme or project;
- day-to-day management of the project and monitoring the progress made in providing the required deliverables or products;
- the review and approval process of all the main deliverables of the programme or project;
- providing reports on the progress made in accordance with the agreed processes;
- dealing with those issues, change requests and exception situations that occur during the course of the programmes and projects;
- closing the programme and/or project in accordance with the organisation's standard processes.

Project or team leader/manager

A project or team leader assists the programme or project manager by taking responsibility for a part of the programme or project. A project or team leader is assigned by each department or team that is involved in the development and installation of the deliverables. Alternatively they may be responsible for a complete stage of a project. Project or team leaders maintain the plan of all the activities that their teams undertake.

This plan is discussed and agreed with the programme and/or project manager and together they resolve any resource conflicts that may arise. The project leader or team leader also assists the programme or project manager in dealing with progress reports, issue and change management and exception situations.

Line or resource manager
Line or resource managers have responsibility for providing the resources to form the programme and/or project development team. They discuss and agree with the programme or project manager the selection, availability and allocation of their staff. They also assist the programme and/or project manager in dealing with resource conflicts.

Programme and/or Project Support Office (PSO)
The PSO is responsible for:

- assisting in administering the corporate planning and masterplan committees by preparing summaries of the information related to resource requirements and usage for past, present and proposed programmes and projects;
- assisting programme and/or project managers when they are preparing plans and deciding the method of approach to be used in the execution of a programme and/or project;
- overseeing the procedures and standards used when managing and undertaking programmes and projects;
- the provision of specialist knowledge and skills in respect of programme and project management and the technical aspects of the programmes and projects.

The PSO has specific responsibility for ensuring that the estimating guidelines, and other components of the programme and project support infrastructure, are regularly reviewed and updated to reflect current and required best practices, standards and techniques used by programme and project managers.

Team members
The team members are responsible for executing the programmes and projects. They also report to the resource or line manager, and the programme or project manager, on:

- *the progress made;*
- *the deliverables produced*
- *the effort used on programmes, projects, and non-project work.*

4. The Programme and Project life cycle and its processes

The programme and project life cycle is typically subdivided into seven processes. These are:

- **identification of the need for the programme or project;**
- **budgeting review;**
- **programme or project initiation;**
- **programme or project feasibility;**
- **programme or project monitoring and control;**
- **programme or project closure;**
- **post programme or post project review.**

The remainder of this chapter provides an overview of these processes that collectively make up the programme or project life cycle.

4.1 Identification of the need for the Programme or Project – Strategic Planning Process

4.1.1 The reason for the process and the benefits it provides

This process starts when the organisation defines its long and short-term business goals and targets, and identifies areas of change or improvement that will be achieved through programmes or projects.

It also provides a prioritisation of the programmes and/or projects that will be included in the organisation's portfolio of programmes and projects – referred to in this chapter as the masterplan portfolio.

4.1.2 Who is involved?

The organisation, having completed its strategic planning, produces the documents in which its business goals and targets are defined. Once they have been reviewed and agreed by the organisation's board, these documents are circulated to the management of the organisation.

The documents are the starting point for any proposed programme or project which is to be included in the masterplan portfolio. The programmes and projects need to be included and identified by the masterplan committee and senior managers, who evaluate whether the current portfolio of programmes and projects will enable the organisation to obtain the agreed business goals and targets. Any shortfall is filled by new programmes and/or projects. This process is operated by the masterplan committee and the organisation's senior and departmental management supported by the PSO.

4.1.3 Involvement and role

Diagram 9

	Approval	Contributes	Responsible
Strategic Planning Committee	X		
Masterplan Committee			X
Senior Managers			X
Departmental Heads			X
PSO		X	

4.1.4 Description of the process

The PSO or the corporate planning function organise a series of meetings with the masterplan committee and the other executive and senior level managers to assess which programmes and/or projects – new or existing – will be needed to achieve the new business goals and targets.

The PSO supports this process by providing information about the existing portfolio of programmes and projects and also estimates of the resources, the effort, or the time-scale of any new programmes or projects. The outcome of these discussions is a list of potential new programmes and projects and a list of existing programmes and projects to be modified or cancelled.

This information can be summarised in a business strategy – programme and project contribution matrix.
Note: This matrix may also include Business as Usual and other activities delivering the business strategy.

*See example document **19**: A business strategy – programme and project contribution matrix.*

4.2 Budgeting Process

4.2.1 The reason for the process and the benefits it provides

This part of the programme or project life cycle ensures that major investments in new and continuing projects are budgeted for. The process enables the organisation to assess the requirements for capital and other resources for the programmes and projects accurately. The process also provides the masterplan committee with a framework within which they can decide whether a project should be commissioned, and what its relative priority should be.

4.2.2 Who is involved?

Senior and departmental managers are responsible for identifying any additional, or continuing, programmes or projects required in the next budget period. Together with the PSO they must accurately assess the capital and other resource requirements needed to realise them.

4.2.3 Involvement and role

Diagram 10

	Approval	Contributes	Responsible
Budgeting Committee	X		
Masterplan Committee			X
Senior Managers			X
Departmental Heads			X
PSO		X	X

4.2.4 Description of the process

All programmes and projects will need to be budgeted for by the relevant budget holder. Once the annual budgeting process commences, each executive, senior or departmental manager who wishes to have a programme or project considered for inclusion in the masterplan portfolio, must ensure that suitable provision for that programme or project has been included in the submissions to the budgeting committee for funds. Assistance in estimating the amount of resources and costs involved is available from the PSO. This budgeting process must also include provision for those programmes and projects that have already commenced.

Only in extraordinary circumstances should programmes or projects that have not been budgeted for be commissioned. In such situations a request for additional budget must be processed through the relevant finance department and management processes.

4.3 Programme and Project Initiation Process

4.3.1 The reason for the process and the benefits it provides
All major investments in new programmes and projects must be reviewed by executive and senior management so that all commissioned programmes and projects support the strategic goals of the organisation. The board, through the masterplan committee, has control of all major investments in new programmes and projects. This process ensures that no programme or project is undertaken without executive-level management approval.

4.3.2 Who is involved?
The programme or project requester, with assistance from a member of staff allocated to provide specialist support, is responsible for preparing a programme or project initiation form (PIF). This is done in conjunction with the relevant executive, senior and departmental managers, finance department, etc., and the PSO.

4.3.3 Involvement and role

Diagram 11

	Approval	Contributes	Responsible
Masterplan Committee	X		
Programme or Project Sponsor	X		
Programme or Project Requester			X
Line Managers		X	
Departmental Heads		X	
Business Analyst		X	
PSO		X	
Finance Department		X	

4.3.4 Description of the process

The programme or project requester who wants authorisation for a new programme or project, asks and agrees with a member of executive-level management that they will act as the programme or project sponsor. The programme or project requester asks the head of business analysis, corporate planning or other relevant departments to supply a member of staff to provide specialist support to complete the programme or project initiation form (PIF). The PIF is also discussed with the finance department who supply any relevant programme or project code and details of the programme or project budget.

*See example document **20**: A programme or project initiation form.*

The PSO reviews the completed form and ensures that it is considered by the masterplan committee who decide:

- **to commission the programme or project once the feasibility study or other quantification or information has been obtained;**
- **the relative priority of the proposed programme or project relative to those in the existing portfolio;**
- **to commission the programme or project immediately;**
- **to put the project on the 'not-started' programmes or projects list; or**
- **to reject the programme or project.**

The programme or project requester, sponsor, or specialist support may attend the meeting either at the request of the masterplan committee, or because the programme or project needs to be explained in greater detail.

The decision taken and relevant factors are recorded on the programme or project initiation form by the PSO. If the programme or project is commissioned or rejected, the masterplan portfolio database is also updated by the PSO. If commissioned, the PSO assists in issuing the relevant documentation which formally commissions the feasibility study.

*See example document **21**: A masterplan portfolio database.*

4.4 Programme or Project Feasibility Studies Process

4.4.1 The reason for the process and the benefits it provides
This process provides sufficient information for executive-level management to ensure that a programme or project supports the strategic goals of the organisation and the investment is valid.

This second review gives a final chance for the masterplan committee to confirm the need for the programme or project and to ensure that no programme or project is executed without their approval.

4.4.2 Who is involved
The programme or project manager allocated to the feasibility study has overall responsibility for this process. The programme or project requester and the PSO assist in this.

4.4.3 Involvement and role

Diagram 12

	Approval	Contributes	Responsible
Masterplan Committee	X		
Project Requester		X	
Line Managers		X	
Departmental Heads		X	
Specialist Support		X	
Programme or Project Manager			X
PSO		X	
Finance Department		X	

4.4.4 Description of the process
The feasibility study is prepared by the team allocated to it by the masterplan committee.

The programme or project manager reviews the documents prepared to support the programme or project initiation form and prepare a plan for the feasibility study.

The programme or project manager then discusses, and agrees, with the relevant resource/line managers, the detailed planning and booking of the resources needed during the feasibility study.

If any major changes are identified to the amount of resources defined in the programme or project initiation form, or the time-scale for the feasibility study, the situation must be discussed with the masterplan committee and the PSO. When the feasibility study is completed it is first checked by the PSO, who may prepare a short summary report to accompany the feasibility study and assist its review by the masterplan committee.

The masterplan committee decides:

- **the priority of the new programme or project relative to the existing masterplan portfolio;**
- **to commission the programme or project;**
- **to commission the programme or project once further information has been obtained;**
- **to put the programme or project on the 'held programmes or projects' list; or**
- **to reject the programme or project.**

The programme or project requester, sponsor, programme or project manager may attend the meeting at the request of the masterplan committee or because the feasibility study, or the programme or project, needs to be explained in greater detail.

See example document **22:** *A feasibility study report.*

4.5   Programme and Project Monitoring and Control Process

4.5.1 The reason for the process and the benefits it provides
This process ensures that the programmes and projects are effectively and efficiently managed, planned, monitored and controlled to an acceptable level, or to the required standard. This avoids repeating known errors, and the organisation can take advantage of the experience and knowledge gained from previous programmes or projects.

It also provides all programme and project managers with suitable forms for these reports, so they do not spend time designing forms, reports or other documents to facilitate the programme or project management process.

This process also provides regular progress reports to the executive-level management so that they can monitor and, if necessary, effect control action on the programme or project. Finally, if a programme or project is failing to meet its targets, processes are in place to notify executive-level management of the need for control action.

4.5.2 Who is involved?

The programme or project manager is responsible for the management and control of the programme or project. The PSO is responsible for advising the programme or project manager on the use and application of the programme and project support infrastructure, and for the collection and analysis of the progress, or other, reports provided by the programme or project manager.

The programme director or project board, resource/line managers and other managers are responsible for ensuring that the programme or project is achieved with the required resources at the agreed time. The masterplan committee is responsible for overseeing the programmes and projects and recommending any strategic direction or remedial action.

4.5.3 Involvement and role

Diagram 13

	Approval	Contributes	Responsible
Masterplan Committee	X		
Project Sponsor			X
Project Requester		X	
Resource/ Line Managers		X	
Departmental Heads		X	
Programme or Project Manager			X
Project Team Members		X	
PSO		X	
Finance Department		X	

4.5.4 Description of the process

4.5.4.1 Step One – Planning

The programme and project support infrastructure provides estimating guidelines and information on the project (or system) development method. The plans are reviewed by the PSO and, if any major differences are identified, the masterplan committee is consulted before further work is carried out.

If the new plans are within the parameters of the original programme or project plan, the programme or project manager discusses with the relevant resource/line manager the availability of the staff required. If any major problems emerge, they are discussed with the programme sponsoring group, director, project board or the masterplan committee.

Having completed the programme or project plan, the programme or project manager plans the first tranche of the programme or project in detail by identifying the specific tasks needed and, in conjunction with the resource/line managers, identifying and booking the resources.

4.5.4.2 Step Two – Reporting Progress

As work continues, the programme or project manager reports progress at prescribed intervals using the agreed progress report form. These reports are collated and analysed by the PSO for circulation to the executive-level management of the organisation. If any changes are required to the bookings made with resource/line managers the programme or project manager agrees these as required.

All members of the organisation involved in the programme or project should complete a time sheet weekly, or to other agreed timescale. This information is collated by the programme or project manager and used to produce the masterplan committee progress report.

*See example document **23**: A progress report to the masterplan committee.*

4.5.4.3 Step Three – Exception Situation

If, when monitoring progress, the programme or project manager identifies that the programme or project is likely to exceed its agreed tolerance, the exception report process is implemented. This consists of a report prepared by the programme or project manager and the PSO for relevant members of the executive-level management so they are aware of the problem, the options to solve it, and the recommended action. Executive-level management provides strategic guidance on what action the programme or project manager should take.

*See example document **24**: An exception report and plan.*

4.5.4.4 Step Four – End of tranche or stage

At the end of each programme tranche or project stage, the programme or project manager prepares an end of programme tranche or project stage report. This report contains a statement of the deliverables that were planned and those actually developed, the planned and actual resources used and costs. The report also contains the detailed plans for the next programme tranche or project stage and an update to the programme or project plan which reflects any changes needed.

The report also identifies any major changes to the business case and the benefits realisation plan for the programme or project that may have been identified.

This report is reviewed with and by the PSO to validate the figures it contains. The programme or project manager, with the programme or project requester or sponsor (or both), and the PSO hold an end of programme tranche or project stage pre-meeting. At this pre-meeting the progress made in the programme or project is discussed, particularly, is the continuation of the programme or project still justified? (The baselined programme or project definition is used as the basis for this review).

If all are satisfied that the programme or project is still within the agreed programme or project definition documents, they sign the end of programme tranche or stage report. The PSO can prepare a short summary report of the meeting which is used at the programme sponsoring group, director or project board meeting to review the tranche or stage. The meeting's decision on the continuing viability of the programme or project is sent to the masterplan committee for ratification or otherwise.

If the meeting agreed that the project is no longer within the programme or project definition document, work on the programme or project is halted while the project or programme sponsor and the PSO report to the masterplan committee. They then discuss the situation and provide strategic guidance to the programme or project manager, the programme or project requester or the sponsor.

*See example document **25**: An end of tranche and stage report.*

4.6 Programme or Project Closure Process

4.6.1 The reason for the process and the benefits it provides
The formal closure of the programme or project helps the organisation formally acknowledge that the programme or project has been handed over to the programme or project requester and all relevant members of the organisation are formally advised, including the masterplan committee.

4.6.2 Who is involved
The programme or project manager together with the programme or project requester and/or sponsor, have overall responsibility for ensuring this process is completed. The PSO and other members of management, who provide information for the report, assist them in this.

4.6.3 Involvement and role

Diagram 14

	Approval	Contributes	Responsible
Masterplan Committee	X		
Project Requester			X
Programme or Project Manager			X
Line Managers		X	
Departmental Heads		X	
Business Analyst			X(or)
PSO		X	
Finance Department		X	

4.6.4 Description of the process
When the programme or project has been completed, the programme or project manager together with the programme or project requester or sponsor, completes a programme or project completion report. The programme or project manager discusses the document with the PSO and all the other managers who have been involved in the programme or project. All the managers are asked to sign the

programme or project completion form to show they know that the programme or project is completed and to add any remarks of use for future programmes or projects.

The programme or project manager, and the programme or project requester or sponsor, also discuss and agree their recommendations for the post programme or post project review. These arrangements include when the review should take place and any specific areas on which they want the review to concentrate.

See example document **26**: *A programme and project closure report.*

4.7 Post-Programme or Post-Project Review Process

4.7.1 The reason for the process and the benefits it provides
All programmes or projects that are part of the masterplan portfolio and have been completed, must undergo a post programme or project review. The review helps the organisation and executive-level management assess the benefits from the programme or project and identify any issues that have emerged since the programme or project was formally closed.

This review provides valuable information to executive-level management about the success, or otherwise, of the organisation's investment in commissioning programmes or projects. It also provides valuable information on the success, or otherwise, of the approach method used in the execution phase so that any lessons learnt are incorporated into future programmes or projects.

4.7.2 Who is involved?
The programme or project manager, or a business analyst, can have overall responsibility for ensuring this process is completed. The programme or project requester or sponsor and the PSO assist them in this.

4.7.3 Involvement and role

Diagram 15

	Approval	Contributes	Responsible
Masterplan Committee	X		
Project Sponsor		X	
Project Requester		X	
Line Managers		X	
Departmental Heads		X	
Programme or Project Manager			X
PSO		X	
Finance Department		X	

4.7.4 Description of the process

The programme or project manager or business analyst, appointed by the masterplan committee to perform the post programme or project review, obtains all the relevant programme or project documents – in particular, any terms of reference or business case – as well as any user requirements and design documents. The review is carried out using these documents with the support of the PSO. Using the programme or project initiation form, the feasibility study, the programme definition or project initiation document, the business case, the benefits realisation plan and the programme or project closure report, they assess whether:

- **the programme or project achieved its aim, objectives and benefits;**
- **any further lessons have emerged since the programme or project was completed;**
- **any of those lessons learnt are such that they should be brought to the attention of executive and senior management, or should be used as the basis of amendments to the programme or project support infrastructure.**

In addition the report must also identify:

- **whether the benefits realisation plan has been implemented;**
- **whether all the benefits contained in the benefits realisation plan have been realised;**

- any failures or problems that have emerged and have not been dealt with;
- any further enhancements or amendments that have been identified;
- any follow on programme or projects that should be considered.

The completed report is then passed to the masterplan committee for their review. The PSO ensures that any required action is implemented.

*See example document **27**: A post-programme and project review report.*

5. The interfaces between the Programme or Project Life Cycle and the Programme and Project Management Methods

The programme or project life cycle provides the mechanism for the most important control documents from the programme or project management life cycle to become part of the organisation's programme and project management methods and processes.

The following diagram describes where this interface occurs and which documents from the programme or project management methods support, or are derived from, the programme or project life cycle.

Diagram 16 **Interfaces between Programme or Project Life Cycle and the Other Methods**

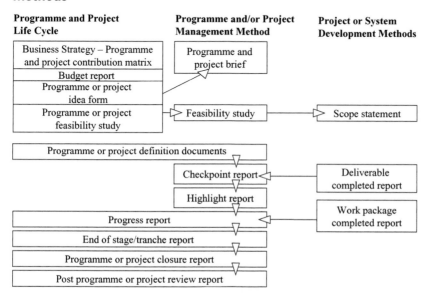

6. Summary

To ensure that the organisation has full control of its investment in programmes and projects it must have an agreed, defined and understood process for their commissioning, monitoring, controlling, closure and review.

The programme or project life cycle provides the interfaces that the programme or project management method needs to receive the relevant strategic guidance.

The processes described in this chapter will need to be tailored by the organisation to reflect its particular needs and business processes.

Without these processes, the organisation cannot be confident that its investment in programmes and projects is under the full control of the executive-level management.

Chapter Eight

Programme and Project Management Methods

1. Introduction

The programme or project life cycle ensures that the organisation selects the correct programmes and projects to achieve its strategic objectives. Programme and project management methods make sure that, during their execution, the programmes and projects are managed appropriately. Therefore, programme and project management methods must interface with the programme or project life cycle and supply some of the documents that life cycle uses.

Diagram 17
Relationship between Programme or Project Life Cycle and Programme and Project Methods

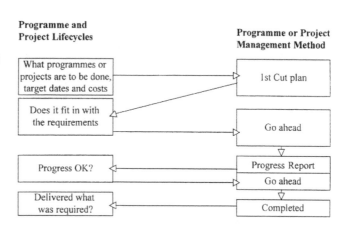

2. Why Programme and Project Management Methods are Needed

2.1 Structured Removal of Uncertainty

All programmes and projects are 'a voyage of discovery'. What is important is that during their execution this uncertainty is regularly re-assessed and gradually reduced. Programme and project management methods advise when re-assessments need to take place and the mechanisms, documents and approval process that are used to reduce uncertainty.

Diagram 18
The Cone of
Uncertainty

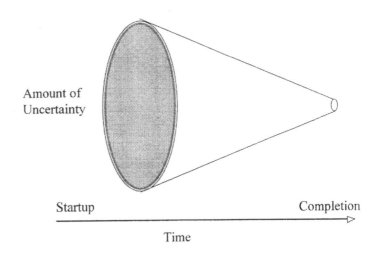

Amount of
Uncertainty

Startup   Completion

Time

2.2 Keeps Programmes and Projects Under Control

Programmes and projects that fail are usually out of control. The use of an effective programme or project management method helps stop this.

All such methods demand that the organisation starts the programme or project under a regime of management control which continues throughout their execution. The methods use a number of interlinking management processes and supporting systems to maintain this control.

2.3 Enables Standard Infrastructure Support

Using a standard approach to the management of an organisation's programmes and projects means that it is possible to support them with a single infrastructure. If the organisation uses a number of different approaches it will, of course, need a number of infrastructures. Justifying and maintaining the cost of one infrastructure is difficult – having to do it many times is almost impossible.

Therefore, the use of a programme and/or project management method which is standard (but tailorable within known limits) means that the organisation can develop a supporting infrastructure which can provide real support to all the methods' users.

2.4 Consistency and Learning from Mistakes

One of the key reasons why structured methods are used is that without a standard approach it is impossible to build any lessons learnt into the management of programmes and projects.

2.5 Training

Another major concern that programme and project methods seek to address is the training of programme and project managers. Unless the organisation develops and implements such methods there is no defined structure on which to base the training of programme and project managers. However, although the methods contain most of the techniques that programme and project managers need to understand and use, they cannot provide the necessary management skills and technical expertise needed to be a programme or project manager.

2.6 Audit

Programmes and projects are substantial investments for most organisations and like any other business activity should be subject to regular audit to assure the organisation that the investment is being wisely spent. The use of a programme or project management method provides the basis for an audit as it contains the management systems to be reviewed.

2.7 Visibility of the Programme and Project Management Process

Finally, the use of a programme and project management method provides the organisation with a visible process for managing the programme or project, which it can follow and understand.

3.   The History of Programme and Project Management Methods

Methods similar to contemporary programme and project management methods have been with us for many years – for example, cookery recipes. The history of mass marketed programme and project management methods started in the late 1970s when, as a result of a major review of IT project failures (which indicated the need for standard project management methods), the UK Government procured licences to use PROMPT (the predecessor of PRINCE) and SSADM.

PROMPT (Project Organisation Management and Planning Techniques) was adopted in 1982 as the standard project management method for the control of Government IT projects. Indeed, without the use of PROMPT, projects were not funded by the Treasury. In June 1989 the CCTA decided to update the method and launched the PRompt INcluding Ccta Enhancements project – PRINCE (PRINCE was changed to PRojects IN Controlled Environments). This upgraded the method and also made it an open method – available for anyone to use without fee. PRINCE Version 2 was started in July 1993 with the aim of making PRINCE applicable to all types of projects and was launched in October 1996.

Since its launch, the use of PRINCE has spread to many types of projects other than those that involve I.T. – throughout the private sector and internationally.

Programme management has yet to evolve fully as a method. However, as with project management, the need for a structured approach to the management of programmes is being addressed in government. The CCTA published a series of books on programme management in 1994 and 1999.

4. The Typical Contents of Programme and Project Management Methods

Programme and project management methods usually contain the following:

- **organisation structure;**
- **process map;**
- **list of deliverables;**
- **deliverable specifications;**
- **techniques.**

The best-constructed methods integrate these components into a single structure, which follows the sequence that they are used in the programme or project. For ease of explanation, this chapter describes them as separate entities, although in most methods they are integrated.

4.1 Organisation Structure

The reason why all such methods contain a recommended organisation structure with prescribed roles and responsibilities is to ensure that:

- **the need for such management involvement is explicit;**
- **the decision making is allocated to the relevant members of the organisation;**
- **the 'right' skills and power are present in the programme or project decision-making structure;**
- **the rule of 9 is avoided– (the typical number of consultations needed to get a decision if these structures are not in place).**

4.1.1 Programme Organisation Structure

A typical programme management organisation is as follows:

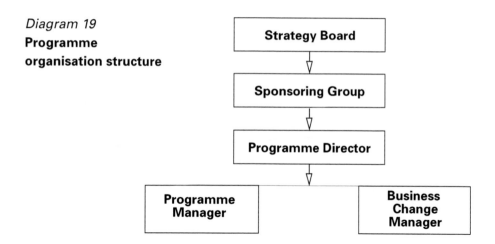

Diagram 19
Programme organisation structure

Strategy Board

Sponsoring Group

Programme Director

Programme Manager

Business Change Manager

Sponsoring Group:
The board-level managers who commission the programme

Programme director or sponsor:
A very senior executive who is the sponsor or champion of the programme– the 'keeper of the programme vision'*

The business change manager
The manager/s responsible for realising the benefits to the organisation of the changes. The 'deliverers of the programme vision'

The programme manager
The manager responsible for the day-to-day management and implementation of the programme through the individual project boards.

The design authority manager (optional role)
The manager/s responsible for ensuring the changes made adhere to the relevant technical standards and policies.

* The keeper of the programme vision is the person(s) who has the vision of what the programme is to achieve and a view of what the organisation will be, and how it will function, when the programme has been completed.

Each member of staff who is allocated one or more of these roles must have a defined and agreed role description. These role descriptions must be regularly reviewed to ensure that they are accurate and up to date, and that the most appropriate person in the organisation has been allocated the role.

4.1.2 Project organisation structure

The typical project management organisation structure comprises three levels:

Diagram 20 **Project organisation structure**

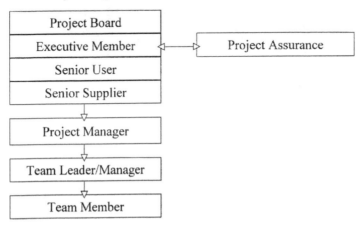

Project board

Typically a minimum of two people are required to fulfil the role of a project board, responsible for the success (or failure) of the project. The members of the board are appointed either by corporate or executive-level management and/or the sponsoring group. Their defined responsibilities and associated tasks (documented) relate to:

- *ensuring ownership of the project;*
- *approving the appointment and responsibilities of the project manager and any persons assigned to the project assurance function;*
- *determining whether the project is, or continues to be, worthwhile;*
- *approving plans and authorising the project to proceed;*
- *ensuring that the project is adequately resourced to*

implement the approved plans;
- *formally accepting the products of the project throughout its existence and at its closure.*

They represent the business, user, and the specialist supplier/provider interests of the particular environment in which the project exists.

Project manager
The role of project manager is defined as someone who is responsible to the project board for the day-to-day management of the project. The project board will delegate authority to the project manager so that decisions, which impact upon the approved timescales and expenditure plans etc., can be made without referral, providing they are within pre-defined limits. This is termed 'control tolerance'.

Project leader/team manager
The project leader/team manager is responsible to the project manager. Their role is defined, documented and assigned to an individual for a stage of the project (possibly to different individuals for different stages). Alternatively, this role could be combined with the project manager role for part, or all, of the project.

4.2 Process Map
As with the organisation structure, both programme and project management methods have a recommended sequence of processes which are subdivided into individual steps. Each of these steps is interlinked with the required deliverables and any of the techniques needed to develop them.

In programme management the following are typical processes or phases:

- **programme identification;**
- **programme definition;**
- **programme execution;**
- **monitoring and control;**
- **benefits realisation;**
- **programme closure and benefits sustainability.**

In project management methods these processes are typically:

- **starting up the project;**
- **initiating the project;**
- **planning;**
- **directing the project;**
- **completing and starting stages;**
- **controlling a stage;**
- **managing product delivery;**
- **closing the project.**

Diagram 21 **Relationship between Programme and Project Management Processes**

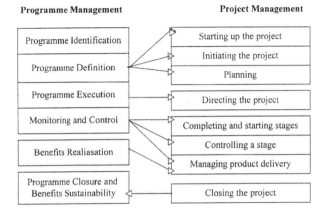

4.3 List of Deliverables

Associated with each of these processes are recommended steps with deliverables accompanied by a deliverable specification. For example, in the programme definition process, the programme management method could recommend the following structure:

Step One
develop and confirm the following deliverables:
investment appraisal and required benefits profile.

Step Two
develop, select and agree the following deliverables:
programme execution options;
benefits realisation and sustainability plan.

Step Three
develop and confirm a programme definition containing:
project profiles, project – programme matrix, programme
definition.

Similarly, the project initiation process in a project management method recommends the following structure:

Step One
develop and agree:
quality plan;
project plan;
defining/refining the business case;
defining/refining the business and project risk identification
and management strategies;
project control structure;
project filing system.

Step Two
develop and agree:
project initiation document.

In both methods, the recommended deliverables are supported with descriptions of the contents and format of each deliverable and, where relevant, a cross-reference to the techniques that should be used in developing them.

4.4 Techniques
Both programme and project management methods provide guidance on which techniques should be used to generate the deliverables.

These techniques include:

- **developing benefits realisation plans;**
- **developing a business case;**
- **planning;**
- **risk management;**
- **issue and change management;**
- **configuration management.**

The methods typically contain an explanation of the basics of the techniques used to develop these deliverables. However, the programme or project manager has to gain a detailed knowledge of these techniques from related training or experience.

5. Interface with the Programme and Project Life Cycles
It will now be obvious that both of these methods interface with the programme or project life cycle described previously.

First, the decision points within the programme or project life cycle coincide with the major processes in each of the programme and project management methods.

Secondly, the documents produced during the programme or project management processes could provide most of the documents needed for the programme and/or project life cycle.

And finally, the techniques used in the programme and project management methods can also be used in the programme or project life cycle.

Diagram 22 **Relationship between Programme or Project Life Cycle and Programme and Project Management Methods**

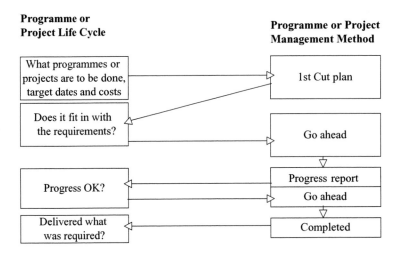

When implementing a PSO and a supporting infrastructure for programmes and projects, it is vital that the design of the infrastructure takes into account these two sets of processes and ensures that they interface efficiently, effectively and economically.

6. Keeping them up to date

Once implemented, it is vital to keep programme and project management methods up to date. This updating involves reviewing the effectiveness and efficiency of each of the components and amending them to reflect the requirements of the organisation. Typically what is found is that, initially, the methods are rigidly applied, but as use and confidence grows, the organisation is able to identify which parts of the methods need this strict application and which do not. Such decisions must be taken in relation to the individual organisation and the type of programmes or projects it undertakes.

The need to update project management methods to reflect any radically new methods of project development is essential. In particular, the growth in the use of sub-components in engineering projects, prefabricated units in the construction industry and rapid application development projects in the IT world, has meant that organisations which use these approaches must amend the techniques used in project management to encompass those used in the projects. In addition, the organisation structure must reflect the devolved decision-making required in these projects.

7. Tuning The Methods

The programme and project management methods described earlier were developed to fit the average programme or project, in the average organisation. It is therefore essential that these methods are tuned to reflect specific programmes or projects.

There are two types of tuning:

- **Macro: Large scale changes**
- **Micro: Small detailed changes**

Only extremely experienced staff, who fully understand the implications of the changes that they are making, should undertake macro-tuning. Usually, the basic structure of processes and the organisation structure is tuned at a macro-level.

The micro-level tuning typically involves redefining one or more of the deliverables, moving a deliverable from one process to another, or amalgamating processes or roles.

What has proved useful for many organisations is to develop and publicise an agreed tailoring approach. This can be a single factor scale – i.e. if the programme or project is of a given size then there are correspondingly things that change – or multi-factored scales can be used, with a range of scaling that can be applied.

Whichever approach is used, it is important that the method is tailored consistently and that the effectiveness of that tailoring is regularly reviewed and, if necessary, amended.

*See example document **28**: The scaling factors to be used on a project management method.*

8. Summary

Most programmes or projects that fail do so because the control systems do not function or are ignored. The key to an effective control system is to use an effective programme or project management method. Such methods must be tailored to reflect the specific needs of a programme or project and regularly updated to reflect new types of projects or organisation requirements.

The programme and project management method must be interfaced with the programme and project life cycles. This ensures that the mechanisms which control the portfolios of programmes and projects are supplied with information to demonstrate that the programmes and projects:

- **are proceeding according to the agreed plan; and**
- **are providing the agreed deliverables.**

Chapter Nine

Project or System Development Methods

1. Introduction

Since time began people have developed things. In addition to the problems of developing something that works, all developers have the additional problems of time, resources and quality. To improve their chances of success, developers have re-used successful ways of working – methods – and adopted new methods necessitated by new technologies or requirements. These methods were traditionally passed on through apprenticeships, education and training processes and documented in books and publications.

project or system development methods are certainly not new, it is only the name – method or methodology – which is new. This chapter looks at:

- **the history and reason for methods;**
- **how they are developed;**
- **their typical components;**
- **how they interface with the programme and project**
  life cycle, and programme and project management methods;
- **how they are used.**

2. The History and Reason for Project or System Development Methods

As an example, I will concentrate on the methods used to develop computer systems. Since the early 1960's there have been millions of people involved in the development of computer-based systems, particularly the development of those supporting commercial applications. When these systems were developed in the 1960's, there was little knowledge of how to approach such a task and some dreadful mistakes were made. Gradually, however, it was recognised that the more successful development projects tended to follow certain phases and steps. These were documented in the 1970's and published by the National Computing Centre (NCC).

Diagram 23 **Relationship between Programme and Project Management Methods and Project or System Development Methods**

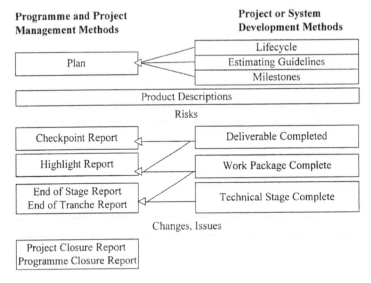

The structure consisted of:

- – **system analysis;**
- – **system design;**
- – **program design;**
- – **program coding.**
- – **program testing;**
- – **system testing;**
- – **acceptance.**

This structure was described as a waterfall method, illustrating how it started narrow at the top and grew wider at the bottom.

However, many systems developers found that this simple structure required enhancements. In particular, the need to supplement it with advice on the processes (which will follow), how to perform them and what the outputs should look like. Meanwhile, other developers preferred to stay within a loose framework and leave the decisions on how it was done and what the outputs looked like to the individual development team.

This hands-off approach worked satisfactorily as long as things were developed on time and to agreed costs, and met the requirements. During the 1970s the requirements for computer systems changed dramatically as they moved from being simple support systems to integral and essential parts of the business process. With this greater importance came greater pressure from the business for these systems to be effective in operation and effectively developed. The management of the organisation also demanded to know the development processes, so that they could be monitored and controlled.

In addition, several major failures of the traditional approach on high-profile projects led managers and developers to seek a more dependable and controlled approach. At the same time the academic and commercial consultancy worlds began to research the benefits from standardising, rationalising and improving these traditional approaches.

By the middle of the 1980's several of the larger consultancies developed complete methods. These methods were developed from their experience in building systems and supplemented by knowledge from the newly emerging branch of computer consultancy – methodology consultants. The commercial companies developed these methods for three purposes:

> **One – it helped their sales process. They could now show the potential client how they would develop the new system and what the phases and outputs would be.**
>
> **Two – their own staff would use the methods when developing the systems and as a result refine and improve the methods.**
>
> **Three – to sell the methods to other companies who had their own in-house development departments with accompanying methodology consultancy.**

In 1987 the UK Government decided that they needed to adopt such a method. They chose the Structured Systems Analysis and Design Method (SSADM), modified from an existing method.

This proved to be a turning point for methods. SSADM was a complete method – it included document standards, techniques and even estimating information for how long each stage would take. Within six months the first computer-based tools to assist the use of methods emerged.

Since then, SSADM has been regularly updated to reflect the needs of today's projects and has been joined by many new methods. One of the most significant was designed to support the use of Rapid Application Development techniques (RAD). Of these, the most famous is the Dynamic Systems Development Method (DSDM).

Today, methods are established – they are part of the education process for students studying computer systems development, they are supported by formal examinations and qualifications and have become integral to the way that computer systems are developed worldwide. The contribution that these methods make to today's sophisticated systems development process cannot be underestimated.

3.   How These Methods are Developed

Project or system development methods are developed from two approaches. Firstly, how we do it now and the second is from research into how it should be done. The two approaches can be combined.

Nearly all the standard waterfall methods that are in use today were initially developed using the first of these approaches. They then used the second approach to improve, or complete, them. The hybrid approach was employed to adapt them to the types of projects or the environment in which they were developed.

Several of the newer methods were developed using the second approach. DSDM, for instance, was first developed in 1994 by the distillation of the experiences of the members of a consortium of consultancy companies, organisations and academic institutions. Together, they constructed a totally new method from the pieces that were available.

Several of the components of these project or system development methods, particularly the techniques and supporting documents, were developed using a slightly different approach – observation and experiment. This approach requires the designer of the component to observe what is currently being used and then try a new output or technique, based on the observed component, but modified to reflect the specific need or requirement.

This approach of observation and experimentation is also used when the need to develop a specially tailored version of the method arises. This need always occurs because the standard method was developed to support the average project in the average organisation. It will not necessarily meet the specific requirements of an organisation or project.

Another approach is employed when it is impossible to meet requirements by tuning or tailoring an existing method. In such cases the approach is one of 'congealed experience'. In this approach the method is built using a large proportion of previous components, but assembled in a different sequence or supplemented with new, or different, techniques and documents. The new method is constructed on the experience of the method's developer.

This type of method construction was used by methodology consultants to construct system development methods for projects that used radically new methods or tools – e.g. 4th Generation Computer Languages – before any practical or academic experience was available.

A final approach used to develop project or system development methods is entirely academically based. A classic example of this type of approach is the development of Euromethod by the EEC in the late 1980's. The purpose of the Euromethod was to provide a method which provided interfaces with all the standard project or system development methods used throughout the EC. Euromethod was constructed from an analysis of the components of the separate methods and by combining them to form a single method.

4.   The Components of a Project or System Development Method

4.1 Typical Components
The contents of each project or system development method vary. However, most of them have the following components:

- **an explanation of the reason for, and when and how to use, the method;**
- **recommended stages or phases;**
- **processes within each of those stages or phases;**
- **steps within each of the processes;**
- **recommend outputs;**
- **recommended techniques to develop these outputs;**
- **roles and responsibilities.**

4.1.1 Reason for, and when and how to use, the method
Almost every method contains an explanation of the purpose of the method and what

types of projects or environments it is designed to be used in. They often give an explanation of the benefits to be gained from its use, why it has the recommended structure of stages or phases, how it links to other project or system development methods and to project and programme management methods.

4.1.2 Recommended stages or phases

The concept of stages or phases is used to subdivide the whole project or system development method into sections. Each of these represents a significant piece of work and indicates where a major decision point in the development process has been reached.

The method also explains the reason for the stage or phase, its start and finish points and why it was placed in its position in the method.

4.1.3 Processes within each of the stages or phases

These methods also describe the processes contained within each of the stages. The definition of these processes contains an explanation of their purpose and their start and finish points. The explanation can also give a summary of the individual steps, outputs and techniques that are to be used. Tuning or tailoring hints are usually provided, particularly in relation to the rearrangement of the processes, steps or outputs. There is also a recommended standard numbering system to identify each of the processes with their relevant stage or phase.

4.1.4 Steps within each of the processes

Each of the processes is then subdivided into steps – again numbered to show which process, stage and phase they belong to. Each of the steps is described in great detail. Some methods include the detailed explanation of the relevant step, while others only give an overview and a cross-reference to other sections of the method where the techniques are described.

The steps also indicate who in the recommended organisation structure is expected to participate in their development and their role. The definition of the steps also includes any interfaces and links with other processes and steps.

4.1.5 Recommended outputs

The format that is used to describe the recommended outputs varies considerably, from a simple description, through to a formal definition with the associated quality criteria, to a full example of the output and a supporting description.

4.1.6 Recommended techniques to develop these outputs

The techniques used to develop the method can be described in great detail or at high level and cross-referenced to a separate section of the method. In early project or system development methods, these descriptions were once so detailed that they overshadowed the description of the rest of the method, resulting in some extremely large methods. The confusion, and eventual separation of the method and the training in the supporting techniques, took a number of releases of the methods to accomplish.

4.1.7 Roles and responsibilities

The inclusion of a recommended management organisation structure with associated roles and responsibilities in the project or system development method was often a major cause of confusion. The reason for the confusion is that when used in conjunction with a project management method (with its own management organisation structure) there was confusion over which of the two structures should be used – in rare instances both were installed – resulting in considerable confusion.

4.2 Other Components

The components described in the previous section are occasionally supplemented with additional components. The inclusion of these additional components came from methods users' demands or were inserted by organisations purely for commercial advantage.

4.2.1 Estimating guidelines

A number of methods include estimating guidelines. These guidelines are high-level and use simple measures that can be used to estimate prior to work being undertaken. For example, in the construction industry there are published tables of the cost and time required to lay a square metre of bricks and also for a complete house. In I.T. an early SSADM estimating system used the number of processes that the system was to include as one of the main measures. However, these estimating systems could be extremely sophisticated when incorporated into, and with, software tools.

4.2.2 Quality control review methods

A number of the methods also include a recommendation of which outputs need to undergo a form of quality control review and the techniques to be used. Like the inclusion of the management organisation structure, this often caused confusion when used in conjunction with the project management method. The general rule is to use the programme or project management method, but take into account the recommendations of the project or system development method.

4.2.3 Short cuts

Several of the methods include advice on permissible short cuts. For example, one I.T. method explained how to move direct from its outputs to a first cut data base design for a specific fourth generation computer language. These short cuts were added in response to demands from the users of the method.

4.2.4 Interfaces with other methods

The growing number of methods has meant that there is a need to explain how the method interfaces with other methods. In some instances there is a direct relationship between the two methods – for example, the Hoskyn's PRISM methods included one for a feasibility study which was interfaced with the one used for the main system development.

5. The Interfaces between the Project or System Development Method and the Programme and Project Life Cycle

The project or system development method provides the delivery mechanism to deliver the programme or project. As a consequence all project or system development methods must interface with the programme and project life cycle. This section explains where these interfaces occur and their use.

Diagram 24 **Relationship between Programme and Project Life Cycle and Project or System Development Methods**

Programme and Project Lifecycle	Project or System Development Methods
Feasibility Study	Feasibility Study
Programme Definition Statement	Programme Initiation Document
Organisation Structure	Organisation Structure
	Plans
	Method of Approach
Risk Analysis	Risk Analysis
	Configuration Management Plan
	Workpackage or Deliverable Specification
	Activity or Product Specification
Progress Reports	Progress Reporting
	Checkpoints
End of Stage Report	End of Stage Report
End of Project Report	End of Project Report

5.1 The Interfaces between the Project or System Development Method and the Programme or Project Life Cycle Control Documents

The interface between these first occurs when the programme, or project, idea is completed at the start of the programme or project life cycle. Here the programme or project requester explains, in high-level terms, the method of approach to be used and estimates the potential size and costs of the programme or project. The project or system development method is also used during the investigations performed in the feasibility study, to provide the high-level plan of the potential programme or project.

During the execution of the project, the progress monitoring and control will also interface with the project or system development method in that the end of the stage, or major technical milestones in the method can also be used in the progress monitoring.

Similarly, at the end of the programme or project, in the programme or project closure report and the post-programme or project review, the effectiveness of the project or system development method and its use is reviewed. The lessons learnt from the reviews and reports must be documented for application in the project or system development method, and thus the method becomes the repository for this knowledge.

5.2 Interfacing the Project or System Development Method with the Programme or Project Management Method

Programme or project management methods control development, so there are many interfaces with project or system development methods. The major interfaces are:

- **the feasibility study;**
- **the programme definition or project initiation document;**
- **organisation structure;**
  plans,
  method of approach,
  risk analysis,
  quality plan,
  configuration management plan.
- **work package or deliverable specification;**
- **activity or product specifications;**
- **progress reporting;**
  checkpoint reports,

highlight reports,
end of stage,
end of project.

5.2.1 The feasibility study

The feasibility study makes use of the information available in the project or system development method when explaining the options available to the organisation to deliver the programme or project.

Firstly, the project or system development method may provide the basis of the high-level plan, its estimated cost and the resources needed. Second, it can give the stages or phases and, third, it can provide a list of the major deliverables. Depending on the type of method used it can also provide recommendations for:

- **who should have what role in the programme or project management organisation structure;**
- **what the arrangements are for quality and configuration management.**

5.2.2 The programme definition or project initiation document

The preparation of the programme and project plan and the description of, and reason for, selecting that particular method of approach can be almost totally based on the information contained in these methods. (Some organisations have extended the traditional format of the methods into a partially completed set of plans complete with network diagrams, schedules and Gantt charts to assist in this process).

In addition, the information provided by the project or system development method can help in defining the management organisation structures and which members of the organisation have what role. It is particularly important here to ensure that a good fit is achieved between this structure's requirements and those from the programme or project management methods. In the unlikely event of any major clashes, the recommendation of the programme or project management method organisation structure must take precedence.

The project or system development method can also help considerably when assessing the risks to the successful completion of the project, as the project or system development method describes what is needed to make the project a success. Any compromises or shortfalls to this in a specific programme or project can give rise to an increase in the potential risks to its success.

The recommendations in the project or system development method for numbering each activity, deliverable, and stage or phase, can provide the basis of the configuration management method. Likewise, the recommendations for which of the deliverables in the project or system development method are subject to what sort of quality review process and the availability of product descriptions, can provide a major part of the quality plan.

*See example document **29**: A project initiation document.*

5.2.3 Work package or deliverable specification

As the programme or project begins execution, there is a need to supply the development team with definitions of the deliverables that are needed. Most project or system development methods provide a definition of these deliverables. The programme or project manager must tailor these to meet the specific requirements of the programme or project.

In addition to this assistance, the project or system development methods often include a definition and explanation of the recommended techniques to develop a deliverable. This can be supplemented with a definition of the output, its contents or format and even a worked example, providing major assistance to the programme or project team.

5.2.4 Progress reporting

The definition of the stages or phases, the major deliverables, the work packages and the products or activities contained in the project or system development method can be used as monitoring points for the programme or project. The stages or phases in the project or system development methods can also be considered as potential stages or phases in the projects themselves. However, it is important to note that simply using these as the stages in a project is incorrect, as the decision of where stages occur is dependent on a number of factors of which the technical development is only one.

The work packages, or major deliverables, identified in the project or system development methods are, however, potential milestones. They should be reported in the highlight and end-of-stage reports, while the products can be used in, or as the basis of, the checkpoint reports.

When preparing end of project stage and closure reports, the programme or project manager reviews the effectiveness and accuracy of the project or system development method in the light of experience. These reviews are critical to the long-term use of project or system development methods because they provide the basis on which they can be regularly reviewed and updated. If these reviews and updates are not performed, the project or system development methods can quickly fall into disuse and disrepair.

6. Use and Abuse of Project or System Development Methods
The project or system development method can provide great assistance to the programme or project manager and team. There are, however, several potential dangers.

The first of these is in the selection of the method itself. The guidance provided in the introduction to the project or system development method, concerning its applicability to certain types of projects, must be taken very seriously.

It is also vital that these methods are not just used slavishly with the 'brain in neutral'. All such methods reflect a typical situation, therefore tailoring and tuning is nearly always needed.

Advice provided by the developers of the methods and experiences from previous projects (obtained via the end of project closure reports) is an essential component in this tuning.

All project or system development methods should be subjected to a process of continual review and updating and must be built into the review process of the organisation's programme and project support infrastructures. These reviews, and the methods, should be driven and owned by the users of the methods – not the PSO. The PSO should only facilitate the process.

7. Summary
The whole of the programme and project support infrastructure should be designed as a single entity and all the life cycles and methods must interface efficiently and effectively. The project or system development methods are an integral part of that structure. They can be extremely useful in providing the linkage for a number of other components of the programme and project support infrastructure – particularly template plans, definitions and examples of deliverables and the basis of the estimating systems.

In order for the methods to be useable, they must relate as closely as possible to the programme and projects being undertaken. Experience has shown that organisations which try to operate their development process with only one project or system development method have great difficulties in obtaining the full benefits that such methods can provide. The most successful organisations are those with a number of such methods, each closely aligned to the types of projects they undertake. Such variations can have a single-parent method or be derivatives of several methods, but what is important is that the users of the method view them as useful and use them, rather than reinventing the wheel every time.

Chapter Ten

Infrastructure to Support Project or System Development Methods

1. Introduction

To obtain the added value benefits from project or system development methods, it is vital that they are supported by an appropriate infrastructure.

This chapter examines:

- **the need for a supporting infrastructure;**
- **what is the aim or function of the infrastructure;**
- **what are the components of the infrastructure;**
- **how these components should be developed; and**
- **how to keep them up to date.**

2. The Need for a Supporting Infrastructure

The use of project or system development methods can assist the organisation in a number of ways, most importantly they assist the programme and project manager to build their plans and specify tasks and deliverables. Project or system development methods also provide the framework to pass the lessons learnt in one programme or project to the next – assuring the organisation that they are managing their programmes and projects in an effective and efficient manner.

However, there is often a lack of enthusiasm from the project or programme managers for the methods. Although they accept that the use of such methods is a good thing, deploying them is not easy. This is often because they are only provided with a single method, which they are expected to tune at both macro and micro-levels, to meet the specific requirements of their programme or project. In addition, the methods are usually not part of an integrated support infrastructure and are just a list of the things to be done.

So, to make them attractive to use instead of a hindrance, the methods must be supported by an infrastructure which is integrated with all the tools and systems used by the programme and project managers, such as template plans, template documents, estimating guidelines, etc.

The supporting infrastructure must also be easy to use and provide real added value to the programme or project managers. An example of such added value is the provision of a library of deliverables from previous programmes or projects that can be re-used.

In addition, the methods need a supporting infrastructure to help training. Often the programme or project manager is given the project or system development method and expected to know how to use it instinctively, sometimes with dire consequences.

3. What is the Aim and Function of the Infrastructure?

The aim and function of this infrastructure are to provide the programme and project manager with as much help as possible in planning, monitoring, controlling and executing the programme or project.

To achieve this, it must provide assistance in the form of a set of interlinked support tools and information systems.

Such infrastructures, if properly designed and implemented, should not just support the programme and project managers. They can also support many other parts of the organisation including human resources, finance and accounts, business units and resource managers. To achieve this holistic support, the infrastructure can be implemented in sections, although it must have been designed originally as a complete structure.

Therefore, when designing the infrastructure, the design team must realise that the support infrastructure is an organisation-wide service, not just restricted to programme and project managers. This means that when identifying the requirements for the infrastructure, they include those from the other parts of the organisation. Infrastructures designed and implemented in this way have a greater chance of becoming integrated into the normal business process of the organisation and have a level of relevance and importance that cannot be ignored by programme or project managers and the organisation as a whole.

However, it must be remembered that the presence of a comprehensive infrastructure does not undermine the need for professional programme or project managers.

4. What are the Components of the Infrastructure?

The following section describes the typical components of an infrastructure to support project or system development methods. The decision as to which of the following components are required must be included in the design of the whole infrastructure to support programmes and projects.

The components described in this section are:

- **multi-system project or system development methods;**
- **templates plans;**
- **development method tools;**
- **data dictionary of tasks/deliverables;**
- **templates for deliverables;**
- **estimating guidelines;**
- **library of deliverables;**
- **skills database;**
- **deliverable/staff database.**

4.1 Multi-Project or System Development Methods

The most essential part of the supporting infrastructure is to provide a range of project or system development methods that align as closely as possible to the types of programmes or projects undertaken by the organisation. This may require up to 20 such methods. The reason for providing a range of methods, is to reduce or eliminate the need for a programme or project manager to macro-tune the method to fit an individual programme or project (leaving only the micro-tuning). To gain the maximum benefit from the use of such methods and to provide an interface with other components in the infrastructure, it is essential that these methods use common naming and numbering conventions for their constituent parts.

To achieve this it is recommended that a data dictionary is created of the deliverables and tasks, with an accompanying numbering system. The data dictionary must include a list of which of the methods use a deliverable or task and an accompanying specification for the item.

The data dictionary is vital. It ensures consistency across the methods and provides the basis for the interconnections with other components in the infrastructure. This data dictionary can be established in a paper format, as a spreadsheet or small database application. Diagram 25 overleaf gives an example.

Diagram25 **Data Dictionary of Tasks**

Data Dictionary WBS No	Description	Document Reference	A - Standard	B - Migration	C - Feasibil	D - Enhance	F - RAD	G – Pack Impl	H - Selection	I – Small	J – Multisub	K - Release	L - Impl	M - Simple	N-Books	O - Incremental
PI-0000	**PROJECT INITIATION FORM**				*				*					*		
PI-1000	Description / Objectives				*				*							
PI-1050	Internal / Departmental Approval / Support memo.				*				*							
PI-1100	Project Sponsor Approval				*				*							
PI-1109	Milestone Idea Sponsored and passed to Project Office				*				*							
PI-1120	Project Office Review Sponsored Idea				*				*							
PI-1130	Business Analyst for Project Initiation Completion appointed	Projref-BA			*				*							
PI-1139	Milestone Business Analyst Appointed				*				*							
PI-1150	Statement of Benefits				*				*							
PI-1200	Market Assessment				*				*							
PI-1250	List Project Expert				*				*							
PI-1300	Project Estimates				*				*							
PI-1350	Detailed Plan & Estimates for Feasibility Study				*				*							
PI-1400	Reviewed Form / Reference No. by Project Office				*				*							
PI-1450	Completed Project Initiation Form Issued	Projref-PIF			*				*							
PI-1500	Masterplan Committee Agenda Item				*				*							
PI-1592	Master Plan Committee Go/No Go for Feasibility				*				*							
PI-1600	Appointment memo. for Project Manager for Feasibility Study	Projref-PM			*				*							

Diagram25a **List of Project or System Development Methods**

Ref	Description	Template Ref	Project Idea Form	Feasibility	Project Definition	Analysis	Design	Development	Testing	Implementation	Close Out	Post Project
A	Standard Development	TEMPLATE.MPP			*	*	*	*	*	*	*	*
B	Migration	MIGRATE.MPP	*	*	*	**	*	*	*	*	*	*
C	Initiation & Feasibility	PICFEAS.MPP		**	**	**					*	
D	Enhancements & Fault Fixes	ENHANCE.MPP					**	*	*	*	*	
E	WEB Development	WEB.MPP									*	
F	RAD	RAD.MPP	*	**	*	*			*	*	*	*
G	Package Implementation	PACKIMPL.MPP			*	**	**	**	*	*	*	*
H	Product Evaluation	SELECTION.MPP					**	**			*	
I	Small Project	SMALLPRJ.MPP			*	**			*		*	
J	Multi Sub Project	MULTISUB.MPP			*	*	**	**	*		**	*
K	Member Release	RELEASE.MPP			*	*	**	**	*	*	*	*
L	Implementation	IMPLEMENT.MPP					*	**	**	**	**	*
M	Simple	SIMPLE.MPP	**	**	**	**	**	**		**	*	**
N	Books/ Brochures	BOOKS.MPP					**	**	**	**		
O	Incremental	INCREMENTAL.MPP			*			**		**	*	*
P	Programme	PROGRAMME.MPP			*		**	**			*	*
	Standard Resource Pool	EURORES.MPP										

Key
* = Standard Phase
** = Modified for type of Project

119

Diagram25b **Data Dictionary**

Data Dictionary/ WBS No	Description	Template-Docref	A - Standard	B - Migration	C - Feasibl	D - Enhance	F - RAD	G - PackImpl	H - Selection	I - Small	J - Multisub	K - Release	L - Impl	M - Simple	N - Books	O - [Incremental]
			Used in which methods													
DE-9901	End of Design Phase Report	Projref-EoDES	*	*		*	*	*		*	*	*	*			*
DV-9901	End of Phase Report	Projref-EoDEV	*	*		*	*	*		*	*	*	*			*
FE-9901	End of Phase Report	Projref-EoF			*									*		
AN-9901	End of Analysis Phase Report	Projref-EofAN	*	*		*	*	*		*	*	*	*			*
IM-9901	End of Phase Report	Projref-EoIMP	*	*		*	*	*		*	*	*	*			*
PC-9901	End of Phase Report	Projref-EoPC	*	*		*	*	*		*	*	*	*			*
PR-9901	End of Phase Report	Projref-EoPIR	*	*		*	*	*		*	*	*	*			*
TE-9905	End of Phase Report	Projref-EoTES				*			*	*		*				
AN-5900	Approved Full Analysis Report	Projref-FAR-1.0	*	*	*	*	*	*		*	*	*	*		*	
FE-7300	Approved Feasibility Study	Projref-FS-1.0	*	*		*	*		*							
PC-1900	Approved Project Closure Report	Projref-PC-1.0	*	*		*	*	*		*	*	*	*			*
PD-1900	Approved Final PDD	Projref-PDD-1.0	*	*	*	*	*	*	*	*	*	*	*			
PI-1450	Completed Project Idea Form Issued	Projref-PIF			*											
PR-1900	Approved Post Project Implementation Review Report	Projref-PIR-1.0	*	*					*							
PI-1130	Business Analyst for Project Idea Completion appointed	Projref-BA							*							
CM-2400	Draft Brochures	Projref-BR-0.1	*	*												*
CM-2900	Approved Brochures	Projref-BR-1.0	*	*												*
DV-7580	First Draft Development Department Documents	Projref-DD-0.1		*												
DV-7590	Approved Development Department Documents	Projref-DD-1.0		*												
DV-4850	Draft Release Package	Projref-DR(n)-0.1				*					*	*	*		*	*
DV-4900	Approved Release Package to CTG	Projref-DR(n)-1.0				*					*	*	*		*	*
AN-5850	Draft Full Analysis Report Review	Projref-FAR-0.1	*	*		*	*	*		*						
FE-7550	Appointment memo. for Project Manager for Project	Projref-FPM	1		*	*			*							
FE-6100	Draft Feasibility Report	Projref-FR-0.1	*	*	*				*							
FE-6850	Issued Draft Feasibility Report	Projref-FR-1.0	*	*	*		*		*							
AN-1850	Issued Full Requirements Analysis Report	Projref-FRA	*			*	*					*	*			*
FE-7250	Second Draft Feasibility Study	Projref-FS-0.1			*				*							
DE-1900	Approved Full System Design Report	Projref-FSD(n)-1.0	*			*				*		*	*			*
DV-5850	Draft Implementation / Roll Out / Migration Plan	Projref-IRM-0.1	*			*				*		*	*			*

4.2 Templates Plans

To support the methods, a set of template plans should be available in all the programme and project planning software tools, word processing documents and spreadsheet formats used in the organisation. They should also have the relevant skill or resource codes pre-allocated to the component parts. The plans should be provided at three levels:

- level one: programme/project
- level two: project phase
- level three: work package,deliverable or task level.

To ensure these plans interface with other components of the infrastructure, they must use the same numbering and naming conventions as those contained in the data dictionary.

4.3 Development Method Tools

Another vital component of the project or system development methods' support infrastructure is development method tools. These tools take a wide variety of forms. The simplest can be a spreadsheet used to perform a specific task or process, for example, a spreadsheet can calculate the net present value when preparing a business case, while there are more sophisticated tools to support activities such as business benchmarking or analysis. There may also be extremely sophisticated software tools to support specific activities such as computer aided design tools for site layouts. All such tools must be integrated not only with each other but also with the other parts of the project or system development method. Such integration can take the form of ensuring that all the software tools provided use the same terminology as the methods or have any method standards (for example drawing conventions and rules) already incorporated.

4.4 Data Dictionary of Tasks/Deliverables

The data dictionary described earlier in this section can be regarded as the centre point of the support infrastructure. As well as ensuring consistency in the naming and numbering of the deliverables and tasks in the development process, it also provides links to other parts of the infrastructure described in this section.

In addition to this linkage, it also enables the organisation to regularly review the costs and methods used, as the data dictionary can show the existing costs and resources devoted to these standard activities. It can also identify where improvement projects should be commissioned to reduce the expenditure on these activities in the future.

The data dictionary provides great assistance when the organisation needs a new or updated project or system development method because the programme or project manager can 'pick and mix' from the existing components to provide components needed for the new method. In addition, if the data dictionary is linked to other parts of the infrastructure, it may be possible to generate a large proportion of the components of the programme or project plans.

Diagram26 **Example Template Plans**

WBS	Description	Template Reference
DE-9901	End of Design Phase Report	Projref-EoDES
DV-9901	End of Phase Report	Projref-EoDEV
FE-9901	End of Phase Report	Projref-EoF
AN-9901	End of Analysis Phase Report	Projref-EofAN
IM-9901	End of Phase Report	Projref-EoIMP
PC-9901	End of Phase Report	Projref-EoPC
PR-9901	End of Phase Report	Projref-EoPIR
TE-9905	End of Phase Report	Projref-EoTES
AN-5900	Approved Full Analysis Report	Projref-FAR-1.0
FE-7300	Approved Feasibility Study	Projref-FS-1.0
PC-1900	Approved Project Closure Report	Projref-PC-1.0
PD-1900	Approved Final PDD	Projref-PDD-1.0
PI-1450	Completed Project Idea Form Issued	Projref-PIF
PR-1900	Approved Post Project Implementation Review Report	Projref-PIR-1.0
PI-1130	Business Analyst for Project Idea Completion appointed	Projref-BA
CM-2400	Draft Brochures	Projref-BR-0.1
CM-2900	Approved Brochures	Projref-BR-1.0
DV-7580	First Draft Development Department Documents	Projref-DD-0.1
DV-7590	Approved Development Department Documents	Projref-DD-1.0
DV-4850	Draft Release Package	Projref-DR(n)-0.1
DV-4900	Approved Release Package to CTG	Projref-DR(n)-1.0
AN-5850	Draft Full Analysis Report Review	Projref-FAR-0.1
FE-7550	Appointment memo. for Project Manager for Project	Projref-FPM
FE-6100	Draft Feasibility Report	Projref-FR-0.1
FE-6850	Issued Draft Feasibility Report	Projref-FR-1.0
AN-1850	Issued Full Requirements Analysis Report	Projref-FRA
FE-7250	Second Draft Feasibility Study	Projref-FS-0.1
DE-1900	Approved Full System Design Report	Projref-FSD(n)-1.0
DV-5850	Draft Implementation / Roll Out / Migration Plan	Projref-IRM-0.1
DV-5900	Approved Implementation / Roll Out / Migration Plan	Projref-IRM-1.0
IM-2850	Draft Installed System Report	Projref-IS-0.1
IM-2900	Approved Installed System Report	Projref-IS-1.0

4.5 Templates For Deliverables

The supporting infrastructure should also contain templates for the deliverables within the project or system development method. These templates provide useful assistance to both the programme and project managers and other processes, for example, in the sales process to explain what will be delivered. They can also provide a useful start in installing a quality management system for the development activities and are extremely useful when incorporated into the training programme for new staff. The templates must be stored using the same reference numbers and names as used in the project or system development method and, of course, the data dictionary.

4.6 Estimating Guidelines

An essential support to the project or system development method is a system of estimating guidelines.

These guidelines need to be available at three levels, providing estimates for:

- **at the highest level, the whole project or system development method;**
- **at the next level, each of the standard stages of the method;**
- **finally, the individual deliverables or tasks.**

It is vital to remember that these are guidelines and therefore will be inaccurate. There are a number of approaches that can be adopted for documenting these guidelines; the best is the nine box matrix. This is used to store nine estimates for small, medium and large sizes of programmes or projects and if they are easy, difficult or very difficult etc.

When preparing these estimating guidelines, it is vital to use appropriate measures for these general terms and that the estimates are consistent, particularly in respect of what is included in the estimate. The better estimating systems include:

- **the total elapsed time or duration; and**
- **the actual pure work effort of each category of resource involved.**

4.7 Library of Deliverables

One of the most valued parts of the infrastructure is the library of deliverables.

The library provides a programme or project manager with a considerable amount of help. It is commonly found that the re-use of a deliverable can reduce the typical

Diagram27 **Estimating Guidelines**

	SMALL 1-2 days	MEDIUM 3-5 days	LARGE 10 days
SIMPLE (based on existing course or material)	6 MAN DAYS	8 MAN DAYS	10 MAN DAYS
MEDIUM (up to 50% new material)	20 MAN DAYS	24 MAN DAYS	32 MAN DAYS
LARGE (all new material)	30 MAN DAYS	45 MAN DAYS	60 MAN DAYS

development time for a deliverable by up to 60%. This is because a previous deliverable provides a template for the new programme or project and shows what is required.

The contents of the library need to be named and referenced to match those of the data dictionary and the project or system development methods. If the same deliverable exists in a number of the project or system development methods then, although it is given the same reference number, a suffix should be added to identify which particular type of project or system development method it relates to.

When initially collecting these documents to form the library, the PSO usually devotes a large amount of effort to get these into a standard format. However, experience has shown that this is a waste of time. Far more benefit is obtained from ensuring the library contains as many examples of deliverables as possible, rather than getting them looking the same.

4.8 Skills Database
Most human resources (HR) departments hold scant information about the detailed skills their staff have as a result of day-to-day work. Similarly, a large number of resource or line managers do not have any formal records of what skills their staff have, and rely on their memory or what their staff tell them. The PSO can help both the HR and line or resource managers by holding such records centrally. These records should include deliverables or tasks staff have worked on and details of any training or skill enhancement they have undertaken. The PSO is in an ideal position to collect this information as it has access to programme and project plans .

The information should be held in a similar structure to that of the data dictionary for deliverables, except here the records refer to the members of staff – the attributes of the record are their skills and information about what they did in the programme and project. This information can then be used in a large number of management processes including planning training and skills enhancement, appraisal reviews etc.

Diagram28 **Staff Skills Database**

Skill Block	Detail Skill	Business Analysis Staff						
		RJF	DEM	JWK	DLP	CLM	JWM	GD
Project Start Up								
	Project Initiation Forms	X						X
	Project Estimation	X	X	X	X	X	X	
	Data Analysis	X			X	X	X	
	Method of Approach	X		X	X			X
	Infrastructure	X	X	X		X		X
	Feasibility Study Reports	X		X	X		X	
Project Initation		X		X			X	X
	Project Manager	X	X					
	Project Planning		X			X		
	Project Organisation structure	X					X	X
	Product Descriptions	X	X		X		X	X
	Risk Analysis	X				X	X	X

4.9 Deliverable/Staff Database

The provision of a database of which members of staff worked on what deliverable on which programme or project can also be of great benefit to a number of departments. This information can be vital to the programme, project and line or resource managers when they are preparing programme and project plans. The information can also be vital when the organisation is either preparing or executing exception situation plans and can enable the organisation to analyse what experience its staff has and to define training accordingly.

5. How to Develop the Infrastructure

The design and development of the supporting infrastructure is best achieved by managing it as a project. Failure to recognise that this is a project and manage it accordingly will result in delay or failure.

The PSO must be constructed to an agreed design. The purpose of that design is to provide an infrastructure that will support the organisation; it is the organisation which is the owner, not the PSO.

The difficulties to be faced in such a project are just like any other project. What is important is that it is recognised as a project. A lack of recognition is, regrettably, very common. The reason for this lack of awareness is best illustrated in the 'plan the plan' experience given to all new Hoskyn's (now part of Gemini Ernst Young) consultants.

Diagram29 **Deliverable Staff Database**

WBS	Description	RJF	DEM	JWK	DLP	CLM	JWM	GD
DE-9901	End of Design Phase Report	X	X		X		XX	XX
DV-9901	End of Phase Report	X						XX
FE-9901	End of Phase Report	X	X	X	X	X	XXXX	
AN-9901	End of Analysis Phase Report	X				X	X	
IM-9901	End of Phase Report	X		X				
PC-9901	End of Phase Report	X	X	XX		X		XX
PR-9901	End of Phase Report	X			X		X	
TE-9905	End of Phase Report	X		XX			X	XX
AN-5900	Approved Full Analysis Report	X	X		X	X		
FE-7300	Approved Feasibility Study							
PC-1900	Approved Project Closure Report	X		XX		X	X	XX
PD-1900	Approved Final PDD	X			X			
PI-1450	Completed Project Idea Form Issued	X				X	XXX	XX
PR-1900	Approved Post Project Implementation Review Report			XX	X			
PI-1130	Business Analyst for Project Idea Completion appointed				X	X		
CM-2400	Draft Brochures		X		X			X
CM-2900	Approved Brochures		X		X	X	X	XX
DV-7580	First Draft Development Department Documents				X			
DV-7590	Approved Development Department Documents		X	XXX		X	X	X
DV-4850	Draft Release Package	X	X		X			
DV-4900	Approved Release Package to CTG	X	X	XXX	XXX			
AN-5850	Draft Full Analysis Report Review	X	X			X	X	X
FE-7550	Appointment memo. for Project Manager for Project	X	X					
FE-6100	Draft Feasibility Report	X	X	XXX	X	X	XX	X
FE-6850	Issued Draft Feasibility Report		X		X			
AN-1850	Issued Full Requirements Analysis Report	X	X		X			X
FE-7250	Second Draft Feasibility Study		X					
DE-1900	Approved Full System Design Report	X	X	X	X		XX	
DV-5850	Draft Implementation / Roll Out / Migration Plan						X	
DV-5900	Approved Implementation / Roll Out / Migration Plan			X	X	XX		
IM-2850	Draft Installed System Report			X				
IM-2900	Approved Installed System Report							

As part of their basic training they are asked by their manager to prepare a plan for a feasibility study. The new consultant starts work on constructing the plan. After a few minutes their boss is back demanding to know where the plan is and when it will be ready. The new consultant replies that they are working on it and will have it available as soon as possible. After many iterations of this the boss asks: 'Where is your plan for the development of the plan?' Thus the new consultant learns that if the job is a plan then you need a plan for developing the plan.

Similarly, don't forget to apply programme or project management approaches and disciplines.

5.1 The Structure of the PSO Implementation Project

There are many ways that such a project could be structured. However there are a few basic rules that need to be followed to help maximise the chance of success.

5.1.1 Create a design for the infrastructure

The creation of a design for all elements of the infrastructure is critical. Just as critical is to ensure that the organisation understands, and shares, the vision of this new infrastructure and takes ownership of it – as it does with all other business support functions such as finance and accounts.

To achieve this successfully the project manager will need both to educate and to inform the organisation about the purpose, benefits and contents of the infrastructure – just like any other project. Thus the design process should ensure that as many of the users of the method as possible are involved in the specification and design activities.

The design process must include the opportunity for the potential users to be educated about what a PSO infrastructure can provide. Therefore the design process will probably need to be carried out through a series of workshops or meetings. Failure to recognise this, and to rush through the design stage, will result in substantial change requests to the project.

5.1.2 Use open or national standards

A very common mistake is for the project team to work on the basis that bespoke is best. Experience has shown that the benefits (if there are any) provided by this approach are hardly ever realised. In addition, a bespoke approach costs considerably more time and resources to build and maintain. It is far better to use open or national standards – particularly for programme and project management methods and project or system development methods.

In addition, the use of an open method means it is easier for new staff with relevant skills to be recruited, there are a greater number of suppliers of support services and there may be a user group where experiences and information can be shared.

5.1.3 Macro-tune bought-in components
If any components of the infrastructure are 'bought in', for example national or open standards etc., there is no point in spending effort in micro-tuning these before they are included in the infrastructure.

However macro-tuning is important. This is because the macro-tuning will ensure that these components link with, or use, terminology that is in common use in the organisation, speeding up their acceptance. If micro-tuning is carried out before staff have experience in the use of the standard, the tuning will rapidly become out of date. This is due to the learning curve effect – until the organisation has used it, it does not know how it wants to use it. Therefore, micro-tuning before initial use is a complete waste of time.

5.1.4 Follow the 80/20 rule
When designing how the project should implement the new infrastructure, it is important to follow the 80/20 rule. This means: implement the 80% of the infrastructure that provides the most benefit to the organisation first – which typically only takes about 20% of the effort needed for the whole thing. It is also important to provide those components of the infrastructure whose functionality supports 80% of its end users.

This will mean that the infrastructure starts providing real benefits very quickly (gain before pain), proving that the PSO infrastructure is a worthwhile project and should receive the full support of the organisation.

5.1.5 Value added components first
The choice of which component to develop and implement first must always follow the principle of providing value added components first. This means those parts of the infrastructure which are acknowledged by the organisation as representing real benefits or gains. Typically these are elements of the infrastructure that improve or support the strategic and tactical decision-making. A common mistake when implementing this structure is to assume that the most important task is to support the programme and project manager first. It is vital to remember there is generally more benefit from doing the right programmes and projects than doing them right!

5.1.6 Re-use existing components

An important approach to follow is: re-use rather than redevelop. All support infrastructures will need to be updated as they are used to reflect the specific requirements of a programme or project. As a consequence there is little point in spending considerable effort in redeveloping the components of the infrastructure so that they are 'right' because in reality they never will be. Therefore, the infrastructure should be developed to provide a useable solution as quickly as possible.

The fastest way to provide this is to re-use as much of the existing information and components as possible when creating the infrastructure and amend them as a result of use. The only adjustment recommended is to bring the components in line with any data dictionary standard numbering or naming conventions.

5.1.7 Sell the gain, remove the pain

The overriding principle is gain first, pain later. Organisations will accept that the infrastructure will need to be installed in phases and they will also understand that at the start the infrastructure will not be as complete or as accurate as it will be, providing they:

- **receive benefits early;**
- **understand and accept that this approach is being used.**

The PSO project must provide the benefits and ensure that the organisation recognises the benefits that have been obtained.

It is worth building into the PSO project an assessment of the attitude changes and communication aspects needed, both to ensure the organisation recognises the benefits, and to and ensure that relevant actions are included in the project plan.

6. Keeping the Infrastructure up to date

The need for a regular review and maintenance of the infrastructure should be included in the project documentation and also considered in the design and development activities. For example, if the programme and project management methods are reviewed by the programme and project managers who use them, then it would be prudent to use these members of staff in any redevelopment activities. Also, it is important to ensure they understand that they will be expected to help in the ongoing regular review and maintenance of the methods.

The following section provides some guidance on how to keep the infrastructure up to date and how these points should be included in the PSO infrastructure implementation project.

6.1 Review Periods

The programme and project support infrastructure should be operated under a regime of continual review and updating. However, it needs to have a full review approximately every eighteen months. This review should examine what parts of the infrastructure are being used currently, what elements are not being used and also what new or re-engineered elements should be included.

In addition to this formal review process, the infrastructure should be designed to be regularly updated on a self-maintenance basis. This self-maintenance is, for example, at the end of the programme or project when the PSO, on behalf of the programme or project manager:

- **includes the deliverable in the deliverable library;**
- **updates the skills and deliverable/staff databases;**
- **updates the estimating guidelines.**

Such regular reviews should be thought about and designed into the processes and procedures of the programme and project support infrastructure during the implementation project.

6.2 Audit Use and Keep Figures

Another important feature to consider and include in the design of the infrastructure is the need to be able to audit the use of the infrastructure and to quantify that use.

The information needed to support the eighteen-month review process should be considered and, during the programme and project support infrastructure design project, mechanisms and procedures installed that will provide the information needed to perform the reviews.

These statistics will also help verify the business case upon which the project was based and provide valuable evidence that the PSO is continuing to provide value for money services.

6.3 Measure Success (and Failures) of Support Provided

As for audit information there is a vital need to provide information on the successes and failures of the support infrastructure. To collect this information effectively and efficiently it is important that it is included in the design of the infrastructure.

The collection of information could become part of the procedure by which users gain access to the infrastructure, or included in the end of programme or project closure reports or post programme or project review process.

What is important is that this is designed into the process at the start and not just 'tacked on' at a later stage.

6.4 Encourage Users to Identify and Recommend Changes

It is vitally important for the long-term use of the infrastructure for its users to own it. This transfer of ownership can only be achieved if the users know that when they identify and recommend changes, these are gratefully received and dealt with efficiently and effectively.

As with the other parts of this section, it is essential that not only are the processes to achieve this built into the design for the infrastructure, but the attitude of the PSO staff and users must be in agreement. In particular, members of the PSO must view these changes as an opportunity to extend the life of the PSO (and their job) – they should not view them as an encumbrance or nuisance.

6.5 Look Forward as Well as Back

Most infrastructures will be developed to support the programmes and projects of today and yesterday, not normally of tomorrow.

When designing the infrastructure, the need to support future programmes and projects must be taken into account. This can mean that the infrastructure will need to be available in a format that can be easily re-used and reconfigured. Also, the maintenance processes must include the ability to look forward.

This will need to be included in the terms of reference and budgetary provision for the PSO; the organisation must be aware that it will need to invest in forward planning for the programmes and projects of tomorrow.

6.6 Look For More Automated and/or Logical Structure

Another function to keep the infrastructure up to date is to increase the use of automated tools and to provide the infrastructure as a logical PSO rather than a physical one.

Although initially the use of integrated support software tools may not be deployed, they should be considered in the design so that when they are deployed, minimal changes to the processes and procedures are required.

To achieve this, it is important that during the development process the requirements for, and required functionality of, such tools are examined and defined and a possible architecture for such an environment defined.

The concept of providing as much of the infrastructure in a logical form, i.e. with minimal human intervention, should be incorporated into the design of the infrastructure and its processes. As with the automation aspects, it is important that this is considered during the design of the infrastructure. For example, it can be incorporated into the procedure for updating the data dictionary with a new element.

6.7 Identify Hot Spots for Further Development Projects

While researching and designing the infrastructure it is certain that other areas of concerns (Hot Spots) are identified. These should be documented and included in the end of project report for inclusion in a further project. Concerns that may emerge are:

- **interfacing the infrastructure with other departments' systems;**
- **providing information from the infrastructure to other departments;**
- **extending the infrastructure to cover the activities of other departments.**

It is important that the programme and project support infrastructure project remains on course and only extends into other areas under control as it is to easy to over-respond to such hot spots.

6.8 Sell Its Use to Others

As well as developing the infrastructure, it is also extremely important to use the infrastructure development process to assist in selling the concept and benefits of the PSO infrastructure to other parts of the organisation. This can be accomplished, for example, in the design process, by involving other departments in the identification of the requirements and the management of the project itself. This is a painless way of selling and can achieve substantial results.

On one such project the inclusion of the accounting department in the requirements specification workshop not only identified further uses of the information in the budgeting process, it also broke down barriers that had been present for many years between the two departments concerned.

7. Summary

Without an efficient and effective infrastructure to support them, project or system development methods stand little chance of fulfilling their maximum potential.

The need to design and develop a supporting infrastructure is paramount. The development project used to design and implement this infrastructure helps ensure that the organisation understands what the programme and project support infrastructure is trying to achieve and the benefits it will provide.

Chapter Eleven

Other Programme and Project Support Services

1. Introduction

Having implemented a successful PSO the organisation often identifies other activities for which it could provide support services.

This chapter examines why the PSO should consider providing other support services and what form this additional support could take for:

- **programme and project life cycle;**
- **programme and project management methods;**
- **programme and project managers;**
- **programmes and projects;**
- **the organisation in general.**

2. Why Should the PSO Provide Other Services?

Before looking at the detail of what other services the PSO could provide, it is worth considering why the PSO should do this rather than any other department in an organisation.

2.1 Economies of Scale

This term describes the way in which a lower unit cost can be achieved with increased levels of output. The term was first used in manufacturing to support the concepts of mass production. However, it also reflects the fact that adding activities to an existing department can result in a lower unit cost per output than setting up a new department.

Thus in the case of the PSO, it could take on other activities related to the functions it already provides to programmes and projects without major increases to the number of managers or other overheads.

2.2 Logical or Actual Links With Other Activities

Another reason for extending PSO services is that of linking up activities logically or physically because they share the same source information. However, care must be taken as the PSO may end up running everything. Nevertheless, adopting this approach with care can yield considerable benefits as it helps eliminate duplicated data (and possible mistakes) and overlapping, or duplicated, functionality.

2.3 One Stop Shop

One of the most common additional services is the provision of a one stop shop for all programme and project management services. This is particularly attractive to organisations because, in today's complex organisation structures, particularly those using matrix management methods, it can be extremely difficult to identify who is responsible for what.

2.4 Who Else Has or Could Provide the Information?

A similar reason to that of logical or actual links is that of who else has, or could, provide the information. If designed and implemented to meet the organisation's needs for programme or project support, it is extremely likely that the PSO infrastructure already contains some of the information needed to provide the new support service, or could be extended with a little additional effort to include that information.

2.5 Existing Links with Programmes and Projects

Providing any new service or function can be problematic because the new team will need to establish relationships and understandings with other managers. The PSO already has existing links with programme and project managers, so it will be easier for the PSO, rather than a new group, to deal with them.

3. Programme and Project Life Cycle Support

The first area where these additional services could be provided is that of the programme and project management life cycle. The following section examines the possible areas of support that could be provided by the PSO.

3.1 Custodian and Maintenance of Life Cycles

The programme and project life cycle will need to be supported to ensure the life cycle is regularly reviewed and the supporting standards maintained. This ensures they continue to reflect the requirements of the organisation and interface with the relevant business functions and processes.

3.2 Custodian of Life Cycles Supporting Methods and Processes

The PSO can also maintain the methods and processes used to support the life cycles. For example, the method of developing the business case and the supporting approval processes, and the links to the organisation's finance and budgeting systems, must be regularly maintained to ensure they reflect changes in discount rates and accounting and budgeting processes.

3.3 Portfolio Management Support (Masterplan Committee)

The processes and standards used by the organisation to support the management of its portfolio of programmes, projects, and business-as-usual, sickness, holiday and authorised absence activities can also be maintained by the PSO. For example, the organisation will need to amend or update the codes or other categorisations applied to these areas and the PSO can ensure that the information contained in this process continues to support the associated business processes.

3.4 Custodian of Records and Documents (Configuration Management)

The use of the programme and project life cycle by the organisation will generate considerable correspondence and other records and documents. The PSO could easily extend the support it provides into these areas with the provision of an information database and the configuration management of those documents and records. For example, it may provide a database which records the history, current situation and progress information on all the programmes and projects in the portfolio.

3.5 High-Level Estimating Guidelines and Information

A natural extension to the support of the programmes and projects is the extraction of estimating information (metrics) and other information to assist business processes. For example, the PSO can provide information about a programme or project's duration and resources to the methods and engineering section to identify which types of programmes or projects could benefit from methods re-engineering activities.

3.6 Benchmarks and Other Performance Measures Publication

There is a wide range of other information that can be extracted from a programme's or project's records that would be of use to other departments. For example, benchmark and other performance measures could be supplied to support the annual report process, or could be used to compare the operation of the organisation with others. The information could also be used to support sales and marketing activities.

4. Programme and Project Management Method Support

The PSO could also provide additional services to support the programme and project management methods.

In examining these possible additional services, this section makes no assumptions about what may have already been included in the PSO as part of the orginal design process.

4.1 Custodian and Maintenance of the Methods

Once the programme and project management methods have been installed, it will be necessary to maintain and update them. The maintenance and update activities include ensuring that the methods will support forthcoming programmes and projects, updating them to reflect the contents of the lessons learnt reports, and any changes to the methods that they were based on e.g. PRINCE to PRINCE2. Although the PSO may be the custodian and responsible for the maintenance, it is vital that the updates are carried out by the users of the methods to ensure that ownership of the methods remains with them on behalf of the organisation. The PSO should facilitate the maintenance and updating, not be responsible for the content.

4.2 Custodian and Maintenance of Supporting Processes

In a similar way the PSO should also ensure that the supporting processes are updated. In particular, the PSO must ensure that the interfaces between the programme and project management method processes and the organisation's business processes are kept in step. This is because business processes often change to reflect new requirements and operational processes.

4.2 Custodian and Maintenance of Supporting Standards and Templates

The programme and project management methods and processes are supported by standards and templates that will need to be regularly maintained and updated. These updates may be identified as part of the regular reporting process at the end of a programme tranche or a project stage. The need to update them can also be identified through the programme or project issue or change process. What is important is that the full effects of these issues or changes are considered before they are implemented, as it is easy to inadvertently affect other components in the PSO infrastructure when making minor amendments. Also, such all changes must be discussed and agreed with the users of the revised standards and templates.

4.3 Custodian of Records and Documents (Configuration Management)
The PSO could provide custodianship of records and documents from programmes and projects. Programmes and projects generate a considerable amount of records and documents, all of which will need to be subjected to configuration management. It may be more economic for the PSO to provide this service on behalf of all the programmes and projects.

4.3 Estimating Guidelines and Information
The PSO could also take over the maintenance and updating of the estimating guidelines or metrics and other information from the programmes or projects. As with some of the other services described in this section, it is essential that the users of this information are involved in its maintenance and updating.

4.4 Benchmarks and Other Performance Measures Publication
A well designed PSO infrastructure can provide a number of benchmarks or other performance measures. As with all the other components of the PSO infrastructure it is important this information is kept up to date. The PSO should take charge of this process by regularly auditing its knowledge database of who has what information, when, for what purpose and for what deliverables. This review may need to be carried out every few months during the initial PSO set-up, moving to an annual cycle once it has been fully established.

5. Programme and Project Manager Support
One of the most common areas in which the PSO provides additional services is in supporting programme and project managers. The range of additional services in this area is extremely large, and this section concentrates on those which have proved to give added value.

5.1 Consultancy, Coaching and Mentoring
Providing consultancy, coaching and mentoring to programme or project managers is a very popular additional service. The PSO can either supply this service or organise the provision of these services through third-party suppliers. In some organisations this service is extended to the provision of a skills group leader whose role is to review and identify ways of improving the skills of the existing programme or project managers.

There is a variation on this, where the PSO maintains a register of those members of the organisation who can provide these services or have specialist skills in programme or project management, such as the organisation's project planning software.

5.2 Sources of Training and Qualifications

There is a wide range of training and qualifications available for programme and project managers. The PSO could become the knowledge centre for this information and maintain a detailed database on behalf of line and resource managers and the human resources or training departments. If such a database is established, it is vital that the PSO informs all relevant members of the organisation that they provide this service.

5.3 Deliverable Production (Subcontracted to the PSO)

This is becoming increasingly common in large organisations. The PSO acts as an internal consultancy – the programme or project manager asks the PSO to quote for a particular deliverable and, if happy with the quote, it is given the work. Some PSOs combine this service with those in previous sections and offer the service using external contractors as well as their own staff.

5.4 Research and Information Services

A large number of programmes and projects will require research and information services. Examples of such services are identifying benchmarks in other organisations, identifying products or services that may be required or commissioning research into new methods of operating existing processes. As before, the PSO could either supply these services or provide them under contract through third-party suppliers.

5.5 Procurement of Resources

A number of PSOs have extended their services into the procurement of resources for programmes or projects. This type of service is usually deployed in those organisations that undertake programmes or projects that require a large proportion of their resources to be provided from outside the organisation.

This service could include finding various resources, but leaving the final decision of which to use to the programme or project manager. The service could also support the ordering and purchasing process, by performing the process for the programme or project manager, or facilitating it through relevant departments. Another support service could be the overseeing and managing of the procurement delivery process. This support typically involves chasing the supplier for overdue items, checking the delivery was as required and certifying the delivery note for payment.

5.6 Subcontract of Processes (e.g. Configuration Management, Planning Etc.)

The final area of support to programme and project managers is that of sub-contracting some of the processes used by the programme or project managers to the PSO. This type of PSO service is particularly common in those organisations which operate on a centralised basis, as they then exploit the economies of scale and the benefits of central control that the service can provide.

6. Programme and Project Support

This section examines the additional services that can be supplied direct to the programmes or projects. For many organisations a number of these will have been included in the original terms of reference for the PSO.

6.1 Administration Support

This is one of the most common additional services the PSO supplies. These services can include secretarial services, meetings, hotel and travel arrangements, filing and all types of general support. It is extremely useful to the programme or project manager and the organisation. However, providing this type of service can typecast the PSO as an administration function. To prevent this, it is advisable to put this type of support function as a separate service within the PSO and to insist that it is paid for out of the programme or project budget.

6.2 Process Support (e.g. Risk Management, Planning Etc.)

Supporting these processes, particularly those which require specialist input such as risk management and planning, should also be considered. This support can simply be advice or actually performing functions for the programme or project. As with other services, the justifications for centralising these services are the economies of scale, standardisation and the benefits of having all the information in one place. However, the programme or project manager must make sure to keep control of these centrally provided services.

6.3 Information on Planning and Other Tools

Most organisations use standard planning and other tools. However, there may be the need to deploy non-standard or additional tools in special situations. The PSO can support this by maintaining information and even copies of the more specialist tools. They can also keep information on which staff in the organisation have used these tools. In addition, the PSO could store copies of any tests or other evaluations of such tools which are in the public domain, or any specialist information system that can be consulted about the tools.

6.4 Standards, Templates, Examples, etc.

Nearly all PSOs provide some form of service in respect of standards, templates and examples. It is important that this service is regularly reviewed and updated to ensure that performance is at the required level.

6.5 Resource and Asset Registers

The final area discussed in this section is the maintenance and updating of resource and asset registers. Many organisations do not keep an itemised inventory of the hardware, software, and other assets deployed to use and support their business. The Year 2K problems highlighted this when many organisations found they had no central register of hardware and software.

By keeping and updating these registers, the PSO can provide a useful service not only to the programme and project managers, but also these registers can be useful throughout the organisation. The number and types of assets included in these registers will vary widely, as with the other information sources mentioned earlier in this section. It is important that all other relevant parts of the organisation are aware of these registers so that they are not duplicated or contradictory.

7. Support to Other Parts of the Organisation

This section concentrates on those other parts of the organisation regularly supported by the PSO. Experience has shown that when the PSO has extended into these areas, it is renamed, or its activities are split into a new business function such as corporate planning support.

7.1 Corporate Planning

One of the important areas of support provided to the corporate planning function is the provision of information on the current and projected portfolio of the organisation's activities. To further support this process, the PSO can also supply information on typical durations and resources required for all the activities in the portfolio. It is important that the organisation knows the total workload including non-productive work – sickness, holidays, authorised absence, etc. – so the PSO can provide estimating guidelines and other benchmarks for corporate planning based on the whole picture – the reality.

7.2 Operational Support

Another important area for support is the day-to-day operations. At its simplest, this can be the provision of information on non-project work – sometimes called business-as-usual or non-productive work. This information can be used to support the annual budgeting and manpower processes, or to define benchmarks that can identify where business process re-engineering might be usefully deployed.

7.3 Sales Process

One of the most critical business functions is sales. The sales function always needs to have information on what would be the likely cost, delivery date, etc. for prospective sales opportunities. The PSO can assist this by providing information on the portfolio of current activities and also high-level estimates of how much time or resources the current or proposed activities, programmes or projects will take.

7.4 Human Resources

Considerable additional support services can be provided to the human resources (HR) department. Most human resources departments have little access to the details of the work undertaken by the development and business-as-usual teams. It is very useful to HR if the PSO maintains a deliverable/staff database, identifying what deliverables have been developed by which members of staff and which members of staff undertake what business-as-usual activities. In addition to supporting the HR departments, this can also assist line or resource managers in the staff appraisal and career development processes.

7.5 Finance and Accounts

The finance and accounts departments can also be supported by the provision of additional services from the PSO. Of particular interest is information that can be used to support expenditure, planning, monitoring and also the estimating guidelines (metrics) and benchmarks. These departments may also want to use information collected by the time sheet system to raise invoices – to internal or external clients. The PSO could also provide, as a major service, a forward projection of programme and project cost outcomes. This information comes from the progress reports and associated analysis, produced by the programme and project managers.

8. Summary

There is a wide range of additional services that the PSO can provide. What is important is that these additional services must be:
- **asked for; and**
- **valued.**

If this is not the case, the PSO can become regarded as a dumping ground and not the vital business support function that it is. It is important that all the services provided by the PSO are measured, monitored and publicised to the organisation – the publication of what has been provided and achieved from the PSO's support is vital. There is always a need to sell the PSO to the organisation; never take it for granted that the organisation will understand what the PSO provides.

When extending the services of the PSO, look for logical holes in the current support systems in the whole organisation that must be addressed, not just those associated with programme and project support. And finally, ensure that all extensions to PSO services are included in an updated business case and terms of reference for the PSO.

Chapter Twelve

PSO and Programme and Project Support Tools

1. Introduction

This chapter looks at:

- **why the PSO needs support tools;**
- **why programme and project managers need support tools;**
- **the types of tools available;**
- **what functionality is provided by these tools;**
- **how to identify and define the need for these tools;**
- **how to select the tools that are right for the organisation.**

2. Why the PSO Needs Support Tools

Before looking at the types of tools available and what they do, it is worth examining why tools are needed.

2.1 To Automate Repetitive Manual Processes

One of the most important functions tools perform for the PSO is that of automating repetitive tasks. A typical example of this is the collation of the progress reports and plans into a report for the whole portfolio.

It is important to consider when examining tools to perform these activities – are they cost beneficial? To perform these activities automatically, the information provided to the automation process must be consistent in both format and quality. However, there is a high probability that the successful completion of the automated process will require human intervention. Therefore it is vital to include this additional cost in the cost benefit analysis of such tools and not be over-optimistic about the efficiency of the technology.

2.2 To Perform Complex Calculations and Analysis

The PSO requires tools to perform complex calculations and analysis. Examples of this include the projection of potential outcomes from a programme's or project's progress data, the development of earned value graphs and other graphical representations of progress information.

Once again, it is important to realistically assess the costs and benefits of the tools to support or automate these processes. This must include the value of having information which at present is not available and the benefit of making better decisions.

2.3 To Integrate Information from Different Sources into the Infrastructure

It is very likely that the PSO will have to receive and integrate information from a variety of sources regarding the portfolio of programmes, projects and activities. These sources could include all operational staff throughout the organisation, and therefore the integration of the information provided to the PSO into a report for senior management can be extremely labour intensive. Again, if the PSO is to be successful in deploying tools to automate this process, standard reporting methods, formats and content will be required. The introduction, and enforcement, of these standards can be extremely time consuming, and therefore the cost benefits of this type of tool must be assessed realistically.

2.4 To Provide Graphical and Other Management Reports

The conversion of the information collected from the progress reporting process into graphical and other management reports by the PSO can also be labour intensive. Before looking for automated tools to provide these, direct from the source data, it is essential to examine the option of manually inputting the source data into a specialist stand-alone graphics tool.

2.5 To Provide Information On-Line

In addition to the provision of information on paper, there is an increasing need to provide the information on-line through Inter-, Intra-, and extranet media. Again, this can be manually prepared by the PSO and placed into an electronic format. The key benefits to the organisation of having this information produced directly by the tools are that there is a reduced chance of errors and the information is available in a shorter timescale. It is vital that the real worth of these benefits are assessed in a realistic business case.

2.6 To Ease Retrieval and Communication of Information

Even if the PSO has been designed and implemented to provide information to the organisation to a prescribed format, it is likely that there will be a strong demand to increase the services it provides and improve its performance. The deployment of tools to achieve these improvements can also provide other benefits in the form of aiding the organisation to make better informed or quicker decisions.

With the number of tools available, it is vital to perform a realistic cost/benefit analysis. Quite often this analysis will show that unless there are follow-on benefits in the organisation, the tools are not cost justified in efficiency gains in the PSO.

3. The Need for, and Types of, Support Tools for Programme and Project Managers

What tools should be provided to support the organisation's programme or project managers? The selection process for these tools can be led, or influenced, by the PSO. It is important that the decision to adopt a specific tool, and agreement of the supporting business case, should be made by the organisation – not just the PSO.

3.1 Programme and Project Management – Process Support

The use of tools to provide a supporting infrastructure for programme and project managers to follow a defined process or procedure (the latest version of PRINCE is entirely process orientated) is becoming increasingly important. Such tools must provide the programme or project manager with the best available information and advice about the programme and project method, in a format that is computer friendly.

Initially organisations developed paper or computer Help file systems to support the use and maintenance of these processes. Later versions of computer software-based support tools included more proactive help; indeed, some almost demanded that a process be followed. Now a new generation of tools is emerging which not only directs and assists the user through the processes, but also interlinks with other tools. Typically these tools include facilities such as:

- **a process map;**
- **definitions of the objectives of the process;**
- **descriptions of the various roles involved in the process and their responsibilities;**
- **examples of the deliverables from the processes and sub-processes;**
- **links with other tools.**

3.2 Programme and Project Planning – Light, Medium and Heavyweight

All programmes and projects must have plans of some type. It is not economic to develop complex plans manually, therefore the need for planning tools to support this process is vital.

Planning tools have been in place since the late 1970s. They allow the programme or project manager to create, either from existing plans or from new, a plan for the programme or project.

The tools enable information about progress made to be put into the plan and to show achievement and expenditure as compared with that planned, to identify any discrepancies and to assist in identifying what control action may be required.

Their sophistication varies with cost – the simplest cost less. However, a facility has now emerged which enables a user to hold plans in a variety of open database formats, so that plans from other tools may be combined together in a single repository for reporting purposes. In addition, it is possible to link these tools, directly or through a repository, with other tools such as those used for risk assessment.

Typically, these tools provide:

- **definitions of the programme or project's deliverables, tasks and activities;**
- **the sequence of their production;**
- **the resources needed to complete the deliverables, tasks and activities;**
- **the definition of the critical path;**
- **the auto-scheduling of resources to a defined algorithm;**
- **the ability to smooth or level the resources over one or more programmes or projects and the ability to input progress and expenditure;**
- **display and output of planned and actual situation reports.**

3.3 Progress Reporting and Time sheets

These enable the programme and project plans to be kept up to date. The programme and project managers need to collect information about the progress made and expenditure incurred. In a large project this can be an enormous task.

The types of tools available to support this process can be either freestanding (not part of a planning tool) or integrated with the planning tool. These types of tools enable reporting on information from all over the organisation, on the progress made and resources expended. The reports can go to the PSO or other relevant management functions for collation and are then transformed into management reports and incorporated into the programme or project plans.

These tools can be either push or pull. The push type of tool presents the user with a list of what they are supposed to be doing (according to some form of plan) which they either confirm or amend to reflect what has been done. In the pull type, the user completes a blank sheet.

The main functions provided by this type of tool are:

- **reporting on activities performed as compared to activities planned;**
- **reporting on activities performed that were not planned;**
- **a facility for vetting or approving reports before they are submitted to update the relevant plans.**

3.4 Risk Management

The risk management process demands considerable amounts of effort to operate and requires access to a wide database of information. As a consequence a number of software tools have been developed to assist the programme and project manager.

There are two main types of risk assessment methods available – quantitative and qualitative. The risk tools support the assessment process and/or the management actions that are commissioned. Those that only support the assessment process allow users to include their own risk model and register of risks, and can have links with word processing tools and project planning tools which present the information in alternative formats.

The risk tools used to support the management process are a register of the risks and their control actions and are used to provide reports on what action has, or has not, been completed.

3.5 Methods and Estimating

When preparing the programme and project plans the programme and project manager needs access to information on project or systems development methods and estimating guidelines.

The tools that support this are often incorporated with others such as the process support or the planning tools. These tools typically provide the ability to store or re-engineer information gained from previous programmes or projects in a format that can be used to assist with planning other programmes and projects. The tools take plans from completed programmes and projects and analyse the information into a new project or system development method, complete with estimating guidelines. They also allow the programme or project manager to take one of the new standard methods as the basis of the next plan, and to populate that plan with estimates based on information obtained from previous programmes or projects.

3.6 Configuration Management

The successful management of the configuration of deliverables and the programme and project management documentation can present considerable difficulties. These difficulties include the amount of effort needed to deal with the creation, maintenance and updating of the records regarding configuration items and ensuring that the records and items are securely and accurately filed.

Tools to support this activity are relatively new. This type of tool is designed to automate the recording of information about the configuration items and their storage and to ensure that any changes made to those items are controlled.

Some of the tools available, in addition to providing this information in the form of a register, also allow for the storage of the items themselves so that master copies are controlled by, and contained in, the software tool.

3.7 Product or Deliverable Library or Catalogues

The programme and project manager often finds access to previous deliverables of valuable assistance. However, before they can utilise the previous deliverables, they must be aware of their existence and location.

Support tools for this are often supplied as part of another tool, particularly the process, estimating and methods tools. These provide a catalogue or data dictionary which enables the user to find relevant examples or deliverables from other programmes and projects, so they can use them as templates. The key to the successful use of these tools is the establishment of the supporting infrastructure – i.e. the use of standard names and numbers for the deliverables across all programmes and projects so they can be quickly and easily identified.

It is possible to build a simple tool to perform this function using standard databases and similar application generation tools.

3.8 Quality Review

Both types of quality review processes can be supported by software tools. The first type of quality review examines the whole programme or project, and uses process and auditing tools. These are applied to the programme's or project's processes to ensure that they are conforming to the relevant standards.

Tools can also be used to support the second type of quality review, which ensures outputs, deliverables or products conform to their specification. The tool provides early warning of a review, monitors the quality process and keeps records of the faults found during the process.

3.9 Cost and Procurement Management

Most of the programmes and projects undertaken necessitate the procurement of products or services. The programme and project manager must keep track of the procurement process and the related expenditure. In some programmes and projects this can almost be a full time job. Therefore any assistance provided to assist tracking the progress of a procurement can be extremely useful.

Support for this aspect of programme and project management is relatively new. Many of the programme and project planning tools currently available can include costs of items purchased, and specialist add-on tools enable the programme or project manager to monitor expenditure. These often use an open database and some allow links with other tools, such as the planning software. In addition, several work-flow management tools have now emerged which provide valuable assistance in monitoring the progress of procurement.

3.10 Programme and Project Management Training

Training of the programme and project managers is traditionally achieved through a combination of formal training and experience. This conventional training can mean that the programme or project manager will be absent for a number of weeks. This form of training is costly and can be inconvenient.

However, training courses can now be provided over Intranets and the Internet. These can replace or supplement formal training; some also support the training process needed to obtain qualifications – such as the ISEB Certificate in Project Management.

3.11 Getting the right tools

Programme and project managers have a wide range of tools to assist them in their role. It must be remembered, however, that as with all packages these tools will at best meet 80% of their needs. The trick is to ensure that the 80% of needs met are those which are the most relevant and useful.

It is becoming increasingly difficult to distinguish between the types of tools described. This expansion and convergence will doubtless continue to increase – it is probably the only way for the tools' suppliers to differentiate their product from their rivals. This will make the selection of the right product even more difficult.

4 The Functionality Supported by the Tools

To help the organisation identify what are the right tools for their specific needs, they must consider two aspects of support. The first is the direct support to the individual processes described in the previous section. The second aspect is the added value functionality that can be supported or provided by the tools. Taking into account both these aspects ensures that the selection of tools is based on a wide consideration of relevant factors.

This section examines these added value areas and why they must be considered as part of the decision process.

4.1 Portfolio Management

The first additional area to be looked at is that of the support to, or provision of, portfolio management.

The ability to combine or collate the various programmes and projects into a single entity, perhaps in the form of a plan or a table, can be extremely useful. Some planning tools already have this facility. However, generally it requires a separate tool to perform the process. Specialist tools which perform this activity often also provide additional features, such as links to other tools which can analyse the data and present it in a graphical format, or export it to, or import it from, time sheet systems.

4.2 Generation and Use of Template Plans

One of the most valued additional support services is the ability to save previous programme or project plans as templates to be used for the next programme or project. This can be provided by the planning software, or by process or methods engineering tools.

4.3 Progress Monitoring (and Some Analysis)

The ability to support progress monitoring by providing analysis or prediction functionality is extremely beneficial to an organisation. This analysis toolkit should include the ability to calculate earned value charts by a variety of methods and also to provide costs and schedule variance charts or graphs as required.

4.4 Keeping Track of the Paperwork and Deliverables

Nearly every programme or project will generate a considerable amount of paperwork and deliverables. This paperwork represents a large proportion of the value generated by the programme or project and as such should be valued and supported by tools which store them efficiently and effectively. This is not only important for the programmes and projects while they are being executed, it is vital for the organisation to store it for future programmes and projects. The PSO can organise the filing and storage of such paperwork and deliverables, either in their physical form or in an electronic document format.

4.5 Analysis of the Database and Graphical Reports and Tables

A large number of tools are based on open databases or allow export of the information they hold into an open database. This is particularly important as it is very likely that the analysis and presentation software, incorporated into the normal programme and project management support tools, is not capable of providing the required reports. That is why the organisation must select tools which either allow the use of such standalone analysis and graphical tools, or can export the information to such tools.

4.6 What If and What Now/Next Analysis

As with the analysis and graphical tools, the organisation must consider how it will perform 'what if' analysis with the information held in the infrastructure. In many circumstances this functionality will need to be provided by tools other than those used by the programme or project manager.

As before, it is important to ensure that it is possible to deploy such tools with those used by the programme or project manager, or to export/import the information into 'what if' tools.

5. Identifying and Defining the Need for Programme and Project Management Support Tools

The range of programme and project management support tools is considerable. It is important to remember when considering the purchase of these tools that there must be a business case for what is a substantial investment. Such investments are substantial not only due to the cost of the software, but also because of the costs of training and installing the processes and standards that support their use. It is also important to assess the additional costs that may be incurred if the tools do not provide support to other parts of the infrastructure.

This section looks at what should be considered when contemplating this investment and the areas that should feature in the business case made to support their purchase.

All of the benefits in this section of the chapter will most certainly need to be discussed and agreed before they are included in the business case. In particular these benefits must also be recognised by the organisation as addressing a real problem.

Any business case that includes the words, better, improved or reduced, will need to be substantiated with benchmarks or performance figures for the before and after scenarios. The value of those improvements must also be explained in terms of the benefits the organisation will achieve due to the improvement in the performance.

5.1 Efficiency Gains
The first area that should be investigated is that of efficiency gains. The business case must ensure that its claims in this area can be substantiated.

5.1.1 Reduction in effort
To calculate the benefits achieved through a reduction in effort, it is necessary to calculate the effort (in man-days) that is, or would be, needed to perform the required functionality without the new software. The key part of this phrase is the required

functionality, not the functionality that the tool will provide. It is all too easy to make a false deduction of the benefits unless there is a defined functionality that the tool is to support. If the functionality that the tool will provide is not performed at present, then it is necessary to agree an estimate of what that effort would be if it were performed. The estimate must be agreed with the members of the organisation who will have to justify the investment or live with the consequences of any budget reduction in manpower that may ensue.

5.1.2 Reduction in time

Often, the programme of project manager will have information some time before it is made available to the relevant end user. Reduction in time referred to here is the reduction in this time lag. While this cannot be counted as a benefit, the reduction in cost obtained from detecting problems earlier, or exercising control action, can be costed and included in the business case. As with the previous section it is important to agree these benefits with the relevant managers before they are included in the business case. For this sort of benefit to be considered as valid or important, the organisation must recognise that the current delay is causing a problem.

5.1.2 Improved use of resources

Any possible benefits from improved use of resources must be identified. Particular attention should be paid to the potential reduction in the need for contractors or other supplementary resources to deal with overload situations, because the organisation has better forecasting information. Again the organisation must regard this a problem that needs to be fixed if it is to be included in the business case for new software tools.

5.1.3 Information or reports currently not available

For a number of organisations, this is the area of benefit that is the main focus of the business case. In preparing the benefits statement it is vital to assess what it would cost to provide the information or report without the new software. As in previous sections, if this functionality is not at present provided, it is important to prepare an agreed estimate of what it would cost if it was prepared manually.

When comparing the manual cost to that of a software package, remember to include in the cost of the software solution the implementation of any necessary standards. This costing must also include the costs of the inevitable manual intervention to put right any inconsistencies in the use of the standards and the consequential impact on the software and the production of the reports.

5.1.4 Improved visibility and communication

This area is again difficult to quantify. If it is to be included, the assessment of the benefit should be based on the cost of providing visibility and communication without the use of software tools and/or proposed knock on benefits – for example cost avoidance or error reductions.

5.1.5 Better information

This presupposes that the current information is in some way deficient. The justification of the expenditure to improve this situation must not be simply based on the avoidance of cost in producing the improved information manually. There must also be a benefit to the organisation from the provision of improved information – without such a benefit there is little chance of the organisation recognising the worth of the improvement.

5.1.6 Improved accuracy

Many of the most important business decisions are made on scant or inaccurate information. This comes as a big surprise to a lot of managers who believe that it is vital that as detailed and accurate information as possible should always be provided. However, what is important is that there is some information and that its limitations or inaccuracies are known. Improved accuracy, like better information, is only valid if there is a recognised need for it and that the improved accuracy provides benefits for the organisation. As with the previous section the improved accuracy can result in a reduction in the costs of bought in resources or reductions in internal staff costs and purchases.

5.1.7 Improved punctuality

The provision of improved punctuality of reports and information is not a real benefit unless currently poor punctuality is causing the organisation a problem. There are, however, exceptions to this, when the provision of the information is essential to the long-term survival of the organisation, or is viewed as a vital part of a long-term strategy or business goal or, in exceptional circumstances, where there is a a legal or statutory reason. In these cases it is valid to use the cost avoidance method of evaluating the benefit that the deployment of the software will provide.

6 Selecting the Support Tools

This can be the most difficult decision and in other ways the simplest. It is difficult because the implications of selecting the 'wrong' tools can be disasterous.

It is the simplest because the PSO should not take the decision; they should facilitate and support the decision-making process which must be led by the organisation and the users of the tools.

This section describes some of the important factors that should be considered during this process.

6.1 It's a Business Decision – Not One of The Heart

The first, and the most important, consideration is to ensure that the selection is based on a business decision and not one of the heart. The decision on which tools are selected and purchased must be founded on business economics and an impartial assessment of the tools' capabilities, as compared to a defined and agreed requirement. Too often this is viewed as a specialist decision and given to the PSO to deal with 'as they understand these things'. Would the selection of a new accounting system be treated in a similar fashion? The answer is no – because the organisation understands the importance of getting this right. To get the organisation to recognise the importance of selecting the software is the first step in ensuring that it really is a business decision.

6.2 Choice Based on Your Design

The most important part of the selection process is the preparation of the design which identifies the areas of the programme, project management and PSO infrastructure the software tools must initially support. The design should also be used to identify which other areas will be supported (through possible extension of functionality or additional tools) when the PSO implementation project is completed. It is vital to ensure that both of these aspects are considered, to ensure that the selection process is carried out on as wide a basis as possible.

6.3 Research the Market

The selection process must be based on a comprehensive study of the tools available. In order that this list is as comprehensive as possible, it is necessary to conduct desk research to identify possible suppliers. An excellent source for this is the magazine *Project Manager Today*, which publishes regular reviews on new or updated tools and also provides an annual Sourcebook and Guide to the features of products. It is also worth attending project management exhibitions and conferences.

This research could reveal a large number of potential tools and suppliers. It is important that such a large list is narrowed down. This is achieved by using the design to weed out those tools that will not support the whole of the design. This is important because 'changing software horses' in mid-course can not only be very expensive, it also seriously dents the reputation of whoever chose them!

6.5 Look for Tools That are Integrated and Non-Proprietary

Having weeded out out non-starters, the next stage selects only tools which allow integration with others. In addition, it is essential to ensure that the potential toolset uses a database that does not lock the organisation into that supplier. If it does use a proprietary database, it is vital that the software tool provides an efficient and effective export/import mechanism to and from other open databases.

6.6 Cost the Whole Purchase (Software and Tailoring and Maintenance)

The next step is to ensure that the full cost of the potential purchase is obtained. Most suppliers of this type of software tend to gloss over the start-up and tailoring costs, the training and ongoing support cost. It is also important to ensure that the costing obtained to support the decision process covers both the requirements now and when the system is fully deployed. Full risk and sensitivity analysis should be performed to ensure there are no nasty surprises when the number of users expands to X or when Y sites are involved.

6.7 Buy to Fit in With the Organisation's Technical Infrastructure

One of the final aspects to look at is how well the prospective tool fits in with the organisation's technical infrastructure. For example, will the network take the strain of the new tools? Will the tools work efficiently over your network? Many of these tools can put a heavy demand on a network, particularly when a large number of users are on-line at the same time.

This aspect will need careful research and it is vital that someone with relevant skills and experience assesses it. Indeed it is worth having a trial of the potential software before finally committing the organisation to a decision.

6.8 Consider Do-It-Yourself!

The option of 'do-it- yourself' must also be considered. The organisation could build a central database which will hold all the relevant data and has interface tools which connect it to the other tools used to support programme and project managers. If the organisation is technically competent to develop such a central database,it can achieve considerable benefits – not just in cost savings, but also because it is not tied to a specific supplier.

7. Summary

The main thing to remember about this process is that software tool procurement should be treated in a similar way to any other procurement decision. It must have a business case and the software must be selected on the basis of how well it meets the requirements now and in the future. The most common mistakes organisations make are that they fail to assess the whole costs or check how well the tools will operate in their own technical environment. It is equally important to consider the 'do it yourself' option. If the organisation can deal with the technical issues, it can provide substantial benefits.

Chapter Thirteen

Dealing with Difficult Situations

1. Introduction

The successful PSO provides services and support that are needed, appreciated and used by programme and project managers and other managers in the organisation involved with programmes and projects.

However, it is very rare that a PSO is so successful that all programme and project managers embrace all the available services and support.

A PSO manager described the difficulty of getting programme and project managers to do this as being like 'herding frogs' or 'pinning jelly to a wall'. This chapter examines how to deal with the problems of getting programme and project managers to use the support and services the PSO provides, and how to deal with any difficult situations arising when one or more managers do not join in. This chapter examines:

- **A typical difficult situation;**
- **How to identify why it emerged;**
- **How the PSO should react;**
- **How to put things right;**
- **A list of dos and don'ts in such a situation.**

All the approaches described in this chapter will require the PSO staff to adopt an open mind to the suggestions and proposals that emerge. It is absolutely vital to remember that:

- **It is better to have 60% of what you believe to be required, used by 100% of the people, than for 100% of what you believe to be required, used by 60% of the people.**

- **Getting programme and project managers all working the same way is the important issue.**

2. The Types of Difficult Situations That Can Arise

A difficult situation can be categorised under four main headings:

- 'Yes but ... '
- 'It can't possibly be'
- 'No it doesn't'
- 'What's the point?'

2.1 'Yes but ...'

This is the kind of difficult situation that occurs where the programme or project manager acknowledges that the principle of the PSO providing support and services is valid, but it does not apply to them. This situation typically involves such items as:

- **The standard programme and project management methods**
- **Standards and templates**
- **Standard processes**
- **Standard tools**

The PSO may well discover that the programme or project manager is using his/her own method. The typical discussion that occurs when this is uncovered includes: 'I think what you provide in the PSO is a good thing, but for my project it isn't what is wanted.'

2.2 It can't possibly be

This is substantially different from the previous category because the programme or project manager does not believe that the PSO could provide services or support that are relevant to them.

This situation can occur with any area of services provided by the PSO, however it typically occurs with:

- **Standard project or system development methods**
- **Estimating guidelines**
- **Standard documents**

The typical discussion that occurs includes: 'How can any standard apply to my programme or project, it is totally different from the rest.'

2.3 'No it doesn't '

This is the kind of response when the programme or project manager does not believe that a particular service provides them with any benefit. It occurs when the PSO claims that what it provides can save the manager time or effort, particularly in respect of:

- **The project management method**
- **The project or system development method**
- **A standard**

Here the programme or project manager will state that the service or support is 'over bureaucratic and doesn't achieve anything worthwhile', or even 'I don't need this because ...'

This situation can emerge at any time, although it is more common when the PSO starts up, or when a new programme or project manager is appointed, or when the programme or project is different from those previously experienced.

2.4 'What's the point ?'
This situation arises when the programme or project manager feels that the particular service or support is not a benefit and also represents a major burden.

It is more likely to occur with those managers who are viewed as 'totally experienced' or have a wide knowledge of the area in which the programme or project is being developed. This is one of the most challenging situations to deal with, because the experience of the manager gives them an air of authority that is recognised not only by the rest of the organisation, but also by the PSO itself.

It can involve any part of the PSO support or services, but most frequently in respect of:

- **The project management method**
- **The project or system development method**
- **Planning and reporting methods and standards**

The programme or project manager will state that: 'This support is for those who are just starting. It doesn't apply to me or this programme because I am too experienced to need them.' It is often linked to one, or more, of the other categories of difficult situations with the manager adding: 'and of course the PSO was not set up for this sort of programme or project.'

These situations can emerge at any time, but are more likely to emerge when a new programme or project manager is appointed or when the programme or project is different from those previously experienced.

What is important about these categories – and no doubt there are more that you could add to the list – is that each of them has a different root cause and therefore needs a different remedy. The remainder of this chapter looks at how the PSO manager and PSO staff identify and resolve a difficult situation.

3. Analyse The Situation

Often the first response to a difficult situation is to attempt an instant fix or to begin a 'deep and meaningful' discussion with the programme or project manager. The important skill is to analyse the situation to uncover the real problem and not just the current symptoms.

3.1 What are they really saying?

The first step in dealing with the difficult situation is to understand what is really being said. You must ensure that you clearly understand the substance of what is being said, rather than the way it is said. Human beings communicate in many ways – the words used, the way they are said, body language – and the PSO manager and staff must recognise this and try to get to the real meaning.

For example 'I am not going to...' must be gently probed to find out what has triggered this response. For example is it:

- **Not having time**
- **Not being persuaded that it is worth doing**
- **Not understanding or misunderstanding**
- **Not being able to do it, etc.**

But the first step is to calm things down. There are a few useful techniques to do this, including listening to them until they run out of steam and then asking them to summarise the problem for you. Another useful technique is to lower the volume of your voice and slow down your speech. Other techniques are described later in the chapter.

3.2 What has caused them to react this way?

In addition to identifying the underlying reason for the problem, it is essential to understand what has now triggered them to react in this way. This is difficult to obtain from the person concerned and usually won't be discovered at the first meeting – they and you need time to reflect on what has been said and to calm the situation.

The spark to such reactions is usually a change in situation that affects the person involved. These changes typically include:

- **A change of their manager or their attitude to them**
- **A change in their own responsibilities**
- **A change in the staff they have been allocated**
- **A change in their personal circumstances**

You may be able to deal with these in a proposed solution to the problem. Equally there will be those that can't be dealt with, but only recognised and partially addressed using containment or mitigation activities.

It is important to have as full a picture as possible of the reasons for the situation so that the most appropriate solution can be designed and implemented.

3.3 Who is the cause of the problem – you or them?
This part of the analysis is the most difficult to perform impartially and dispassionately. You must decide whether you have:

A cultural mismatch;
A lack of understanding; or
A failure, or deficiency, in education or training

A cultural mismatch is where, no matter what you do, there is no chance that the person will change their point of view even partially to accommodate your viewpoint. If you come to this conclusion your options to rectify the situation are severely restricted. However, experience has shown that this cause is very rare and is often misdiagnosed, particularly by inexperienced PSO staff who fail to establish what is really being said and why.

One of the best ways to establish whether a lack of understanding is the root cause of the problem is to ask the person with the grievance to show you the problem. Getting them to show you their problem may result in you identifying that they are right and you are wrong!

You, just like them, are capable of getting it wrong – discovering that you are trying to get them to do something impossible is common. If this occurs, you must be brave enough to recognise where the problem lies and tell the person that this is your conclusion. This honesty often brings a level of respect and trust between the two parties that is difficult to achieve through other means.

Having identified that there is a lack of understanding, the PSO staff can then start the process of designing and implementing the relevant follow on actions.

A failure, or deficiency, in education or training can also be the root of problems. As before, this failure can be on your side; again honesty is the only approach. This type of failure often indicates a major failure in the way that the PSO was designed or implemented. Either the users of the support or services were not involved in their development, or the design process did not ensure that the support or services were designed to meet a real (and recognised) need.

4.   Winning them Over (Motivation Strategies)

The strategies included in this section have been selected because experience has shown them to be the ones most commonly used. Dealing with difficult situations is just like any other form of customer service, except that in the case of the PSO it is vital that the situation ends with you both feeling that you have won.

How you and your staff handle the problem makes all the difference to how both parties feel. A good starting point is to put yourself in the other person's position; understanding their problem and their needs will set you both on the right course to solving the problem.

Small things make the difference, particularly in early encounters. I have met PSO staff who regard programme or project managers who raise issues as an interruption to their true work – they must recognise that this is 'true work'.

Customers (for that's what they are) will return to where they get good service. The way you react to customers is very important and can avert or minimise these difficult situations.

4.1 What's in it for them?

This type of motivation, or selling, strategy concentrates on explaining and defining the benefits that the programme or project manager can get from using the PSO. In order for this strategy to be successful it must be personalised for the individual concerned. An example of this strategy is to identify a problem the individual has and work with them to resolve it, reinforcing this with some form of peer group recognition for the achievements attained.

4.2 Help them to see the benefits

This strategy is high risk and can be very difficult to achieve – it should only be undertaken by very experienced PSO staff. It necessitates getting very close to the individual and giving them personal attention in the form of direct coaching, support or assistance with the use of the PSO. The risk of this strategy is that there is no hiding place if the process produces little or no benefits or if it fails due to a personality clash.

However, if this approach is successful, the results are very impressive and the 'converted' programme or project manager often becomes a champion of the PSO.

4.3 Help them to achieve...

At first glance this strategy looks like the previous one. There is, however, one major difference – it is aimed at building confidence in the PSO in general, rather than dealing with a specific problem. This strategy tackles the problem indirectly by ensuring that the whole support service is appreciated. Therefore, if there is a problem with a single part, it can be traded-off for the overall good.

This is a very honest approach and, as in the previous strategy, must only be undertaken by experienced PSO staff.

5. Motivation And Selling – Really Tricky Cases

This section looks at the trade/craft secrets in dealing with difficult situations. These strategies and tactics should only be deployed by staff experienced in attitude restructuring. The strategies and tactics will need to be implemented through a range of activities that are too numerous to be described here. However, some of the most common approaches are explained.

5.1 Give them a sense of power

This strategy can also be used as a tactic. As a strategy it addresses the difficult situation by empowering the manager to fix the problem, alone or with others. For example, if the manager complains that the programme or project management method does not meet their needs, get them to develop one that will. This strategy can also be used as a tactic by using them to fix a specific problem or by asking them to manage a team that is constructed to solve the problem.

5.2 Personal pride

In this strategy the manager that raised the problem is given credit for identifying the problem and is asked to assist a team to solve the problem, by acting as their mentor or coach. This is different from the previous strategy, as they are given the status of directing the work – a far higher honour than just doing the job.

5.3 Recognition

This strategy works in a similar way by ensuring that the manager is recognised for the contribution made in raising the issue. The strategy is designed to turn the energy, which at present is negative, to a positive one. It revolves around elevating the difficult situation to senior level so that the person who raised the issue is brought to the attention of senior management. Senior management will expect the person who brought the problem to bring also a solution. Thus, by ensuring they are recognised for the problem which they raised, they must turn the negative energy into a positive one – i.e. rectify the situation.

5.4 Peer group recognition

A final strategy is peer group recognition. The PSO can ensure that the difficult situation and the manager who raised it are brought to the attention of their peer group.

The peer group and the manager are then asked to help the PSO solve the problem. As a result, the manager who raised the issue is recognised or associated with the problem and the peer group will look towards that manager to solve, or help solve, the problem.

Also, peer group recognition is a powerful motivator – people prefer to be remembered as helpful rather than negative.

6. Things To, And Not To, Say And Do

There are numerous books written about conflict management. This section only aims to highlight some of the dos and, just as importantly, the don'ts that can help or hinder difficult situations.

6.1 For every action there is an equal reaction

This 'law of motion' can apply to difficult situations. If a programme or project manager says to PSO staff: 'Something does not...', their first reaction is to say: 'Oh yes it does.' This pantomime-sketch situation can exacerbate the problem – the reaction from the PSO can cause a further reaction from the manager and the cycle continues.

The first thing to remember is not to react or defend a situation instinctively. The answer is to listen. This is not easy to accomplish. Often we think we are listening, but in fact we are only hearing part of what is being said. Because we were affected emotionally by some words, we failed to register all of them.

The first thing to do is use active listening – that is listen to the manager and then carefully repeat back what you believe has been said and give them the opportunity to correct any misunderstandings. This repeating back needs to be done with care – with the correct words in the correct tone. The process stops you from jumping in and gives the manager the chance to get it off their chest.

6.2 Key things to Do

- **Let them finish what they are saying without interruption;**
- **Ask questions to ensure you are not confused or misunderstand what they say;**
- **Pay attention to what they say, keep comfortable eye contact and don't let your, or their, eyes wander;**
- **Remain open minded, ready to revise your opinions;**
- **Use feedback and paraphrasing to test your understanding;**
- **Pay attention to non-verbal signals;**
- **Make sure you don't 'tune out' (start thinking about something else) too much!**

6.3 Words and how they are said

There are a number of theories in this area, however what is important is that you consider what you say and, equally important, how you say it.

The tone given to a phrase or sentence can drastically alter its meaning. For example words said in an ironic tone change their meaning totally.

When annoyed we tend to use hard words such as must, always, only, won't, can't and say them in a tone to evoke a reaction from the listener. Skilled orators and performers use this to get a reaction from their audience.

I describe it as the 'accusative tone'. The words usually end with a lifted pitch – on a sort of hook. This tone lifting nearly always evokes a similar response from the listener.

The only way to break this is to respond in a different way than was expected. For example: 'The buses are always late, aren't they?' The expected reply is 'Yes they are. I was waiting...' To change this to a positive response, reply: 'I don't find that the case all the time, sometimes they are good, sometimes they are bad'. The response is saying there may be another viewpoint, with no harsh words or tone.

The chance of changing a conversation with one such round of exchanges is very slim; you will need to repeat this at least twice to shift the discussion.

Similarly, responding in a more aggressive or childlike way will downgrade the conversation until eventually it becomes an argument. So, the key things to remember are:

- **Think about the number of 'hard' words you are using;**
- **Think about the tone in which they are said;**
- **Try to move a conversation to a path where open discussion can take place.**

6.4 Non-verbal communication

Rather than attempt to explain the complete spectrum of non-verbal communication, I will restrict myself to looking at only those elements which are vital in dealing with difficult situations.

Let's start with position or posture. The way to signal that you are not annoyed is to avoid:

- **Tapping your fingers;**
- **Clenching your jaw;**
- **Speaking quickly and/or loudly;**
- **Making jumpy body movements;**
- **Staring.**

What does the programme or project manager's posture tell you? If they feel they are in charge they may:

- **Deliberately interrupt;**
- **Stand with their feet straddled;**
- **Put their hands on their hips;**
- **Fail to step aside for you;**
- **Hold eye contact longer than is comfortable;**
- **Hover, or lean, over you.**

If they are doing this, what do you do?

Do not react (remember the law of motion), feed back to them what they are exhibiting by asking them a question such as: 'Is there a problem I can help you with.' Watch the tone, don't put in the accusative lift .

7. Summary

Having to deal with difficult situations is an inevitable occurrence in a career with the PSO. In the heat of the moment, the instant response is to defend yourself and argue that what you are doing is right. But, behind every one of these difficult situations there is something that must be resolved. In almost every case there is something of substance to address and an opportunity to improve the support and services provided by the PSO. The programme or project manager who raises the issues is your customer – remember, good news about customer service travels, and bad news travels even faster.

In dealing with these situations, ensure you understand the problem and the programme or project manager's viewpoint before you build the solution together, and both emerge as winners.

Chapter Fourteen

Auditing What the PSO Provides

1. Introduction

The purpose of this chapter is not to explain why a PSO is required, but to look at how to audit what the PSO provides to ensure that it will continue to meet the organisation's needs.

Having established and operated PSOs to support current programmes and projects, I have recognised that it is vital to audit the PSO regularly to ensure that not only does it meet current requirements, but it is also prepared for tomorrow's challenges.

2. Step One: Confirm the Reasons for the PSO

There are many reasons why an organisation needs to develop and install a PSO. Before auditing what the PSO provides, there must be a clear understanding of why it was implemented and its current role and portfolio of services.

This step, at its most simple, is to obtain a copy of the PSO's terms of reference. All too often these are lost or so out of date that they must be re-drafted. If re-writing is required, you can use the pointers in the following section which describe the PSO functions and reasons for their existence frequently used by organisations.

2.1 Re-inventing the wheel

The first of these is to avoid re-inventing the wheel. All programmes and projects are by definition transitory – they start and end. This means that the staff involved in the projects and programmes are also transitory, or temporary – they work on one project and may not be involved in the next.

Therefore, the organisation installs procedures, an infrastructure, or a PSO to develop and maintain the programme and project management procedures and perhaps deliverables that are common to all programmes and projects. A classic example of this is the project plan. It is usual for each new project to have a project plan developed on a clean sheet of paper, rather than starting, or using elements, from previous projects. This re-invention is time consuming and generates unnecessary risk; adopting the recycling approach may avoid rediscovering a mistake already gained on previous projects.

2.2 The Cost of Programme and Project Management

The second, and perhaps even more prevalent reason for establishing a PSO, is to obtain a reduction in the costs of the programme and project management function. Organisations seek these reductions by providing procedures, standards and tools which are designed to reduce the amount of effort needed to manage a programme or project. It is advisable to benchmark the cost of programme or project management. These benchmarks usually show that the costs of programme or project management are in the order of 7% to 17% of the total programme or project cost. A PSO can reduce costs to as low as 5%.

Improving the quality, in terms of cost and outcome, of the programme and project is more problematic to quantify. Projects are usually not repeated, therefore it is impossible to prove quantitatively the benefits that a PSO might provide. This benefit can only be quantified in what is known colloquially as 'touchy-feely' terms.

2.3 Retaining Knowledge Gained

Another reason to establish a PSO is to ensure that knowledge gained from the services it supports is owned by someone. Often an organisation will spend considerable time and effort building a PSO, a programme and project support infrastructure, a portfolio of services and then leave them to wither because no one looks after them. This custodial role is usually assigned to the members of an actual, or logical, PSO.

2.4 Terms of Reference

To ensure that the terms of reference for the PSO contain all the relevant information, the tried and trusted acronym BOSCARI always proves useful:

B (Background) *The business environment that the PSO was created to operate within.*

O (Objectives) *The objectives, both qualitative and quantitative, that the PSO is designed to meet.*

S (Scope) *The physical, logical or people boundary within which the PSO operates.*

C (Constraints) *Those constraints of time, money, manpower or* *other restrictions that the PSO works under.*

A (Assumptions) *The assumptions that contribute to the understanding of what (or not) the PSO does e.g. Responsibility for producing all project plans.*

R (Reporting) *The reporting arrangements that apply to the PSO – who do they report what to.*

I (Information) *The information or services that the PSO provides e.g. project life cycle and estimating matrices.*

3. Step Two: What Does the PSO Provide?

The second step when auditing the PSO is to establish, on a realistic basis, what your PSO provides. The audit should take the form of a constructive criticism of each of the services provided by the PSO.

3.1 Standards

For example, in respect of standards, it is advisable to develop a catalogue of the published, unpublished and 'understood' standards that have been developed and make an assessment of each of them in respect of:

- what is the standard;
- when were they developed;
- who developed them;
- what are they designed to achieve;
- are they complete;
- are they actually in use;
- when were they last reviewed and updated;
- do the users like to use them – if not, why not;
- are they vital/essential/useful to the organisation;
- do they meet future requirements?

Note: Normally these are the basic questions to use. However, it is usually necessary to add a few more to accommodate the specific requirements or local working arrangements of the organisation.

All of these standards will need to be subjected to a critical examination to determine if they are complete and comprehensive. There are no checklists in the public domain to help with this assessment. Therefore, it is advisable to seek the help of an experienced programme and project support implementation consultant to help with the audit.

3.2 Programme and Project Management Framework

The programme and project management framework that is provided for use in the organisation should also be examined. Look for the following information:

- **who developed it;**
- **what development environment was it designed to support;**
- **what does it consist of;**
- **is it complete;**
- **is it actually in use;**
- **when was it last reviewed and updated;**
- **do the users like to use it – if not why not;**
- **does it meet future requirements;**
- **is it vital/essential/useful to the organisation?**

Note: A realistic assessment of the use of the existing service can reveal a LIPSO (LIP Service Only) approach to the use of standards and frameworks.

Checking of the programme and project management framework must be performed against a checklist which includes any non-standard features that are required for particular circumstances.

Some of the frameworks in the public domain, such as the CCTA's PRINCE methods for project management and the associated programme management series of books, are a useful start point for a checklist.

However, one of the important things to consider is the appropriateness of the methods. Most of the current methods, including PRINCE, were developed for yesterday's programme and project execution methods, not tomorrow's. Future execution methods may use different approaches.

3.3 Estimating Guidelines

Current estimating information can be difficult to identify. This is because it may not be stored in one place – for example, in some organisations, the information often resides inside the heads of its programme or project management staff. Estimating guidelines should be catalogued and realistically assessed in respect of:

- **who developed them;**
- **what development environment were they designed to support;**

- are they complete;
- are they actually in use;
- when were they last reviewed and updated;
- do the users like to use them – if not why not;
- are they vital/essential/useful to the organisation;
- do they meet future requirements.

Estimating guidelines or databases are much misunderstood. To the inexperienced programme or project manager they seem never to be right and of little use. As a consequence, it is easy for the organisation to decide that their benefits are so minimal that it is not worth having or maintaining them. That's why they are misunderstood! They are really mini OSINTOT (OH Surprise I Never Thought Of That) eliminator machines. They provide a powerful mechanism which avoids missing out complete tasks or deliverables, or failing to consider the complexity of the development.

As with the other services, when assessing their completeness a number of problems can emerge. For example, should the organisation have estimates for everything; with what levels of granularity; what should they contain – cost, time; and which of the many resource M's (Minutes, Men, Machinery, Mortar) should be supported? Strictly apply the 80/20 rule.

3.4 Project or System Development Methods
Another service that can be provided is project or system development methods. Some organisations have up to twenty such development methods due to the extremely wide range of work they undertake. As with the other PSO services these must be catalogued and realistically assessed in respect of:

- who developed them;
- what development environments were they designed to support;
- what do they consist of;
- are they complete;
- are they actually in use;
- when were they last reviewed and updated;
- do the users like to use them – if not why not;
- are they vital/essential/useful to the organisation;
- do they meet future requirements?

As with the estimating section, the purpose of the project or system development method is greatly misunderstood. If the estimating database is the micro-OSINTOT chaser this is the MACRO one. Project or system development methods are there to be used as a start point, not the route. The experienced project manager knows that reference to the method avoids them omitting a major deliverable from their project.

3.5 Consultancy or Body Shop

Some PSOs provide a consultancy or 'body shop' service in the form of assistance to project and programme managers and/or the provision of project management or other project team staff. Such services must also be catalogued and realistically assessed in respect of:

- **who developed them;**
- **what development environments are they capable of supporting;**
- **what does the service consist of;**
- **are they complete;**
- **are they actually in use;**
- **when were they last reviewed and updated;**
- **do the users like to use them – if not why not;**
- **are they vital/essential/useful to the organisation;**
- **do they fully meet future requirements?**

To audit and assess this service is more difficult than the others because it is difficult to separate the audit of the service from the quality of the staff supplied. It is, therefore, advisable to question both areas, but separately.

Some of the questions to use in examining the services provided are:

- **is there a defined and agreed service level for the provision of the service;**
- **does the PSO meet its responsibilities under the service-level agreement;**
- **does the organisation meet its responsibilities under the service-level agreement;**
- **does the PSO offer the full range of consultancy and body-shop services required by programme and project managers?**

In respect of the quality of staff ask:

- do the customers regard the quality of the consultancy or bodyshop services as equal to what would be provided by an external consultancy;
- do the customers regard the consultancy or bodyshop services as value for money;
- do the consultancy or bodyshop services meet the required level of professional standards and competency?

It is vital that this service is catalogued and realistically assessed in respect of:

- who developed it;
- what development environments does it support;
- what does it consist of ;
- is it complete;
- is it actually in use;
- when was the service last reviewed and updated;
- do the users like to use it – if not why not;
- is it vital/essential/useful to the organisation;
- does it fully meet future requirements?

3.6 Senior Management Information

Most PSOs provide an information service to senior managers about programmes and projects. This information can take a variety of forms ranging from simply reporting on progress, to performing full audits of the management and operation of a programme or project and its deliverables.

These information services must also be catalogued and realistically assessed in respect of:

- who developed them;
- what do they consist of;
- are they complete;
- are they actually used by senior management;
- when where they last reviewed and updated;
- do the senior managers like to use them – if not why not;
- are they vital/essential/useful to the organisation;
- do they meet future requirements?

After completing the inventory of the current 'stock' of support services, it is important to examine critically the components of the current PSO programme and project support infrastructure to determine how complete it is.

4. Step Three: What Should The PSO Provide?

The third step in the audit is to identify what services the PSO should provide for the organisation.

Ignore the inevitable question, about whether it is the PSO's duty to supply and maintain services, or if they should be delegated to others, to the final stage of the audit.

In deciding what services the PSO should provide, it is vital that all requirements are examined, from all interested parties. This process is described extremely well in Professor Checkland's books on soft systems analysis. Essentially the technique forces the analyst to look for, and recognise, other people's views as to what services the PSO should supply for the organisation.

Such an analysis can reveal some surprising requirements. A recommended start point is to identify and define the needs of senior management, then those of the programme or project managers, and finally the PSO's view. In most circumstances other views have to be considered, such as internal or external auditors, customers and even suppliers. Failure to identify these requirements, and consequently supplying the wrong service, is a major reason why some programme and project managers do not use the PSO.

5. Step Four: Building the Blueprint for the Future

Having analysed the specific requirements of the organisation, it is possible to start to develop a blueprint, or recommendations, for the changes needed to ensure the PSO is ready to meet these requirements.

One of the biggest problems to overcome when developing and agreeing a vision of the future, is to ensure that all the interested parties have a clear understanding of what is required (proposed) and that they all share the vision.

The most successful approach to building this vision is real-time modelling. This technique demonstrates the existing system of services in the form of a mini-play, identifying new requirements. These are then tested in a second mini-play, which illustrates the new services and how they will be operated.

Not withstanding the above analysis, there are some additional services that should be considered.

5.1 Previous Project Deliverables

One of the most commonly requested additional services from programme and project managers is the catalogue of previous deliverables. These are top of the list because they not only save time – over 60% time saving can be obtained working from a previous example – but they also help avoid OSINTOTs.

To develop this service it is necessary to identify the various types of project deliverables that will be needed by the users of your services.

You may be surprised at what emerges when you ask managers what services are required. For example, a PSO found that one of the most important services it could provide for its project managers was a database to help identify which technical support person could deal with what sort of problems, equipment or software. Another need was for information about who to contact in the procurement branch about their specific requirements and the procedures to be followed.

5.2 Jobs and Role Descriptions

This element of the service portfolio includes other components. The reason for looking at it as a separate component is that when assigning a role, the member of staff wants to know everything entailed in accepting that role. This may seem obvious, but often the PSO delivers it piecemeal from various parts of the PSO service portfolio. For example, the role description may come from the project management method, while other duties such as quality control come from its quality manual.

The services provided must also take into account a number of variants within the role and cater for special organisation structures. Not all duties are described in the job description and therefore it is important to include a service which helps tailor the specific terms of reference for the job.

5.3 Hints and Tips

Not all hints and tips can be contained in the method, indeed it is often advisable not to include them. For example, putting these in the project management organisation structure can stop the job holder tailoring the job description to reflect their own particular project.

The key to making hints and tips easy to use is an efficient structure. It is recommended that the 'rule of six' be followed for such structures. This is based on the fact that the normal human can only manipulate, at best, six things (plus or minus two) in its brain at once. Therefore, structure the hints and tips in a macro to micro-level following the rule of no more than six categories at each level.

An example – Planning and control systems:

Top Level:
- **structuring the plan;**
- **selecting the appropriate life cycle;**
- **tuning the life cycle;**
- **planning tool tips;**
- **deciding the granularity of the resources to be included;**
- **deciding on the minimum size of each component of the plan.**

Second level.
Structuring the plan:
- **select essential components of the plan;**
- **decide how many stages to have;**
- **link the plan to other projects;**
- **link the project to a programme;**
- **link the plan to the management control systems; and business cycles of the organisation; etc.**

5.4 Techniques

Most programme and project managers will have undergone training for their job – either formal or on the job. However, it is useful for the PSO to provide, in its service portfolio, assistance with the common project management tasks.

The service can take the form of previous deliverables and complete projects, training packages or even a consultancy service to develop deliverables on behalf of the programme or project manager. These techniques can be supported by specialist tools – with appropriate tool training provided from the PSO or specialist organisations.

It is vital that the contents of this service are kept up to date, particularly in respect of the PSO's business case. Often the programme or project manager finds that deliverables have to be completed more than once because the standard forms and procedures were not up to date.

6. Step Five: The Report

The final step in the audit is the report. There is an old consultancy adage that many a good assignment is wrecked by the report. Constructing the report is not a mechanical action, it must be developed to meet both the requirements of the authors and, more importantly, those of its audience. There is no standard structure to be used. For example, some organisations do not want any form of criticism included in their reports, just a vision of the future. Others may want a history of why they are at the position they are, before giving the vision of the future.

What is vital is that the report is designed to meet a defined purpose or aim and then planned as a whole. The most successful way of achieving this is to plan the whole report, not just chapter by chapter.

This technique starts by defining and agreeing the purpose or aim of the published report. The next step is to decide the sections of the report so that it builds logically towards that aim or purpose.

The size, in terms of page numbers, of the report is then determined by assessing the possible reading time the recipients will be prepared to give the report. Next, the total number of pages are allocated to the various sections in proportion to their importance in 'making the case'.

The final step is to identify, in bullet format, the paragraphs for each of the sections, including only those facts or opinions that will be useful in 'making the case'.

The detailed writing of the report can then be undertaken. Using this technique ensures a sharply focused report that can be constructed in a very short time.

When constructing the recommendations for change section, it is important that all the options of providing the services are considered, including the use of a logical PSO. This concept is being increasingly adopted by those organisations who have advanced to at least level two of the software process maturity model.

7. Summary

A major audit of the PSO needs to be performed on a regular basis, approximately every three years, or when a significant new type of project or programme emerges. Between these major audits, it is worth reviewing the report on an annual basis to identify if a full audit is required and to refresh the organisation's memory as to what the PSO was designed to provide.

Chapter Fifteen

Preparing the PSO for Future Programmes and Projects

1. Introduction

The current business environment of rapidly changing marketplaces has led organisations to continually revise their business processes to ensure that they are effective and efficient. When changes to the business and business processes are required, the organisation usually implements the changes through interrelated programmes and/or projects.

In order that these programmes and/or projects are executed effectively and efficiently, it is vital that the organisation has developed and adopted a comprehensive and relevant programme and project support infrastructure.

This chapter looks at what is needed to ensure that future programmes ans projects are adequately supported by the PSO and what occurs if they are not.

2. Today's Programme and Project Support Infrastructures

Before looking at the future, it is important to understand the environment that existing programme and project support infrastructures were designed for.

2.1 Evolution From Construction Projects

The first, and most important, part of this understanding comes from the environment in which current programme and project support infrastructures were developed. The approaches most commonly used have their roots firmly based in the construction industry. Thus the programme and project support infrastructures reflect this environment, including:

- **an agreed specification of what has to be delivered;**
- **detailed specifications and drawings of what must be developed;**

- **modular construction;**
- **time pressure on the development process;**
- **a long-term, fixed-timescale business case.**

This environment has undoubtedly affected the way such projects are directed and managed. However, as projects of the future will not necessarily be developed in this environment, it will be necessary to review and update the programme and project support infrastructures.

2.2 Method dependent

The basis of the current programme and project support infrastructures are programme and project management methods, which were developed on the concepts of:

- **efficiency in build effort;**
- **the programme or project manager is 'king';**
- **command-type structures;**
- **control orientation/drive.**

The efficiency in build effort is reflected in the almost universal use of the project network technique and the accompanying resource smoothing techniques. Equally common is the fact that this technique is used on only one aspect of the project – its duration. Research carried out by Middlesex University took a multi-dimensional view of projects by developing networks for at least three dimensions: costs, human resources and tasks. The final network being a combination of these separate viewpoints. Perhaps tomorrow's projects may need networks based on maximising the efficiency of user input or the quality of deliverables. What is important to remember is that today's programme and project management methods, and hence the programme and project support infrastructures, are based on efficiency in build effort.

The concept of the 'programme or project manager is king' is based on a construction programme or project's need for a simple command structure. The programme or project manager in the typical construction programme or project is always supported by a further level of day-to-day management. This next level may include the clerk of works, foreman and also the heads of the various trades employed on the project. Each of these heads of trades is left to manage the work of the team and to be the spokesman on that area for the project manager. This approach is not always followed in I.T. programmes or projects, as the programme or project manager often undertakes development activities. However, the chance of the programme or project getting out of control rapidly increases with the amount of development work undertaken by the programme or project manager.

The command structure found in the typical construction programme or project, starts with the customer who is assisted by his own independent specialist advisor. This specialist gives advice on both the technical aspects of the project specification and the quality of the development, by the programme or project team, of the deliverables.

The designer or architect of the programme or project further supplements the top level decision making team. This person can also have a role in the development activities by giving direction to the programme or project team (through the programme or project manager).

This tripartite team structure is often found in I.T. programmes or projects. However, it is important to remember that this structure was designed to meet the requirements and challenges of this specific environment and must be adjusted to reflect the demands of any new environment.

Another of the main foundations of today's programme and project management methods, and hence the programme or project support infrastructures, is the high degree of formalisation. This is rooted in today's methods, where the programme or project has as its basis a contract with a series of subcontracts. This occurs because most of these programmes or projects involve the payment of invoices (or the release of further funds) on the delivery of the programme or project, or tranches, stages or deliverables. As a consequence all such payments are made only after a formal agreement of:

- **what is to be produced;**
- **where;**
- **when;**
- **how (or the quality standards it must conform to)**
- **the measurement of the successful completion (which triggers the payment of the agreed amount); also:**
- **how the contract will deal with exception situations and changes to the agreed work;**
- **how this work will be commissioned;**
- **how it will be measured;**
- **how it will be paid for.**

The final aspect to consider is the control orientation of most programme or project management and programme or project support systems. As illustrated previously, this stems from the need of construction projects to have formalised control points. These control points are used for two main purposes. The first is to ensure that the development activities have been completed to the required technical standard, so that subsequent work can be performed safely, and with the knowledge that the previous work has been completed. The second reason is that it is at these control points that contracts and subcontracts are completed and payments made.

By examining the roots of the support infrastructure, we discover if the current programme or project support infrastructure has been designed for today's or yesterday's programmes and projects. If the support infrastructure does not fit today's programme and project environment, then you must ensure that it is redeveloped.

3. Lessons From The Past

The first step in preparing for the future is to identify what aspects of programme or project management we have already identified as a threat to the project's success, and ensure that they are dealt with in the new infrastructure.

Analysis of programme and project failures has shown that the most important aspects to control are the requirements. It is vital to include, at the programme or project's initiation, training and education for all team members. This is to ensure that they understand the environment the project is to support, and users understand what the project will or could offer.

The second major area of potential failure is unrealistic estimating. To counteract this, attend seminars or other events where new methods are discussed and apply the information to rebuilding the current estimating guidelines.

One important issue to be addressed is the size, novelty, and complexity of the new programme or project. This is important, as undertaking something that is substantially different from that carried out in the past does cause problems with the project or system development methods and can put severe pressure on those methods – particularly the organisation and reporting structures. Again, look at what others have done and rebuild the system and methods before the event – not during the project.

The attitude of the organisation can cause problems and potential project failure. Organisations must shift their attitude towards programmes and projects, and learn to regard them as business-led initiatives, rather than technical initiatives, owned by the development team. It is important to ensure that programme and project management methods are reviewed and updated to meet the demands of such changes. Such changes can increase the need for a communication strategy to be installed at the beginning of the project, or for the organisation and reporting structures of the programme and project management methods to be substantially modified.

The experience of the organisation and the team in dealing with the type of project is also an important potential cause of failure. Additional training and education may be needed before the project to equip the team with new disciplines. Also assess the effect that a new situation will have on the time taken to use new techniques, or to develop the new deliverables. The 'learning curve' can be quite steep in such circumstances.

The effect of the learning curve is that the time taken to perform a task may be substantially increased when faced with new challenges. Indeed industry uses figures that start at double the normal time, reducing to the normal time only after many iterations.

The final aspect is how the project or programme will affect the organisation. If it will substantially change the organisation, it is essential once again to ensure that the project or system development and programme or project management methods have been updated to deal with these changes. This is also likely to affect the programme's or project's communication strategy, deliverables and organisation structures.

4. Current and Future Working Methods

Working methods are also important to consider when preparing the PSO for the programmes and projects of the future. Those used today were first developed in a completely different job environment. This environment was typified by in-house project teams consisting of full-time employees with the occasional contractor. Today's environment may be very different with projects utilising a mixture of internal and external staff, often off site. The organisation itself may also be embracing the concept of homeworking and part-time staff. All these factors demand changes in both the project or system development and programme or project management methods, as well as the attitude of managers, to ensure that new working methods are managed to maximum benefit.

The final issue is that of the 'age bubble'. Those in their fifties probably represent the most experienced group of staff. The organisation must ensure that today's programmes or projects include sufficient opportunities for this group to pass on their skills and knowledge to the next generation.

5. The Technology Trends

Technologies used today are considerably different from those used when the current systems and methods were developed. While changes in technology do not necessarily affect these methods, it is still important to assess whether they need to be amended.

One of the main issues is the size and complexity of today's computer programmes. Size in itself is not the problem – the concern is how to keep such complex programmes under appropriate levels of configuration control? In smaller projects the role of configuration librarian or manager is only a part-time job, using fairly simple support systems – card indexes or a simple database. But complex programmes and projects require a higher level of configuration management and sophisticated support tools. More complex configuration management methods can influence both the systems development and programme or project management methods.

The increased use of Internet technology can also substantially amend the development activities. For example, it is now possible to hold interactive design sessions over the Internet; post, collect and deal with time sheets on a remote basis; disperse system documents over many sites, etc. While the technology in itself may not change the methods, it can radically affect how these processes are performed in the organisation and may require the introduction of new skills and techniques.

Another major factor to consider is the now almost total integration between telephone and business systems. Integration brings new opportunities for radically different forms of work organisation structures to be contemplated as part of the new business system design aspects of the project. This is an area that will continue to grow in importance so it is essential to understand what opportunities and benefits this convergence will provide.

Also, do not ignore the impact of faster computer processing and cheaper data storage systems. The explosion of work flow programmes and projects, and the use of images as an every day part of the working environment, have been facilitated by the growth in the speed and capacity of these systems.

This explosion enables completely different ways to manage and store documents. We have still to identify all the ways in which this technology can help, but it is essential to assess potential benefits as they could mean the difference between an organisation's surviving or failing.

6. Business Trends

One of the key areas of change facing us is the increasing number of programmes or projects that are facilitating, or actually driving, the integration of business entities. These business process re-engineering programmes and projects are driven by business benefits and executed through a programme of projects and initiatives.

These benefits-driven programmes and projects require a different management approach – the programme or project will not be complete until the benefits have been achieved. Indeed, during a programme or project's development, the most important aspect of the monitoring process concerns the benefits realised – not the expenditure or the delivery of the component parts. This requires a more dynamic approach to the strategic direction and management of the programme or project and can lead to its being structured in relation to the benefits realisation process, rather than the development process. It can also mean that the organisation structure remains in place long after the deliverables have been completed to ensure that the benefits have been realised.

Another major trend is the de-centralisation of business entities and decision making. This can dramatically affect the number of variations of the same product, programmes or projects. It may also lead to a significant increase in the number of customers, or members of the organisation, who are involved in its strategic direction.

Programme and project managers of these types of programme and projects typically spend more time embroiled in internal politics than in 'conventional' programme or project duties. This will require increased support from the programme or project support infrastructure and a restructuring of traditional roles and responsibilities to reflect these working arrangements.

The increase in work flow and offshore development methods is also having an effect. Consider, for instance, the time difference experienced when development, or even the end customer, operates in a totally different time zone. It can be an advantage – arriving in the morning to find the work completed overnight, or a hindrance – being unable to talk to the developer until 10 o'clock at night. These sorts of business trends need to be considered and the system development and programme or project management methods modified accordingly.

Finally, what is the next major new programme or project over the horizon? We've faced the Millennium Bug and EURO programmes. Perhaps the next will be liberalisation of the phone systems or data networks. What is certain is that there will be advance signs for the wise to look out for – is your PSO designed to look for them and modify its approach to programmes and projects?

7. The PSO Must Be Prepared

Re-definition of programme or project or system development methods is vital – failure to use the right tool may not only damage what you are working on, it might even damage your career.

To persuade the organisation to invest in researching and developing new structures in advance can be difficult. Making a business case for such investments is never easy because the investment is designed to avoid problems that have not occurred. However, the organisation must be made aware that the lack of suitable programme and project support infrastructure can severely limit the organisation's ability to exploit opportunities. These opportunities may be to use offshore development, work flow methods, the Internet, or the use of more flexible working arrangements.

It is important to emphasise existing limitations on the types of projects that can be undertaken. A lack of support to the programme or project team and the programme or project manager may mean that a programme or project has to be outsourced. The expertise gained during the development of the programme or project is lost to the organisation and in many cases this experience is as important or valuable as the deliverable itself.

However, the most substantive argument for a PSO is to increase the chance of success. Every year the surveys carried out by the Standish Group and other research organisations find that up to 30% of all projects are cancelled and a further 20-30% overrun to the extent that they are no longer viable and the benefits they are supposed to deliver are never achieved.

Research also shows that projects with unfamiliar project or system development methods or technology produce the most common failures. It is impossible always to avoid failure, but to undertake a project without conducting the suggested reviews is taking an unnecessarily high risk. Remember, with a programme or project there is only one chance to get it right and many to get it wrong. Failure to prepare for these events can also limit the careers of the PSO staff; it is better to have brought matters to the attention of the organisation – if they fail to react, at least the PSO told them.

8. Summary

It is vital that the PSO ensures that the organisation has relevant project or systems development and programme or project management methods to support the projects of tomorrow. Today's programme and project support infrastructures may be a good foundation, but without updating them to meet the challenges and opportunities of future programmes and projects, the PSO will become redundant.

The organisation must be convinced of the need to update continually the PSO staff's skills and techniques. Programme and project management support as a profession must always strive to reinvent itself to reflect a changing world; otherwise it will become obsolete.

Chapter Sixteen

Supporting Fast Moving E-Programmes and Projects

1. Introduction

Today's Programme and Project Support Offices (PSOs) have proved their worth in supporting organisations, programmes and projects. However, the advent of E-programmes and projects is causing many organisations to reconsider the traditional roles of the PSO.

This chapter looks at some of the main challenges that need to be addressed and provides help in deciding how to enhance the PSO to support fast moving E-programmes and projects.

2. Why today's PSO might not be able to cope

2.1 Based on the concept – you do, we check

Many of today's PSOs work on the basis that the programme or project manager does something and the PSO checks or gives advice on what has or should have been done. These models were put into place largely because organisations felt that if the PSO did anything more to help the programme or project manager, then they would be usurping his or her responsibilities. In some organisations this method of operation has resulted in the PSO becoming regarded as a 'police force'.

This approach also supports the concept that programme or project managers are 'kings or queens' of all they manage. This autocratic style is a result of the need to keep lines of responsibility clear. However, it forces the programme or project manager to become an expert in all the supporting techniques and tools such as programme and project management methods, development methods, configuration management methods, etc. Just like the first car drivers, they are expected to be expert mechanics as well as drivers. Today, in E-programmes and projects, the situation is very different.

2.2 Works at 'arms length' from the programme or project

A large number of today's PSOs work at 'arms length' from the programmes or projects and are not directly involved in them. In some organisations the PSO provides some services such as planning, or progress data collection, but they are not part of the team, they are outsiders who are allowed in to perform specific tasks. In some organisations these are very low value-added tasks such as minute taking or chasing deliveries or materials that have been ordered.

2.3 Provides help not HELP

This is somewhat of an overlap of the first two sections in that the PSO is largely seen as providing the sort of help that is best described as advice only, not the other extreme of help, i.e., doing the job or taking an active involvement in what has to be done. This again is related to the general role of the PSO in that they are to one side of the programme or project – they are only involved, not committed to its success.

Using the analogy described earlier, the PSO would tell the driver what is wrong with the car but would not help either to put it right or show how to continue while containing the problem.

2.4 Skills and experience of the staff

This perhaps holds the key to some of the restrictions or problems identified earlier – where do the PSO staff acquire the relevant skills and knowledge – and what is that skill and knowledge?

The majority of today's PSO staff have had little or no formal training for the PSO role. They may have had some programme and project management training, or training in specialist methods such as PRINCE or Managing Successful Programmes. However such training is directed towards programme and project managers, not those that support them. As an example, it is often found that such courses do not explain in depth why a formal organisation structure is needed and how to develop one to fit a specific organisation or programme or project.

3. What are the problems?

3.1 The pace of the development

The biggest problem that E-programmes and projects present is the sheer speed at which they are commissioned and delivered. With conventional programmes and projects there is not usually the same urgency and there is time to consider what is to be done, why it is needed and its business case. However, with high tech, fast track projects and programmes there is no time 'because if we don't have this now our competitors will be there and will take the marketplace.'

Whether this is the reality or not – and history shows that the second comer usually reaps the real reward – this is no answer to most organisations, they feel they must respond to these pressures.

This means that the traditional model used for PSO support is too slow and is seen as a hindrance, i.e., waiting to get project management documents approved before the project starts, etc.

3.2 Cross-function programmes and projects
One of the common features of E-programmes and projects is that they almost inevitability have a cross-business function.

CASE STUDY

A recent programme under taken by T- Motion (a WAP phone system supplier) involved the following departments or functions:

- *Marketing – working on the product and the market*
- *Legal services – ensuring the services were not subject to legal constraints*
- *Procurement – to identify sources of services etc.*
- *Infrastructure/Service Delivery Department – could this new product be carried on the existing infrastructure?*
- *Finance and accounts – to determine prices etc.*
- *Development*
- *Marketing – again to deal with the CRM aspects and the launch*
- *Customer support department – training in the new project*
- *Development and testing*
- *Infrastructure – changes to existing infrastructure components*

The impact of this was that the programme manager was selected not from specialists, but rather was a departmental manager who understood and had experience of these various departments.

Organisations are appointing these types of staff to the role of programme or project manager because they believe that they stand a far better chance of delivering the required programme or project than the specialist programme or project manager. However, such people will require more support than the specialist.

3.3 Acceptable right now, not 100% later

This requirement is the mantra of the E-programme or project. Such pressure means that the processes used to support the programmes or projects must be quick and also be seen to add value from the start. As a consequence organisations are questioning the traditional role of the PSO: should it still be a guardian role? Can they afford this both from the cost of providing the service and the delays that it may introduce into the process?

In an article in *Computer Weekly* (7 September 2000) Anne Gurton reported she had found that 'a structured, methodical approach is essential, if the details are rushed or overlooked, the impact can resonate throughout all departments. Speed is necessary, but not at the expense of security or quality'.

Thus what is required of today's PSO is the ability to meet these requirements within the mantra of 'acceptable now not 100% later'.

3.4 Today's programme and project managers

In a previous section some of the changes that today's E-programme and project managers face were discussed. In addition to the pressures of having a large number of departments to deal with and the need to get an acceptable system in place, they also have to face the reality that the sheer pace of the development means that they no longer have the luxury of working towards a clear and defined objective.

In the British Computer Society's Computer Bulletin of September 2000, Phil Davies encapsulated this with the following words: 'E- Commerce projects are about creativity, improvisation, flair and intuition, and a traditional project manager may be unable to cope with the loss of control that this entails'.

'They must first adopt an evolutionary strategy and at the same time maintain a vision of the general direction of an e-commerce strategy for the organisation and its business end-users, partners and other stakeholders.'

Programme and project managers will need to change to cope with this, or their careers may well finish before their first programme or project finishes.

3.5 No-one has time to read big documents

Because of the pace of these types of programmes and projects no one has time to read big documents. This affects two aspects. Firstly, the size of the programme and project management documents that are required and used. Secondly, the size of the programme or project management method documents that support programme and project managers.

This means that the existing programme and project management processes will need to be revisited and trimmed back to their real 'nugget' state. Each of the standard documents must be looked at and reassessed to ensure that each piece of information earns its keep – there's no room for any fat.

Also the processes and standards need to be trimmed back so they are easy to read, quick to assimilate and to easy to digest. If they are not they will not be used and the 'baby may be thrown out with the bath water'!

3.6 Testing and integration is of greater importance

The final piece of the jigsaw to consider is that testing and integration is of even greater importance. This is because of the total reliance on the technology and the fact that without it there is no product. This means that the testing phase of the project takes on a greater importance. Add to this the frequent changes to the infrastructure because of the rapid deployment of new and improved products and services, and the infrastructure management team become the crucial part of the development chain.

Most programme and project managers have little understanding of this process in the current development environment – in the new environment not only must they understand the process, they must regard it as a critical part of the programme or project.

4. Programme and Project Support

4.1 Explaining the programme and project management processes

So what sort of support is actually needed? The first area to address is the need to be able to explain the programme and project management processes.

If the organisation, and in particular the programme and project managers, have little time to spend on understanding the need for the processes and how they operate, then the PSO must be ready and able to do so when required. The need to be able to explain the reason for these processes is paramount; the PSO will not be able to simply respond with the words 'cos it's the rules'. The managers will need to be convinced. Therefore, the PSO must be able to explain these in a way that is rapidly assimilated and understood. For many of the existing PSO staff, new skills and increased understanding and knowledge will be prerequisite if they are to provide this sort of service.

4.2 Advice and guidance as required

The new breed of programme and project managers will require advice and guidance in both new ways and different time frames. It requires a practical based approach from the PSO, in other words, doing things for them. This is summed up by one programme manager who said 'By the time you have explained it to me and I really understand it you could have done it. So what's the point? Please do this for me'. So this new form of advice and guidance is one based around practical help.

The other new feature is that this advice and guidance are needed before the event and ideally 'just in time' rather than retrospectively. This is not possible unless the PSO is far closer to the programmes or projects than it is now. At present PSOs would not be aware of what advice and guidance is required because they are not totally up to date with the status of the programme or project, or with the programme or project manager's thinking.

4.3 Preparation of project management documents

Experience has shown that for a programme and project to stand any chance of being under control, then it must ensure that the documents and understandings on which this control is to be based are both defined and accurate. In addition it is vital to update these documents to reflect the changes made as the programme and project progresses.

This aspect of programme and project management is one that programme and project managers find difficult. It is difficult on three counts: firstly, because they do a task (i.e., preparing these documents) only once for each programme or project, and a relearning exercise is required the next time it is needed. Secondly, they prepare the documents on the basis of their own experience and as a consequence may not be including knowledge or understanding gained from other programmes and projects undertaken by the organisation. Finally, because they do this exercise so infrequently, it takes a lot of effort and time at a point in the programme or project where they need to be discussing and forming the vision of the programme or project with others affected by, or who will affect, the project.

4.4 Investigation and support services

Some of the programme and project support services required more directly are those of investigation and general support. This relates to such activities as identifying the availability of resources needed. If assistance is provided by the PSO in this process it means that not only is it done (quite often it gets forgotten!), but it also means that, because the PSO knows what other programmes and project are being undertaken, current workload undertaken by the organisation can be taken into account. This aspect is particularly important in respect of the resources required and used to carry out the testing of the programme or project deliverables and their integration into the infrastructure.

4.5 Planning and monitoring services

Another of the major services where the support required from the PSO is different is that of planning and monitoring of progress and expenditure.

The really important and challenging part of developing any plan is the thinking on which it is based. In an E-programme or project the programme or project manager will probably be new to this process and may have limited amounts of time to devote to it.

PSOs in such an environment are not only helping programme and project managers by guiding them through the thought processes, they are also supporting them by developing the plans for them. After all, how many Project Workbench or Microsoft Project experts do you need? This form of HELP also means that plans are developed consistently and to the same amount of detail for all programmes and projects. Maximum use of templates and other quality and productivity aids can be easily adopted; it is far more efficient to have these plans prepared by an expert.

Progress and other monitoring can also be provided as a new service, in particular, the monitoring of benefits achieved. This service offers the programme and project manager (and the organisation) the same sort of benefits that the planning service provides. In particular, the experience gained from monitoring other programmes and

T- Motion -Project Management Lifecycle

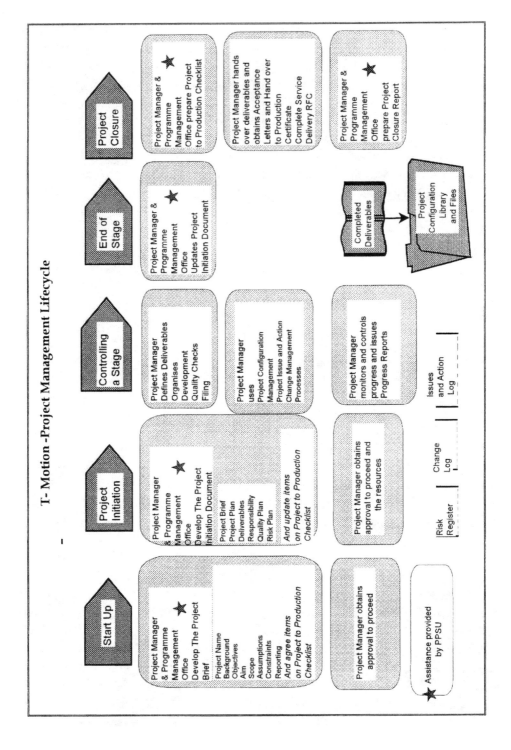

Start Up

Project Manager & Programme Management Office Develop The Project Brief

Project Name
Background
Objectives
Aim
Scope
Assumptions
Constraints
Reporting
And agree items on Project to Production Checklist

Project Manager obtains approval to proceed

Assistance provided by PPSU

Project Initiation

Project Manager & Programme Management Office Develop The Project Initiation Document

Project Brief
Project Plan
Deliverables
Responsibility
Quality Plan
Risk Plan

And update items on Project to Production Checklist

Project Manager obtains approval to proceed and the resources

Risk Register

Controlling a Stage

Project Manager Defines Deliverables Organises Development Quality Checks Filing

Project Manager uses
Project Configuration Management
Project Issue and Action
Change Management Processes

Project Manager monitors and controls progress and issues Progress Reports

Change Log

Issues and Action Log

End of Stage

Project Manager & Programme Management Office Updates Project Initiation Document

Completed Deliverables → Project Configuration Library and Files

Project Closure

Project Manager & Programme Management Office prepare Project to Production Checklist

Project Manager hands over deliverables and obtains Acceptance Letters and Hand over to Production
Certificate
Complete Service Delivery RFC

Project Manager & Programme Management Office prepare Project Closure Report projects means that the right or difficult questions are asked when the information is being gathered and analysed.

5. Programme and Project Methods Support
5.1 Programme and project methods in diagrams
One of the earliest lessons learnt when working in E-programmes and projects is that time is precious. To ensure that the programme and project managers understand the programme and project support processes quickly and efficiently, it is advisable to convert text-based manuals to diagrams.

Having converted a traditional method to this form of presentation, it is clear that:

- **Programme and project managers understand the method much more quickly than from conventional means,**
- **The diagrams are easily tailorable to their specific needs,**
- **It is easy to explain the processes to other managers,**
- **It is easy to produce other diagrams in a similar way for the lower level process, eg., configuration management.**

The exact content of these diagrams will be dependent on each organisation. However, the real-life example shown opposite was designed to show the major steps in the process, the project management deliverables, responsibilities and support services provided.

5.2 Infrastructure
In a similar way the infrastructure provided to assist the programmes and projects must also be revisited and redesigned to provide value added support quickly and efficiently.

There are various delivery mechanisms needed for the various parts of the infrastructure, such as:

- **Programme and project management support processes toolkits,**
- **Deliverable, risk and other libraries,**
- **Hints and tips.**

All need to be revisited and ways identified to deliver these more efficiently and effectively. For example, are the support systems that are provided for the programme and project management process easy and quick to use? Do they not only contain advice and guidance on how to use them, but also contain some embedded added value such as possible risk containment measures or recommended lists of deliverables to be subject to configuration management?

Are the hints and tips identified from previous programmes and projects recycled and available to the programme and project managers at the point at which they are needed? For example, are they included as part of the templates or other standards that are used during the programme or project?

6. The Supporting Infrastructure
6.1 New and relevant programme and project methods
So what should the PSO provide to support an E-programme or project? First of all, it needs to update its programme and project management methods support to reflect the pace and the types of programme and project managers that the organisation is using. These methods need to be slimmed down to the bare bones so that no 'just in case' fat exists. Each part of the method must add value to the process. If it does not, then consider removing it. The presentation of the methods should also be converted to pictures or diagrams supported by notes – even better if they can be delivered by Intranet or other general access methods.

6.2 New and relevant project or system development
The project or system development methods and the supporting infrastructure of standards and templates will need to be updated and supplemented; new ones may have to be built for the new products and services required for E-programmes and projects. It may be possible to use some components from existing methods. Experience has shown, however, that it is usually quicker to prepare new structures than to try to 'shoe horn' what is required into existing ones. It is worth remembering that you will not get them right first time; only experience and a number of programmes and projects will enable you to do that.

6.3 Live Templates
There will also be a need to develop new templates and standards. Again, experience has shown that these need to be developed in a live situation, i.e., take any previous standards and templates and interactively modify them to the new format and content, in conjunction with the programme or project manager. Keep, as far as possible, the structure and framework of the previous documents, but reflect the needs of this new generation of programmes and projects.

This action also applies to the rebuilding of:

- **Programme and project documents,**
- **Programme and project plans,**
- **Registers, logs, quality and configuration management systems.**

Don't forget, however, that these all have to be 'joined up' to form a cohesive infrastructure. One of the key components of such a joined up infrastructure is the use of the concept of a data dictionary. This is used to ensure that all components in the infrastructure are uniquely identified and their history (configuration management no less!) known.

7. Tomorrow's PSO
7.1 *PPSU not PSO*

So what is required for tomorrow's PSO? The first thing, and perhaps an important signal to the organisation that things have changed, is the renaming of the PSO to the Programme and Project Support Unit (PPSU). This new name reflects that it is a support unit not an office, and that its primary function is support not officialdom. The name PSO has for many years caused a problem, particularly for the more go-ahead PSOs. The support unit describes what it does: it works alongside the programme and project managers. If the organisation wants assurance then let it address that properly through a proper audit function, not a half-hearted attempt to control the programme and projects by the PSO which is a tiger with no teeth!

7.2 *With and in the Programmes and Projects*

One of the biggest steps forward is the recognition that the PSO needs to be with and in the programme and projects rather than operating at arms' length. The requirement for an impartial view of what's going on in a programme or project should not be mixed in with the need to provide real support. Failure to separate these functions can cause role confusion not only within the programme and projects, but also inside the PSO itself. Indeed, in a recent consultancy assignment I was asked 'Well, what if the PSO thinks the project manager is doing something wrong?' My reply indicated that the first priority is to get the project back on track and that will only be achieved if the programme or project manager trusts the PSO enough to take its advice and to work with it to sort out the problem.

That's the real benefit; leave shooting the wounded until after the battle – the internal auditors will do that job for you!

7.3 Skilled technicians not minute takers

So what of the PSO staff in this new PPSU? What are they and what skills do they need? The answer is that the staff need to be programme and project support consultants – to be constructive auditors – working alongside the programme and projects as the trusted source of information about the management of programmes and projects in that organisation. Therefore they need to be skilled – as skilled as the Formula One mechanics putting together and providing their drivers (the programme or project managers) with a vehicle that is capable of meeting their requirements, tuning and adjusting it to ensure that it continues to function correctly. Above all, they must be part of the team.

7.4 A career in itself – not just a stop off point on the way to being a programme or project manager

The role of this new professional PPSU/PSO will mean that the people who work in this area can consider themselves in a new career, not just a fill-in job, or simply a step to being a programme or project manager – although this has a great deal of merit. This career will include administration and infrastructure support, through to tuning the various tools and other techniques and systems. At master mechanic status they will be supporting the programme and project manager at the top level.

7.5 Being part of the training of project managers

The final major change is for the PPSU to be considered part of organisational and personnel development plans. Programme, project and other departmental managers will be seconded to the PPSU to gain experience not just about programmes and projects but also about how a support function should be operated. This internal consultancy unit will provide a training ground for tomorrow's business leaders.

Summary

Is the PSO a hindrance in today's E-programmes and projects? The answer is probably yes, unless it is redesigned, reformed and re-skilled to meet the requirements of these types of programmes and projects and the needs of the programme and project managers that are being used to manage and deliver them.

All organisations undertaking E-programmes and projects need to reassess the way their PSO is providing support, and to ensure that it does meet the needs and the environment of today and tomorrow.

Special Interest Groups

The various project management professional bodies have special interest groups for their members. Some are open to both members and non-members. For full details of the groups you can contact the following organisations.

The Association for Project Management

This Association, with over 10,000 members, is the UK focus for project management. Various groups covering a wide range of project management interests. Of particular interest is the Programme Management Group.

Thornton House
150 West Wycombe Road
High Wycombe
HP12 3AE

Tel: 01494 528937

British Computer Society

The BCS has a wide spread of interests including an interest group in project management (PROMS-G).

The British Computer Society
1 Sanford Street, Swindon, Wiltshire SN1 1HJ

PROMS-G The project management special interest group of the BCS
This group is open to non-members of the BCS and has meetings and events on a wide range of topics including evening Schools in the Spring and Autumn.
Secretary
Mike Wright
e-mail mike.wright@siemens.co.uk

The Information Systems Examination Board of the BCS has qualifications in Project Management and Programme & Project Management Office Support.

ISEB Exams Officer,
The British Computer Society, 1 Sanford Street
Swindon, Wiltshire SN1 1HJ

iseb@hq.bcs.org.uk

PRINCE User Group

The PRINCE method has its own user group which has a programme of events including an annual conference.

Contact

c/o PI4 Projects, Murrells House, 6 Murrells Lane, Frimley Road, Camberley, Surrey GU15 2PY

Tel: 0870 901 5583

The Programme Management Specific Interest Group

Supported by the Association for Project Management and the British Computer Society, it promotes the science and discipline of programme management.

Website: www.e-programme.com/progm.htm

SIG Secretary:

Adrian Pyne

Pyne Consulting Limited

Tel: +44 (0)7767 822 842

Email: adrianvap@aol.com

Project Management Institute (UK Chapter)

The UK Chapter is part of the Project Management Institute based in the US. PMI has over 60,000 members.

16 Quennelle Way

Huton

Essex CM13 2RS

Project and Programme Support Office Special Interest Group

A forum for uniting PSO professionals

Website: psoforum.com

Chairman: David Marsh

Email: david.marsh @ m-m-p.co.uk

Example Documents

EXAMPLE 4 PROGRAMME BRIEF

Programme Background

The Board of Amalgamated Utilities have agreed that their business goal is to position the company to be among the foremost of its kind over the next five years by increasing its efficiency, improving its effectiveness, and achieving greater economy. To help meet this goal it has decided that the newly amalgamated organisation should be re-structured into one corporate body.

Programme Aims and Objectives

The aim of the programme is to unify the HR procedures, processes, and IS/IT systems to become multifunctional, covering all levels of personnel and operational activities.

The specific objectives are:

1)   To reduce the management costs to the average level of the benchmarked   organisations or less.

2)   To reduce the cost of product and service marketing to the average level of the benchmarked organisations or less.

3)   To reduce the costs of customer billing and payment processes to average level of the benchmarked organisations or less.

Scope

The programme will address the management, marketing, and accountancy functions. Any links with other functions such as the capital expenditure programme must be documented and defined.

Assumptions that have been identified and agreed

The programme assumes no increased business expansion through further takeovers or amalgamations.

The programme is to be executed and managed using internal resources.

Any changes to existing systems of work will be capable of easy implementation and operation by relatively untrained staff.

The business systems will be able to cope with the expected growth of 5% this year and each successive year for the next 5 years.

Any new business system installed will incur less running costs than the existing system(s) it replaces.

The first tranche of the programme will be completed within 15 months from commencement.

Responsibilities and Reporting Arrangements

Amalgamated Utilities has given overall responsibility for this programme to the Chief Executive M. Eaux who will fulfil the role of Programme Director. Reporting to him will be a programme executive board comprising Ms. Worry, HR Director (who will undertake the role of business change manager), Mr. B Counter, Finance Director and Mr. C. Askey, IT Director (who will form the design authority) and Mr. E. Sparks, Sales and Marketing Director (who will be the programme manager).

The programme executive board has delegated authority to proceed with this programme on behalf of the full Board of Amalgamated Utilities and the programme director.

EXAMPLE 5 PROGRAMME DEFINITION

INTRODUCTION
The purpose of this programme definition statement is to summarise the background to the programme, its scope, its aims and objectives, and the benefits the company will derive from its implementation and the achievement of its business goals.

Following the recent report to the Amalgamated Utilities Board a programme executive board has been appointed to oversee the implementation of the programme. This programme definition statement has been prepared to enable the Board to define the portfolio of projects that will be required to achieve the business goals. It also suggests an appropriate organisation structure to facilitate management and control of the programme.

PROGRAMME BRIEF
Background
The Board of Amalgamated Utilities have agreed that their business goal is to position the Company to be among the foremost of its kind over the next five years by increasing its efficiency, improving its effectiveness, and achieving greater economy. To help meet this goal it has decided that the newly amalgamated organisation should be re-structured into one corporate body.

Programme Aims and Objectives
The aim of the programme is to unify the HR procedures, processes, and IS/IT systems to become multifunctional, covering all levels of personnel and operational activities.

The specific objectives are:

1)   To reduce the management costs to the average level of the benchmarked   organisations or less.
2)   To reduce the cost of product and service marketing to the average level of the benchmarked organisations or less.
3)   To reduce the costs of customer billing and payment processes to average level of the benchmarked organisations or less.

Scope
The programme will address the management, marketing, and accountancy functions. Any links with other functions such as the capital expenditure programme must be documented and defined.

Assumptions That Have Been Identified and Agreed
The programme assumes no increased business expansion through further takeovers or amalgamations.

The programme is to be executed and managed using internal resources.
Any changes to existing systems of work will be capable of easy implementation and operation by relatively untrained staff.

The business systems must be able to cope with the expected growth of 5% this year and each successive year for the next 5 years. Any new business system installed must incur less running costs than the existing system(s) it replaces. The first tranche of the programme will be completed within 15 months from commencement.

Responsibilities and Reporting Arrangements

Amalgamated Utilities has given overall responsibility for this programme to the Chief Executive M. Eaux who will fulfil the role of programme director. Reporting to him will be a programme executive board comprising Ms Worry, HR Director (who will undertake the role of business change manager), Mr. B Counter, Finance Director and Mr. C. Askey, IT Director (who will form the design authority) and Mr. E. Sparks, Sales and Marketing Director (who will be the programme manager).

The programme executive board has delegated authority to proceed with this programme on behalf of the full Board of Amalgamated Utilities and the programme director.

BUSINESS CASE
Programme Scope and Duration
The scope of the programme covers the management, marketing, and accountancy functions.
The programme represents a major investment to achieve a long term goal and as such the programme duration has been agreed as four years.

Options Examined
1) **Improvements to the existing systems**
   This option will involve reviewing all existing manual business processes/systems and organisational structures, investigating possible improvements to unify the currently different water and electricity systems, to remove 'bottlenecks' and reduce overmanning.
2) **Installation of an upgraded computer system and any additional computer systems**
   In addition to Option 1, this option will involve examining existing IT systems and replacement possibilities, and investigating possible computerisation of existing manual systems.
3) **Full Business Process Re-engineering of all three function areas**
   This option will involve reviewing all processes throughout both constituent companies of the amalgamation, radically transforming and improving their effectiveness through fundamentally rethinking their design, their supporting IT systems, and their resourcing.

Risk and Sensitivity Analysis
Option 1
The major risks of option 1 are the potential disruption that could be caused both by the investigative processes themselves, whatever changes may be introduced and the possibility that little significant improvement may be achieved especially when compared with the cost of the effort involved.

Option 2

The major risks of this option are the possibility that the appropriate resources may not be available and the potential disruption of key systems such as the billing and revenue collection systems, any major disruption to which would seriously affect the company's cash flow and financial stability.

Option 3

The major risks of this option are the management challenges in controlling a number of simultaneous projects and in maintaining all the core business functions throughout a period of potential large-scale change. It will have a significant impact on management and staff at all levels and unless the transition is managed competently it will endanger morale.

Recommendation

The majority of the benefits to the company from the programme will come from the reorganisation of management. Such a reorganisation will require a total appraisal of all functions, processes, and their resourcing. Although this carries high risk it is recommended because of the extent of its potential contribution to the overall business goals. The recommendation therefore is to proceed with Option 3.

COSTS AND BENEFITS SUMMARY

OPTION 3	Year 0	Year 1	Year 2	Year 3
COSTS				
Mgt. Objectives				
Project 1	2,700k	300k		
Project 2	3,000k	500k		
Project 3	500k	750k	250k	
Project 4	300k	250k	200k	
Project 6		750k	250k	
Mgt. of Change				
Project 5	175k	200k	200k	225k
Billing & Payment BPR				
Project 7			1,500k	1,500K
Marketing Project				
Project 8			500k	
BENEFITS				
Reduced Mgt. Costs			50.75m	50.75m
Reduced Mktng. Costs				4.5m
Reduced Billing Costs				16.725m

PROGRAMME PLAN
This section contains an outline of the contents of each tranche of the programme.

Tranche 1

Project 1	Reorganisation of 'white-collar' staff	Budget £3m
Project 2	Reorganisation of 'blue-collar' staff	Budget £3.5m
Project 3	Management Information System (Phase 1)	Budget £0.75m
Project 4	Executive Information System (Phase 1)	Budget £0.4m
Project 5	Management of Change	Budget £0.2m

To be completed in 15 months.

Tranche 2

Project 3	Management Information System (Phase 2)	Budget £0.75m
Project 4	Executive Information System (Phase 2)	Budget £0.35m
Project 6	Manual Processes BPR	Budget £1m
Project 5	Management of Change	Budget £0.2m

To be completed in 1 year.

Tranche 3

Project 7	Billing and Payment BPR (Phase 1)	Budget £2m
Project 8	Marketing Reorganisation	Budget £0.5m
Project 5	Management of Change	Budget £0.2m

To be completed in 1 year.

Tranche 4

Project 7	Billing and Payment BPR (Phase 2)	Budget £1m
Project 5	Management of Change	Budget £0.2m

To be completed in 9 months.

QUALITY PLAN FOR THE PROGRAMME
Programme Tranche Terms of Reference
These will be prepared for each tranche of the programme and once agreed will be used to define the specific projects to be undertaken and the programme tranche technical and resource plans.

Project Briefs
These will be created for all projects at the beginning of each tranche.

Project Management and Planning
All projects will be managed using structured methods. Project plans will be prepared on a product-based approach and product descriptions will be prepared for all the products to be developed. These will be agreed with the project board when plans are being prepared and approved.

Project Controls and Reporting Arrangements
Checkpoint reports will be produced every two weeks. Highlight reports will be produced every four weeks and circulated to the project board. Mid-stage assessments will be held if a stage exceeds three months in duration. All other arrangements will be determined during plan preparation.

Project Quality Management

Quality reviews will be undertaken either formally or informally, the level of review and the review teams to be determined by the project management team when creating the plan for the particular stage in which the products are to be produced. All reviews will be fully documented.

Programme Controls and Reporting Arrangements

Monthly programme progress reports will be prepared by the programme manager, agreed with the programme executive board and submitted on their behalf to the programme director. These reports will be compiled from information derived from project board reports. A resource usage and requirements report will also be submitted along with a business benchmarks update report

At the end of each tranche the programme executive board will provide a progress review and action memo for the board of Amalgamated Utilities.

PROGRAMME PREREQUISITES

All members of Amalgamated Utilities who will have a programme or project management role must receive appropriate training.

EXTERNAL DEPENDENCIES

The implementation of the proposed programme will be affected by any change in relevant legislation or any change in government or government policy.

RISK MANAGEMENT PLAN

The risk management process operated in this programme will use a qualitative risk assessment method using the checklist/risk register provided by the programme and project office and supplemented through an unstructured workshop held at the start of each tranche.

The programme and project office together with the programme manger will produce a report for the programme executive board which describes:

The risk identified.
The probability of their occurrence.
An assessment of their impact on the programme.
The agreed action plan to manage, contain, eliminate or insure against that risk.
The arrangements agreed to monitor the effectiveness of the risk actions.

Risk No	The Risk Identified	Probability	Impact	Action Plan	Monitoring Actions
1	Change in government policy	Low	Severe	MD is to hold regular meeting with Ministers	
2	Industrial unrest	High	Severe	Inclusion of management of change project	Attitude surveys
3	Failure to achieve targets	Medium	Medium	Regular review of benefits plan by programme executive board.	Update Benchmarks every 3 months
4	Competition	Medium	High	Monitor competitors, PR campaign.	Competitor review every 3 months distributed to programme executive board.

EXAMPLE 6 BENEFITS REALISATION AND SUSTAINABILITY PLAN

	Benefits Area 1	Benefit Area 2	Benefit Area 3
Description of Benefits	Revenue from Job club	Revenue from Government Services	Decrease operating & running costs
Initial Plan of Areas Affected	Invoicing Accounts Business activity measurement Library operations	Invoicing Accounts Business activity measurement Library operations	Library operations
Agreed Action Plan	1. Agree with LA the payment framework 2. Put in-place infrastructure 3. Transfer Job clubs 4. Activate charge process	1. Agree with GOV the payment framework 2. Put in-place infrastructure 3. Activate service 4. Activate charge process.	1. Business process Reengineering of main operations 2. Relocation project
Responsibility	1. J Smith (Finance Director) 2. S Davis (IT Director) 3. W Purves (Operations Manager).	1. J Smith (Finance Director) 2. S Davis (IT Director) 3. W Purves (Operations Manager).	1. W Purves (Operations Manager) 2. W Purves (Operations Manager) and J Smith (Finance Director)
Achieved to date	1. Process agreed and documented (1). 2. Equipment & ISP installed (2) 3. Transfer plans in place (3)	1. Process agreed and documented (4).	Business Process Reengineering pre-study
Achievements Next period	Transfer of Job clubs - activate payment process	1. Equipment and ISP installed 2. Service Installed 3. Activate payment process.	
Manager responsible for Sustainability	1. W Purves and J Smith 2. S Davis 3. W Purves and J Smith	1. W Purves and J Smith 2. S Davis 3. W Purves and J Smith	1. W Purves (Operations Manager) 2. W Purves (Operations Manager) and J Smith (Finance Director)
Supporting Documents	(1) Agreement with LA over recharge rates (2) Sign off of equipment installed and handed over (3) Plan for training of staff and transfer of job club members	(4) Agreement with LA over recharge rates	

EXAMPLE 7 BENEFITS PROFILE

Benefit and Cost Profile

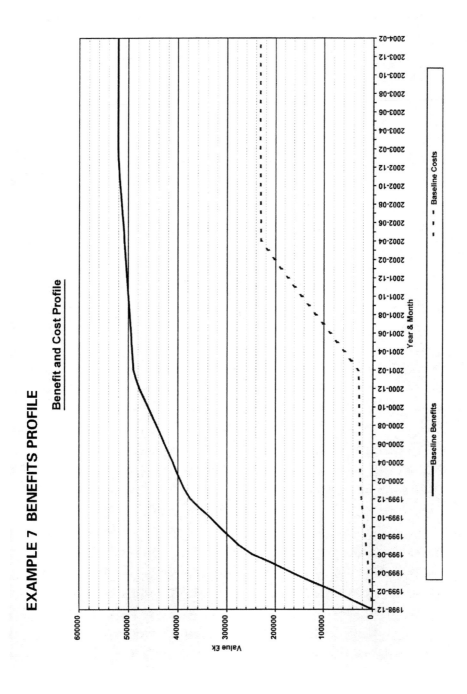

EXAMPLE 8 BLUEPRINT

Background To The Programme

The UK Government has decided to establish a United Library Service - taking over the responsibility from local authorities and moving to a pseudo profit making basis.

(This means that they will receive from either the local authority or the government payments which match the current level of expenditure for the services they are to provider. They therefore can make "profit" by delivering those services at a cost less than that received by them from the local authority or government departments).

The new United Library Service is to receive the same level of funding as the current local government authorities libraries and government departments - however the management team's remit is to reduce the costs of operating the library and other services (see the attached benchmarks).

They are also to expand the membership of each library from 1,200 to 4,000 by offering new services of:

- Internet and Intranet access to on line government information and publications and inquiries.
- Job club services - linked to local and national employment agencies.

The new services will be funded by central government on the basis of usage - therefore greater usage will mean greater funding.

Attachment 1 - Business benchmark data

Benchmark	Current	5-year Target
Library Services		
Av. Number of books per library	333K	600K
Av. Number of members per library	1.2K	4K
Av. Number of books per year per member	15	30
Av. Operational cost per book borrowed	£0.25	£0.15
Av. Cost of procurement and installation per book	£7.5	£2
Av. Price paid per book	£15	£17
Av. Number of books purchased per year per library	300	500
Number of library sites	1,670	1,500
Percentage of the population within one mile of a library	65%	75%
Av. Available capital expenditure per library	£15K	£75K
Av. Capital investment per library (1999 prices)	£200,000	£300,000
Av. Number of staff per library	4.35	4.00
Av. Cost per staff member (1999 prices)	£26,567	£28,356
Av. Cost of repairs/replacement books per branch	£18K	£17K
Av. Length of book loan	10 days	9 days
Av. Reading age of members	12.4yrs	12.9yrs
Government Information Service		
Av. Cost to Government of dealing with each inquiry	£50	£5
Total number of inquiries to Government Dept per year	1,500K	6,000K
Av. Value of information provided per inquiry	£600	£1500
No. of government staff involved in answering inquiries	65,000	15,000
Number of Government Departments with "On-line" information systems	35	108
Av. Cost of a Government employee	£45,000	£45,000
Number of Government employees supporting "On-line" information systems	150	350
Government Job club Services		
Av. Cost of revenue expenditure per Job club member	£18.7	£11.0
Number of Job club (JC) members per year	385K	400K
Av. Time in Job club	6 mths	4 mths
Information sources available for Job club members	3	10
Av. Cost of equipment provided per year per JC member	£30.0	£15.0
Av. Number of Job club members per annum per library	150	250
Av. Cost of Job Seeker Allowance Payments to JC members	£1800	£1200

Business Vision Statement
Aims

The aim of the new United Libraries Service is to become the source of information for 75% of the UK population.

Scope

The information provided by the United Library Service will consist of all published fiction and non fiction books, other publications, government publications, and any available job vacancies publicly known.

Targets

In order that this aim is met in an economic and efficient manner the following targets have been set for the new service:

1. The services must be situated so that they are available within 1 mile of at least 75% of the population.

2. The number of members of each library is to be increased from 1.2K to 4K by extending the services provided to include:
    - Provision of direct access via the Internet and Intranet to UK government departments information and inquiry system's.
    - Relocating local Job clubs to the library (they will use the technology provided for the Internet and Intranet service).
    - Increasing the number of publications available for members at each library from 333K to 600K.

3. Reducing the costs of the operation and provision of:
    - The library service.
    - The Job club Service.
    - Government information and inquiries.

4. Improving the quality of life of the members/general population by:
    - Increasing their average reading age and the number of books read per year.
    - Reducing the time a job seeker spends looking for employment.
    - Expanding the amount of, and access to, government information.

Operational Vision Statement

The United Libraries service will operate as a national organisation with local branches. The purchasing of books and equipment will be carried out centrally as will be the development of all operational processes and systems.

United Libraries will also enter into strategic partnerships with each of the relevant government departments who are to participate in the on line information service.

Each local library will operate all three mainstream services, library, Job club and government information. The staff of each library will be multifunctional and support all three areas of activities. New national qualifications will be introduced to support this new role.

The establishment of United Libraries is also part of the government's project to improve adult literacy – this linkage is through two routes – firstly the reallocation of the libraries to new locations to improve their availability – secondly by increasing the number of reasons of why the public should go to the library.

Culture Change Statement

In order for the full benefits to be obtained, the culture of the new organization must be outward-facing, customer-focused and service-driven. To meet this requirement a substantial change culture/attitude project will be required.

EXAMPLE 9 TRANSITION PLAN

Introduction and Purpose of the Plan
The transition plan is a description of the transition arrangements the organisation expects to use to move from its current business operations to the new environment of the blueprint.

It provides a view across all the programme's projects of the activities that will be needed to effect those changes. The transition plan therefore provides a checklist of those activities that are to be included in the programme's projects. This plan will be updated to reflect the progress made to ensure their continued validity.
The plan is divided into the tranches defined in the programme plan.

Tranche One   Establishing United Libraries Service and Moving the Job clubs
Overview of the Transition
The tranche will involve the design, development and installation of the new management structure for the service. Of particular importance are the finance, accounts and procurement functions. In addition the training of the existing staff to be able to assist the new job club members is also vital to enable the transfer of the job clubs to be made.

Change Management Responsibilities
The changes that need to be achieved in this tranche are the responsibility of two of the main board directors – Mr. M Stone (Operations Director) and Mrs. G Grant (Human Resources Director).

Mr. Stone has specific responsibility for the following aspects:
>   Procurement of the new computers and software.
>   Suitable training is provided for the staff.
>   The business process for cross charging and monitoring job club activities are completed.

Mrs. Grant has specific responsibility for the following aspects:
>   The design and implementation of the new organisation structure.
>   The redesign of the staff grade and payment system.
>   The redefinition of job descriptions.
>   Ensuring new professional qualifications are developed for the new roles.

Organisational Change
The major changes to be achieved in this tranche are:
>   The installation of head office and regional structures.
>   Development and installation of operational monitoring processes
>   The change of librarian role.
>   The management and monitoring of the new job club function.

Change Plans, Phasing and Intermediate Stages
The following plan has been agreed:

Week One to Week Five
Development and agreement of new organisation management structure.
Development of new business processes for monitoring operations.
Briefing staff on changes and the plans for job clubs.

Week Five to Week Twenty
Definition and agreement of new job descriptions, grades and payment systems.
Recruitment and implementation of new organisation structure.
Training of staff in new roles.
Implementation of new computers.
Introduction of new monitoring processes.

Week Twenty to Twenty Eight
Transfer of job club.s
Introduction of job club service monitoring and charging process.

Training Needs
The following major training needs have been identified:
Training of library staff to:
> Support job club members.
> Support of new computer computers and hardware.
> Their new role and that of ULS.
> The performance monitoring process and their role.
Training new ULS staff:
> Role and purpose of ULS.
> The performance monitoring process and their role.
> The operation of job club support.

Capture of Historic Information
The existing records and other information will be safeguarded by the following activities:
> Each library will develop a plan for the identification and reservation of records.
> These plans will be co-ordinated centrally and a unified plan developed for the whole of ULS.

Requirements for Buildings and Services
The existing buildings will need to be surveyed and additional power and telephone points installed to support the new computer services. New services will be required to support the operation of the new computer equipment – this is to be done by an external organisation under contract.

Handover Plans
The two major handovers that need to be achieved in this tranche are:

> Transfer of the financial responsibility for job clubs.
> Transfer of the job club.

Then transfer of the financial responsibility will be dealt with centrally at the head office, the transfer of the job clubs will managed at national level through the regional and local level offices.

The responsibility for the financial handover is Mrs. S Purves (Finance Director) and the job clubs Mr. Stone, assisted by the 6 regional mangers.

Remainder of the Programme
The detailed plans and arrangements for the final two tranches will be defined during Tranche one.

Tranche Two   Extension of Services to Include Government Information
Overview of the Transition
The tranche will involve the updating of the monitoring process to include the provision of the new service, training the staff, and the updating of the computer systems to cope with the new service.

Tranche Three   Streamlining the ULS Business Processes and Re-location
Overview of the Transition
The tranche will involve the redesign, development and installation of new business processes for book purchasing, indexing, and operation of the loan processes. In addition the identification of the revised locations for the libraries and their relocation and refitting.

EXAMPLE 10 BUSINESS CASE

Project Aim

To provide the senior managers of Ace Plumbing Supplies with up to date information on current stocks and sales.

Project Objectives

- To ensure that sales are not made for items not in stock.
- To ensure that slow or non-moving stock is identified on a weekly basis.
- To enable the level of stock held to be reduced by 10%.
- To provide accurate and up to date information on customers and purchases.

Project Scope

The scope of the project is the sales and stock section of Ace Plumbing Supplies.

Project Life

The project is a long term investment and as such the project life has been agreed as four years.

Options Examined

1 Improvements to the existing system
This option will involve improving the existing manual system by updating the records currently held by the sales section and by carrying out a full stock check every week to ensure the stock records are accurate.

2 Installation of a partial computer system
This option will involve installing a computer system to hold details of the stocks held by Ace Plumbing or details of the sales made to its customers.

3 Installation of an integrated sales and stocks computer system
This option is to provide an integrated computer system that will hold details of all stocks and sales made by Ace Plumbing with an on-line interrogation facility.

Risk and Sensitivity Analysis

The majority of the benefits from the project come from the computerisation of the stock control system. This area must be closely controlled. The sales information does not provide substantial benefits and if any problems occur with the project development then this aspect could be removed from the project.

The project is not critical for money however it is important that the benefits are realised. To this end we will extend the development life cycle into benefits realisation and keep the project in place until this product has been completed.

Recommendations

Proceed with Option 3 with a possible reversion to Option 2a if difficulties emerge with the sales section aspects of the project.

COST AND BENEFITS SUMMARY

	Year 0	Year 1	Year 2	Year 3	Year 4
Option 1 Costs					
Consultants to review existing system	10000		10000		
Overtime to update records	3000		3000		
	13000		13000		
Benefits					
Reduction in sales errors	6000	6000	6000	6000	6000
Additional sales	2000	2000	2000	2000	2000
	8000	8000	8000	8000	8000
Option 2 a) Stocks Costs					
Provision of computer system	3000			3000	
Conversion of records	2000				
	5000			3000	
Benefits					
Reduction in stocks	2500	250	250	250	250
Reduction in sales errors	8000	8000	8000	8000	8000
	10500	8250	8250	8250	8250
Option 2b) Sales					
Costs					
Provision of computer system	3000			3000	
Conversion of records	2000				
	5000			3000	
Benefits					
Additional sales	4000	4000	4000	4000	4000
	4000	4000	4000	4000	4000

Option 3 Costs

Provision of computer system	5000			5000	
Conversion of records	5000				
	10000			5000	

Benefits

Reduction in sales errors	8000	8000	8000	8000	8000
Reduction in stocks	2500	250	250	250	250
Additional sales	2000	2000	2000	2000	2000
	12500	10250	10250	10250	10250

COMPARISON

Option 1

Costs	13000			13000	
Benefits	8000	8000	8000	8000	8000
	(5000)	8000	8000	(5000)	8000
Discount Factor	1.0	.934	.877	.826	.781
Net Present Value(NPV)	(5000)	7472	7016	(4130)	6248
Cum NPV	(5000)	2472	9488	5358	11606

Option 2 a)

Costs	5000			3000	
Benefits	10500	8250	8250	8250	8250
	5500	8250	8250	8250	8250
Discount Factor	1.0	.934	.877	.826	.781
Net Present Value	5500	7706	7235	4336	6443
Cum NPV	5500	13206	20441	24777	31220

Option 2 b)

Costs	5000			3000	
Benefits	4000	4000	4000	4000	4000
	1000	4000	4000	1000	4000
Discount Factor	1.0	.934	.877	.826	.781
Net Present Value	1000	3736	3508	826	3124
Cum NPV	1000	4736	8244	9070	12194

Option 3

Costs	10000			5000	
Benefits	12500	10250	10250	10250	10250
	2500	10250	10250	5250	10250
Discount Factor	1.0	.934	.877	.826	.781
Net Present Value	2500	9573	8989	4336	8005
Cum NPV	2500	12073	21062	25398	33403

EXAMPLE 11 DESIGN MANAGEMENT PLAN

Introduction

The design management plan is used to define the programme's overall technical design integrity and to ensure it interfaces with the organisation's plans for infrastructure and support services.

1. Technical Architecture Design

The technical architecture for the United Library Services IT systems is divided into two areas:

1. Management of United Library Services.
2. Operation of the job club and government information services.

1.1 Management of United Library Services.

The design for the IT architecture used to support the management of ULS will consist of a wide area network connecting the branches and regional offices to the head office local area network.

This architecture will consist of ...

1.2 Operation of the Job Club and Government Information Services.

The design for the IT architecture used to support the operation of the Job club and Government Information Services consists of local office-based stand-alone systems linked via an ISP to the Internet.

2. Configuration Management Plan

The configuration of the technical infrastructure will be controlled by the ULS IT Configuration Management process operated by the technical architect. The detailed arrangements are as follows:

3. Policies and Standards to be Applied

The technical policies and standards that are to be applied to the ULS programme are subdivided into:

IT architecture.
Programme deliverables.
Project deliverables.

3.1 IT Architecture
3.2 Programme Deliverables
3.3 Project Deliverables

4. Technical Transition

The only transition arrangements that need to be made are those for phase two of the operation support system (government information services). These arrangements are to ensure that service to the job clubs is maintained, whilst the architecture is upgraded to meet the requirements of this new service as follows:

5.   Quality Plan

The plans for ensuring that the outcome of the development programmes is as required are divided into:

Programme deliverables.
Project deliverables.

5.1   Programme Deliverables

The quality plan for the deliverables from the programmes is ...

5.2   Project Deliverables

The quality plan for the deliverables from the programmes is ...

6.   Arrangements for Updating this Plan

This plan is jointly owned by the relevant operations department and the IT department and will be reviewed at regular intervals and also when major development stages and service levels are achieved. The review points identified are ...

EXAMPLE 12 PROGRAMME (WORK) PLAN

Introduction

The programme (work) plan sets out the schedule of work (the projects and other activities) that will be used to deliver the programme. This plan is part of the programme definition and will be used during the programme in the monitoring and control of progress.

Contents of the Programme (Work) Plan

List of projects and initiatives.

The major outputs, deliverables or products.

The proposed development schedule (Gantt chart).

Resources to be consumed during the programme.

Programme milestones.

List of major project interdependencies.

Example Programme (Work) Plan

The programme is divided into three Tranches

Tranche One	Introduction of automatic questionnaire generation.
Tranche Two	Introduction of greater use of Email and telephone research.
Tranche Three	Introduction of automatic data processing and presentation material.

This structure has been chosen because it ensures that the organisation achieves early benefits in relation to the conversion to the new business processes and reduces the risks of not being able to produce market research data by either using an external organisation or reverting to previous processes until the final Tranche.

EXAMPLE 13 QUALITY PLAN

QUALITY PLAN FOR THE PROGRAMME

Programme Tranche Terms of Reference

These will be prepared for each tranche of the programme and once agreed will be used to define the specific projects to be undertaken and the programme tranche technical and resource plans.

Project Briefs

These will be created for all projects at the beginning of each tranche.

Project Management and Planning

All projects will be managed using the structured project management method. Project plans will be prepared on a product-based approach and product descriptions will be prepared for all the products to be developed. These will be agreed with the project board when plans are being prepared and approved.

Project Controls and Reporting Arrangements

Checkpoint reports will be produced every two weeks. Highlight reports will be produced every four weeks and circulated to the project board. Mid-stage assessments will be held if a stage exceeds three months in duration. All other arrangements will be determined during plan preparation.

Project Quality Management

Quality reviews will be undertaken either formally or informally, the level of review and the review teams to be determined by the project management team when creating the plan for the particular stage in which the products are to be produced. All reviews will be fully documented.

Programme Controls and Reporting Arrangements

Monthly programme progress reports will be prepared by the programme manager, agreed with the programme executive board and submitted on their behalf to the programme director. These reports will be compiled from information derived from project board reports. A resource usage and requirements report will also be submitted along with a business benchmarks update report

At the end of each tranche the programme executive board will provide a progress review and action memo.

PROGRAMME PREREQUISITES

All members of United Libraries Services who will have a programme or project management role must receive appropriate training.

EXTERNAL DEPENDENCIES

The implementation of the proposed programme will be affected by any change in relevant legislation or any change in government or government policy.

EXAMPLE 14 RESOURCING PLAN

Introduction
The resourcing plan is an abstract from the project portfolio and other parts of the programme definition statement in which are identified:

What resources the programme requires.
Who is to provide those resources.
Funding of the required resources.
Service levels and or contractual arrangements needed.

1.   WHAT RESOURCES THE PROGRAMME REQUIRES.
The project and programme plans have identified that the following resources are required.

Tranche One Week One to Twenty Eight

Resource	Quantity	Cost Per Unit	Total Cost
External consultants	400 man days	£850	340,000
Training consultants	400 man days	£750	300,000
Temporary staff	300 man days	£400	120,000
New power and telephone points	1500 of each	£ 650	9,750,000
Computer equipment	1500 sets	£2500	3,750,000
Grand Total			£ 14,260,000

Tranche Two Week Twenty Nine to ....

Resource	Quantity	Cost Per Unit	Total Cost
Grand Total			

Tranche Three

Resource	Quantity	Cost Per Unit	Total Cost
Grand Total			

2.   WHO IS TO PROVIDE THOSE RESOURCES.
The provision of the resources required by the programme have been allocated to the following managers.

Resource	Manager
External consultants	Mr. Stone and the procurement department.
Building and services	Mr. Stone and the procurement and IT departments.
Computer equipment	Mr. Stone and the procurement and IT departments.
Training consultants	Mrs. G Grant and the operations and procurement departments.

3.   FUNDING OF THE REQUIRED RESOURCES.

Resource	Source of Funds
External consultants	Programme Budget
Building and services	Programme Budget.
Computer equipment	IT Budget
Training consultants	HR Budget.

4.   SERVICE LEVELS AND OR CONTRACTUAL ARRANGEMENTS NEEDED

Resource	Service Level and Contractual Arrangements
External consultants	One Months Notice.
Building and services	Within 4 hours of contract – penalty clauses if late.
Computer equipment	Within 4 hours of contract – penalty clauses if late.
Training consultants	One Months Notice.

EXAMPLE 15 RISK MANAGEMENT PLAN

Introduction

The risk management plan has been developed to describe the processes and method that will be used to identify, assess and manage those risks which may affect the programme. This process will be used during the programme to update the following risk management plan at the following points:

> End of each tranche.
> Whenever a programme exception report is produced.
> At the request of the programe executive or board.

The risk management process operated in this programme will use a qualitative risk assessment method using the checklist/risk register provided by the programme and project office and supplemented through an unstructured workshop held at the start of each tranche. The programme and project office together with the programme manager will produce a report for the programme executive board which describes:

> The risk identified.
> The probability of their occurrence.
> An assessment of their impact on the programme.
> The agreed action plan to manage, contain, eliminate or insure against that risk.
> The arrangements agreed to monitor the effectiveness of the risk actions.

Current Risk Register

Risk No	The Risk Identified	Probability	Impact	Action Plan	Monitoring Actions
1	Change in government policy	Low	Severe	MD is to hold regular meeting with Ministers	
2	Industrial unrest	High	Severe	Inclusion of management of change project	Attitude surveys
3	Failure to achieve targets	Medium	Medium	Regular review of benefits plan by programme executive board.	Update benchmarks every 3 months
4	Competition	Medium	High	Monitor competitors, PR campaign.	Competitor review every 3 months distributed to programme executive board.

234

EXAMPLE 16 COMMUNICATIONS PLAN

Introduction

The communication plan defines the strategy that will be followed and the plan for how the programe management team will communicate with the relevant parties, the progress made with the programme. It also defines who will tell what to whom and their delegated authority.

This document is divided into the following sections:

> The communications strategy.
> Monthly communication process.
> Ad Hoc communication process.
> Roles and responsibilities.

1. THE COMMUNICATIONS STRATEGY.

The communication strategy decided by the programme executive board for this programme is based on controlled openness and regular reporting.

This approach has been chosen because of the sensitivity of this programme where it is vital the organisation receives information only from approved sources.

The majority of such reports will be provided by the programme and project office (PPO) and approved by the programme executive board– the only exception to this ad hoc reporting which will be in accordance to the policy set down. This communication strategy will be reviewed at the end of each tranche of the programme and in the case of an exception report raised by the programme manager.

2. MONTHLY COMMUNICATION PROCESS.

The monthly communication process will be the major route by which the programme will communicate information about the programme to the organisation.

The process is as follows:
The project managers will provide summary reports to the (PPO) on the 25th day of each month.

The PPO will prepare the draft progress report and send it to the programme manager by the 27th of the month.

The programme manger will review the report and circulate it to the programme executive board who will authorise (or not) its distribution by the 30th of the month.

The PPO will then circulate the report to the agreed circulation list (see annex 1). The corporate communication department will prepare the news letter from this information – any supplementary information will be requested from the programme manager. (see ad hoc reporting). This newsletter will be circulated to the agreed circulation list (see annex 2).

Any requests to be included on either circulation list must be submitted to the PPO and approved by the programme executive board.

3. AD HOC COMMUNICATION PROCESS.

Any request received for ad hoc information must be referred to the programme manager who will decide whose approval is needed to release the information to that requester. **This process is mandatory for all information requested in addition to that published through the monthly progress reports.**

4.   ROLES AND RESPONSIBILITIES.
The following table describes the roles and responsibilities.

Programme executive board	Approval of monthly report. Approval of special reports. Approval of circulation lists. Approval of major Ads Hoc requests.
Members of the programme executive board	Approval of medium and low importance ad hoc requests (see programme manager)
Programme and project office.	Preparation of all monthly progress reports and once approved their circulation .
Programme manager	Vetting all progress reports. Deciding who must authorise ad hoc reports – Major importance programme executive board, medium importance the programme director, low importance – any member of the programme executive board, clarification – programme manager.

EXAMPLE 17 PROJECT INITIATION DOCUMENT FOR THE XXX PSO PROJECT

Objectives of the Project.

The following project objectives are proposed:

1. Develop and implement a core 'centre of excellence' within XXX to support the programme, project and product management processes and procedures in terms of quality, resource and financial management.

2. Determine and agree the scope and function of the Project Support Office (PSO), i.e. distinguishing between project support and project management office responsibilities.

3. Establish the phases in which the PSO set-up and implementation should be carried out, in line with delivering short term tactical solutions ('quick wins') whilst managing expectations regarding longer term initiatives.

Included

Organisation   Support to senior management.
                       Support to sales management.
                       Support to project management.
                       Support to XXX resource or line managers.

Areas of Focus: Strategic planning.
                       Sales management
                       Project management resource.

Quality Management:
                       Supporting the project management processes and procedures e.g. risk, change, issue, vendor management.

Resource Management:
                       The capture and supply of skills, experience and knowledge for projects as well as activity tracking.

Financial Management:
                       Budgeting, reporting, monitoring and control of costs for projects and business as usual.

Users: Strategic Management.
            Sales management.
            Project Management.

Specifically Excluded

The following are excluded from project but may be included in future phases.

- Quality management.
- Service management.
- Financial management

Implementation – Guiding Principles

Delivery Focused

The project will be structured to ensure the delivery of tangible benefits at key milestones during the course of the project rather than taking a big bang approach to implementation.

Consistency

The project will follow the current version of the XXX project management guide.

Organisational Buy-In

To assist in achieving the required level of buy-in the project will include the development and operation of a communication strategy and plan and an attitude change plan.

These will be used to both communicate what XXX PSO is trying to achieve and to create the support needed to effect the required changes to policy and methodologies.

Approval

In accordance with the project management method the project team will consult with management and obtain approval for any proposed changes to the scope of the project or its project plan.

Approach

It is intended to take a four-phase approach to this project as outlined below:

Phase One: *Provide Support for Senior Management*

No	Task
1	Design & agree format of new reports
2	Extend existing sales portfolio into a full project portfolio database
3	Set up and introduce use of psuedo projects for business as usual activities

No	Task
4	Set up and introduce pseudo projects for sickness, holiday and authorised absence.
5	Identify project types to be used in estimating matrices and system development methodologies database
6	Populate estimates database
7	Introduce new management reports

Phase Two: *Project Management Support*

No	Task
1.	Set up constructive audit function
2.	Update project management methodology
3.	Update system development methodologies and plans
4.	Update (as required) resource management plans with, business as usual and authorised absence
5.	Develop and introduce (as required) new senior management reports
6.	Develop data dictionary
7.	Build detailed level estimating database
8.	Develop and implement library of workpackages and deliverables
9.	Development of Benchmarks for common workpackages and products
10.	Support Software tools supplier to introduce links between project plans and resource management plans

Phase Three*: Enhancing Sales Support System*

No	Task
1	Extend existing sales portfolio to include over the horizon projects.
2	Develop and provide tailored versions of senior management reports on forward resource usage.
3	Develop and provide estimates for the most commonly occurring projects.

Phase Four: *Enhancing the Resource Management System*

No	Task
1	Extend existing resource management system to include details of skills and competencies and history of workpackages and products delivered.
2	Develop special views to enable resource and line managers to utilise the new information.

Issues

- Input from XXX and project management will be required for this initial work, and a budget will be required for external consultancy resources.

This is a critical as it will form the basis for defining and agreeing the most suitable way forward for the PSO implementation.

- Project responsibilities – XXXX will manage the PSO establishment project.

- There are a number of variables that will affect the timing on the delivery of the project including scope, resourcing, short and long-term priorities and existing levels of other project activity.

- The initial design will provide as complete as possible a description of all the proposed functions and processes – However these will be implemented in phases. The contents of the phases will be selected on the basis of those that fulfil the following criteria "maximum gain to XXX – minimum pain involved in implementation".

EXAMPLE 18 TERMS OF REFERENCE FOR MASTERPLAN COMMITTEE

1.   PURPOSE OF THIS DOCUMENT

To describe the purpose, objectives and role of XXXXX masterplan committee in order for executive management to agree on its inception and its membership.

2.   AIMS AND OBJECTIVES OF THE MASTERPLAN COMMITTEE
Aim

To recommend to the Board a masterplan portfolio that will assist XXXX to achieve its required strategic goals and direction and to oversee the management and delivery of that portfolio.

Objectives

1. To demonstrate to the Board (via a masterplan) that the portfolio is meeting it's agreed strategic requirements and direction by.

   - Reporting on a monthly basis the contents of and progress made in the completion of the portfolio.

   - Implementing the Board's decisions to commission, cancel or redirect a project.

   - Proposing to the Board the initial prioritization of the projects in the portfolio and to ensure any subsequent changes to those priorities are implemented by line and or resource managers.

2. To ensure and demonstrate to the Board that XXXXX has sufficient resources to deliver its agreed portfolio by.

   - Regularly reporting to the Board on the ability of the existing XXXXX resources to deliver the agreed portfolio and to recommend any remedial action that is needed.

   - Regularly reviewing the short term (the coming year) and long term (3 years) resource requirements needed to complete the portfolio.

3. To ensure and demonstrate to the Board that the delivery of the portfolio is being effectively managed by:

   - Reporting to the Board on the effectiveness of the management and delivery of the portfolio.

   - Ensuring projects are initiated and managed in accordance with the agreed processes.

   - Authorizing the initiation of a project (up to and including the production of the feasibility study report).

   - Reviewing feasibility study reports from each project and to recommend to the Board if it should proceed or removed from the portfolio (Go- No).

   - Regularly reviewing each project's progress and where appropriate e.g.

Where the project has or will exceed its agreed timescale or costs.
Where the project does not have the resources it requires.
The feasibility study shows that the project is not viable.
A major technical problem has emerged that cannot be dealt with.

To make recommendations to the Board for any action that is needed.

3.   **THE CONSTITUTION AND MEMBERSHIP OF THE MASTERPLAN COMMITTEE**

Constitution

The masterplan committee (MPC) is formed - within the limits set by the Board - to ensure that all projects within XXXXX are effectively monitored and controlled through the agreement and updating of the masterplan and associated documents.

Note: responsibility for the tactical allocation (on a daily or short term basis) of specific resources remains the responsibility of line managers.

The MPC will meet every two weeks or once a month to formally review, update and approve the masterplan.

Membership

The MPC has the following representation:

At least one representative from xxx representative(s) should be able to represent xxxxxx with their requirements for new product and services, and enhancements to those that already exist.

At least one representative from xxxx- representative(s) should be of significant standing with the xxxx organisation and understand the operational impact, internally and externally, of each new development, or represent operational project requests.

At least one representative from xxxx - representative(s) should be responsible for ensuring that XXXX uses its resources effectively and helping with the financial cost control of projects.

Project support office manager - ensures the relevant documents are available, processes have been implemented and to assist the chairman with the management and administration of the meeting.

4.   **ROLES AND RESPONSIBILITIES OF THE MEMBERS**

The MPC has four classes of members:

Chairman
Members
Project support office manager
Requested attendee

The chairman role

- To chair the meeting,

- To ensure that meetings are run to an acceptable standard and that all decisions are accurately recorded,
- To represent the masterplan committee at the Board,
- To ensure that all subsequent actions are carried out effectively and efficiently.

The chairman and members jointly

- Ensure that the masterplan takes account of the strategy and constraints set by XXXX Board, e.g. project budget limits and reporting requirements.
- Review project ideas and grant approval where justified for those projects to proceed to a feasibility study
- Based on the feasibility study report, the project definition, and defined budgets recommend to Board whether a project should be commissioned.
- Confirm that projects in the masterplan have been successfully completed.
- Provide regular reports to the Board and department heads as required.
- Recommend to Board where control action needs to be taken e.g. Closing projects, changing priorities, reallocating funds and resources, or allowing a longer time to complete.

Project support office manager

- Organise the necessary documents and administration activities to support the MPC meetings
- Ensure that the decisions made are accurately recorded and any subsequent actions are carried out.
- Ensure reports and other documents are prepared as required.

Visiting Member

- Provides specialist input to the MPC as requested
- Provides papers and other documents as required.

5.   PURPOSE OF MEETINGS
The committee meets once a month or fortnightly to:

1. Look at all project requests and decide which should proceed to feasibility and to review project feasibility reports to recommend to Board which projects should be commissioned.

2. To review the masterplan portfolio to see if any project should be recommended to the Board for closure or redirected to reflect changes in priority or business need.

3. To review the status of each project through the progress reports provided by each project manager.

6.   INTERFACES TO OTHER COMMITTEES AND BUSINESS UNITS

The masterplan committee will prepare recommendations to the Board for XXXX yearly budget process on staffing and other resourcing issues on both long-term (3 years) and short-term (within 1 year) requirements. The MPC will, if necessary, make requests during the year to the Board for the release of additional resources.

The MPC reports on a regular basis on the status of the masterplan and XXXX masterplan portfolio to the Board.

The MPC interacts with line managers, project managers

The MPC will also interact with corporate planning and control for project cost control and HR on resource issues. The exact nature of these interactions will be determined when the by the masterplan committee is in place.

7. OVERVIEW OF THE MPC PROCESSES

The primary role of the masterplan committee is during the 'initiation' and 'feasibility' phases of the project lifecycle. The actions taken during these two phases are described below.

Project Initiation Phase

When a member of staff identifies that a new project or programme is needed they complete a project request form. This is a simple one page form containing the following:

- sponsor or requester name; project title, high level scope, rationale, objectives, market date; link to corporate objectives; benefits and competitive assessment,

- The project request, once approved, is given a project ID and included in the masterplan as a project held for recommendation by the masterplan committee,

- The project request is passed to the projects committee who use their specialised knowledge to complete the project initiation report and provide the following:

> Assumptions; high level member, system and departmental impacts; total project cost estimation, and detailed costs for feasibility.

Based on this information, the MPC completes the report and decides on GO/NO for feasibility; on relative priority; and nominates the project manager or business analyst to conduct the feasibility study. Any comments from the sponsor/requester are also included in the report.

Project Feasibility Phase

Once approved by the masterplan committee, the project manager, analyst, and project requester work together to produce the project initiation document, and business justification (down to the business case level if necessary).

The project initiation document includes: service description and business requirements; impact analysis (member, system, operational, organisational); solution proposal and risk analysis; a high level plan covering all project phases; budget requirement; project structure; a detailed plan for the analysis phase.

When reviewing the master plan portfolio, the committee will look for held projects that could be combined with new project requests, recommend cancellation of projects that are no longer required, or do not make business sense, and start any held or pending projects that they can.

The committee uses the master plan to help them in this process as well as the portfolio and progress reports.

8.   DOCUMENT VERSION HISTORY

Business justification will describe the qualitative and quantitative benefits of the project, down to a detailed business case if necessary.

The project manager, analyst, and project requester prepare a project feasibility report, which includes the project definition and business justification. The master plan committee reviews the feasibility report and provides recommendations on project go/no go, planning, priority, responsibilities, and reporting. Any comments from the sponsor/requester are also included in the report. The feasibility report with the recommendations of the MPC goes to the Board for decision.

The project initiation document with its detailed plan and resource allocation will be first approved by the projects committee as a quality control unit.

The committee looks at all new project requests, ensures that they are really needed and decides what priority is to be given. Feasibility reports are prepared and if this means other projects are to be suspended, or stopped, or de-prioritised, this is provided as recommendations to the Board.

EXAMPLE 19 BUSINESS STRATEGY, PROGRAMME/PROJECT CONTRIBUTION MATRIX

Business Strategy	To obtain 30% of the companies sales via E Commerce within 3 years.		
	Programme /Project	Contribution- Benefits	% Contribution to Strategy
1.	Project 1 Research report on options to introduce E Commerce. (To identify if the company should have its own Web site , use an ISP or other companies sites (shopping mall)	Infrastructure To all the projects and programmes. Assessed as 10% contribution.	10%
2.	Programme 1 To design and install new computer systems for the warehouse to operate internet as well as conventional orders.	Delivery of main functionality. Assessed as 25%	25%
3.	Programme 2 Management of attitude changes needed. (To cover both internal and external changes including customer attitudes).	Infrastructure To all the projects and programmes. Assessed as 20% contribution	15%
4.	Programme 3 Design of Internet Site and conversion of stock control systems to work with Internet orders. (The development of the site and also the interface between the site software and the warehouse stock control (see programme 1)	Delivery of main functionality. Assessed as 25%	25%
5.	Programme 4 Development and launch of new marketing policy. (New point of sale materials, advertising)	Infrastructure To all the projects and programmes. Assessed as 10% contribution	10%
6.	Project 2 New Sales Information program. (To enable sales trend data to be extracted automatically.)	Marginal benefit. Assessed at 5%	5%
7.	Programme 5 Sales by credit card. (To provide the ability to handle credit card sales electronically.	Infrastructure To all the projects and programmes. Assessed as 10% contribution	10%

EXAMPLE 20 PROGRAMME OR PROJECT INITIATION FORM

PROGRAMME OR PROJECT SUBMISSION FORM

Submission No:	User Department/s:
Programme or Project Initiator:	Date Submitted:

Reason for/Description of Submission

PROGRAMME OR PROJECT DETAILS

Programme or Project ID:

Programme or Project Title:

Programme or Project Manager:	Programme or Project Sponsor:

Scope

Objectives

Benefits

Dependencies/Constraints

Estimated Start Date:	Estimated Completion Date:

COMMISSIONING RECORD

Masterplan Committee Meeting	Decision Taken Hold/Commission Process/Reject Priority	Reason (where appropriate)

COST ESTIMATE

	Consultancy	Internal	Bought In	Equipment	Total
Capital					
Revenue					
Budget Codes			Total Cost	£	

APPROVALS

	Masterplan Committee	Sponsor
Name		
Signature		
Date		

EXAMPLE 21 MASTER PLAN PORTFOLIO DATABASE

Initial Ref No.	FS Ref. No.	Prog Or Proj. Code	Corp. Obj No.	Title	Date Included in Masterplan	Programme/Project Requestor	Programme/Project Sponsor	Programme/Project Manager	Baseline Start	Actual Start	Baseline End	Planned End	Baseline Man Days	Man Days Used	Baseline Cost	Actual Cost	Status Red Amber Green

EXAMPLE 22 FEASIBILITY STUDY REPORT

Proposed Project XXXXXXXX

Feasibility Study
Internal

1.   Document Control
1.1. Sign-off Details

Document Name	Owner	Version Date
Feasibility Study	Master-Plan Committee	

Original Author	Department	Date Written

Sign-off Authorities	Role	Date	Signature

1.2.   Distribution List

Name	Role	Reason
	Business Owner	Content Owner
	Input & Review	Key Reviewer
	Input & Review	Key Reviewer

1.3.   Contributors

Name	Role	Contribution
	Business Owner	Contents
	Input & Review	Contents
	Input & Review	Contents

1.4.   Reviewers

Name	Role	Sections Reviewed
	Business Owner	All
	Review	All
	Review	All

1.5.   Version History

Version No	Version Date	Requester of Change	Ref. Document
0.0 Draft			

1.6.   Document Change Mechanism

- Any requirement for change must be addressed to the author.

- For documents with draft status, the author may make changes at will.

- For documents with controlled status, the Sign-off authorities must approve changes.

250

Table of Contents

2. PROPOSAL SUMMARY SHEET

2.1. Project Identification

Project Idea Ref:
Project Code:
Corporate objective:

2.2. Project Responsibilities

Project Sponsor:
Business Owner:
Project Manager:

2.3. Deliverables Summary

3. MANAGEMENT SUMMARY

3.1. Project Purpose

3.2. Major Deliverables

3.3. Financial Case

3.3.1. *Revenue*

3.3.2. *Return on Investment*

4. ALTERNATIVE APPROACHES / BUSINESS CASES

Complete alternative analysis for each project alternative.

4.1. Alternatives Summary

Alternative	Description	Benefits	Cost
Alternative 1			
Alternative 2			
Alternative 3			

4.2.   Alternative 1 - .

        4.2.1.   ***Costs vs. Realisable Benefits***
        4.2.2.   ***Impacts***
        4.2.3.   ***Risks***

4.3.   Alternative 2 -

        4.3.1.   ***Costs vs. Realisable Benefits***
        4.3.2.   ***Impacts***
        4.3.3.   ***Risks***

4.4.   Alternative 3 -

        4.4.1.   ***Costs vs. Realisable Benefits***
        4.4.2.   ***Impacts***
        4.4.3.   ***Risks***

5.   Impact Analysis of Recommended Option

The recommended option is Alternative XX

5.1.   Customers/Users

5.2.   IT & Support Staff

5.3.   Operations/Support Staff

5.4.   Third Party Suppliers/Software Houses

5.5.   Legal

5.6.   Sponsoring Department

6.   Organisation

6.1   Decision-making Bodies

6.1.1. Masterplan Committee

The masterPlan committee includes managers coming from the various divisions and departments of XXXXX. The masterplan committee's purpose is to make the interface between executive management and the project committee.

Main tasks are:

- approval to go ahead after each phase of the project based on the various deliverables ('project idea', 'feasibility report', ...) and based on budget considerations.
- put priorities on the various projects.
- solve issues escalated by the project committee.
- review closure of the projects.

252

6.1.2. *Project Committee*

The Project Committee include managers of the several IT departments.
Main tasks are:

- review project definition before passing on to masterplan committee.
- track progress of all projects.
- solve resources conflicts and other issues reported by project managers.
- review project closure.
- escalate issues to IT management committee and to masterplan committee.

6.1.3. *Sponsoring Department*

6.2.   Team Organisation

6.2.1. *Project Team*

The following is the team organisation:

6.2.2. *Project Sponsor*

The project sponsor is responsible for helping ensure the final success of the project.
He/she participates in the definition of the requirements.

For this project, XXXXXX is the sponsor. The project requester is XXXXXX.

6.2.3. *Project Manager*

For this project, the project manager is XXXXXX from XXXXXXX.

The project manager has overall responsibility for the complete project, across all departments involved, for resource commitment, project schedule, control and budget follow-up.

He/she tracks the progress of the tasks performed by each department and reports progress and issues to the project committee.

He/she participates in the approval process of all main deliverables.

For this project, a monthly meeting will be held to review progress.

6.2.4. *Specialist Skills Required for the Project*

6.3.   Management Control

6.3.1. *Project Reports*

The project manager will prepare a weekly project status report for the project sponsor copied to the project support office.

6.3.2. *Statement of Change Control*

No changes to the project will be considered by the project manager without written request. All change requests must be:

- submitted to the project committee for tracking.
- approved by the project sponsor.
- approved by the project business owner and/or customers.
- approved by the project committee.

The project manager has full management authority to action such requests providing they do not:

- extend the project scope.
- extend agreed time-scales.
- exceed the budget by more than agreed contingency.

7.   PROJECT PLAN OF RECOMMENDED OPTION

7.1.   Milestones

Extract from Microsoft Project by selecting milestones in the Gantt Chart view

7.2.   Gantt Chart

Extract from Microsoft Project

7.3.   Resource Requirements

8.   APPENDIX A - PROPOSED CONTENTS/FUNCTIONS/SERVICES TO BE PROVIDED BY THE PROJECT

EXAMPLE 23 PROGRESS REPORT TO MASTER PLAN COMMITTEE

Summary of Programme and Project Progress Report									
						TO DATE			
Ref. Number	Current Phase	Unresolved Programme or Project Threatening Issues	Plan/Actual Resources %	Plan/Actual Spend %	Plan/Actual Milestones %	Plan/Actual Delivery %	Overall Assessment of Project Status	Red Amber Green

EXAMPLE 24 PROFORMA EXCEPTION REPORT AND PLAN

EXCEPTION REPORT	From:	To:			
Why This Report is Needed					

PRODUCTS AFFECTED IN THIS STAGE					
Product ID	**Due to Start**	**Due to Finish**	**Impact of Problem**		
			Time	**Cost**	**Comments**

OTHER PRODUCTS/PROJECTS AFFECTED					
Product ID	**Due to Start**	**Due to Finish**	**Impact of Problem**		
			Time	**Cost**	**Comments**

OPTIONS CONSIDERED	Effect on Problem	COST		Comments
		Time	**Resources**	
1.				
2.				
3.				

RECOMMENDATION AND REASONS:

EXAMPLE 25A END OF PROGRAMME TRANCHE REPORT

To: The Programme Board

From: Jan McClelland

Subject: End-Tranche Report

Introduction
This paper summarises the reports, presentations and agreements made at the end-tranche meeting held at the office of Philip Henry 12 February 2000.

Programme Managers Report
The programme is running approximately 3 weeks later. This is due to delays experienced on project two earlier in the tranche when resources were not available and we had to recruit and train new staff to carry out part of the business process re-engineering. This had a knock on effect on projects 3,4,6 and ultimately the whole programme.

This has delayed the benefits that were planned for this tranche and as a consequence special funding arrangement were needed to match the shortfall of funds the delay caused.

In addition the communication and attitudinal change plan had not proved to be substantial enough in that several cases of actual sabotage had occurred which were traced back to disaffected staff. This had caused minor problems but were indicative that more work was needed in this area if the second and more demanding tranche of the programme was to be successful.

Benefits Realisation/Sustainability Plan
The plan has been updated to reflect the agreement and plans that that have been agreed during this tranche and the benefits that are planned to be raised when we complete this tranche.

The report will be updated once these benefits have been obtained.

At present the programme has not realised any benefits.

(see appendix 1)

Programme Plan

The programme plan has been updated and is now as follows:

Tranche Two

Project 6   Completion of project.
Project 10   Commenced.

Year Three of the Programme

Project 7   Completion of project.

End of Tranche Two
Implementation of cross charging administrative processes for government information systems service.
Benefits realised £ 261,000K

Tranche Three

Project 8   Completion of project.
Project 9   Completion of project.

Year Four of the Programme

Project 11   Commenced.
Project 12   Commenced.

End of Tranche Three
Operation of administrative processes to support cross charging for government information systems (reduction in staff in government departments) implementation of business process re-engineering - Part One - Purchasing of books and new operational processes.
Benefits realised £11,025 K (part)

Tranche Four

Project 10   Completion of project.
Project 11   Completion of project.
Project 12   Completion of project.
Project 3   Completion of project.

End of Tranche Four
Implementation of business process re-engineering - Part Two - Relocation aspects.
Benefits realised £11,025 K (part)

EXAMPLE 25B END OF PROJECT STAGE REPORT

To: **The Masterplan Committee**
                  The Project Sponsor
                  The Project Requester
                  The Project Board
                  Project Support Office

From: **Mr P Farmer**
                  Project Manager

End-Stage Report

Project Managers Report

The project was still within the original project plan although a number of amendments have been made to the project initiation document. These have been approved by the project sponsor and the masterplan committee and are included in the current version (number 4) of the project initiation document.

The major uncertainty left in the project was the conversion of the existing stock and sales records. To reduce this uncertainty the project manager requested that some of the staff were asked to assist the team who were to key in the data into the database during September. The manager of department X agreed to arrange this and the project plan is to be amended to reflect the increase in user involvement.

Project Team Report

User Aspects

The only item raised by the user department was concerned with the number of deliverable descriptions that she had been asked to review for the next Stage. The project manager had explained that this was an exceptional Stage as it had contained a lot more user deliverables than previous phases and this had resulted in the user department- having to vet approx. 20 deliverable descriptions in the last 3 weeks. It was agreed that if the project manager felt that such a workload was likely to occur again then she would ask the manager of department x to appoint a further person to the project team role to help out.

Product Quality Reviews

The project team leader reports that all the product quality reviews scheduled for the stage had been completed and only two deliverables had remedial work still outstanding. The project team leader (who attended the review of Deliverable 3) said that he felt that it could have been reviewed informally. He had examined the records to see why it had been selected for a formal review and it appears as if the project manager had not correctly applied the checklist of the factors for selecting formal versus informal reviews. The project sponsor and project manager have discussed this and reviewed the agreed level of reviews for the next stage of the project to ensure that the checklist was being correctly applied and that it did reflect the needs of this project.

Project Issue Status

Three 3 project issue reports had been received and had all been processed. An analysis of all the project issues received to date will be prepared in the next two weeks to see if any trends were emerging. This will be presented at the next mid-stage meeting.

Standards

The use of the deliverable descriptions from the system development handbook has helped in setting the standards required in the quality criteria. In respect of the standards used for project management it had been requested by several of the users for the distribution of the monthly progress summary report to be amended to include them. The project manager and sponsor have discussed this and it has been agreed to amend the distribution list to include these people.

The Project Plan

The only changes to the project plan (version 5) from that agreed in the previous stage were that the data conversion and take on deliverables had been allocated additional user resources (see item 2).

The project sponsor has approved the new plan but pointed out that as there was only 13 days tolerance left any further time slippage would resort in them having to request additional time from the masterplan committee. The project sponsor has stressed that he is to be informed if the project manager felt that the project would go outside of the remaining tolerance.

The Business Case

The business case has been updated to reflect the costs incurred to date and also the updated benefits that were identified during the last stage. The project sponsor has asked the user department x to investigate the claimed increased benefits and report on this at the next mid-stage meeting.

Business Risk Assessment

A review of the risk assessment had been carried out. There were no new risks identified and the containment strategy has worked well. The overall level of risk for the project was still medium due to the development work being dependent on the new version of the operating system that was due for release in September.

Next Stage Plan

The plan for the next stage is attached. It is different from that in version 4 of the project plan as follows:

Deliverable 12 was no longer required due to the user specification being frozen by the project sponsor at the last end-stage report

Total duration of the stage is less 3 days and the resources required less 24-man days.

A new deliverable has been identified as being required this is shown as deliverable 97. It is a trial of the data conversion software that will be carried out in this stage to identify any problems that may arise when the full conversion takes place.

The changes in this plan from the project plan had been included in both the updated risk assessment and business case.

Approval to proceed

Formal approval of the project board, sponsor and masterplan committee is requested for the project to proceed.

EXAMPLE 26A PROGRAMME CLOSURE REPORT

To: The Programme Board
From: The Programme Manager

Programme Closure Report – United Libraries Service

INTRODUCTION

The purpose of this report is to describe the reasons why the programme has been closed and the arrangements that have been put into place to realise and sustain the benefits.

The report also describes the lessons learnt during the programme.

This report is divided into five sections:

Section One is a review of this programme against its objectives, its plan and the effectiveness of the programme management processes and standards. In addition it contains statistics for the following functions:

> Planning and control.
> Exception reports

Section Two contains the Lessons Learnt that are pertinent to this programme only and should not be taken as a global change to the programme management method on future programmes.

Section Three contains the Lessons Learnt that are pertinent to all future programmes and should be applied as a global change to the programme management method.

Section Four describes the arrangements that have been put into place to realise and sustain the benefits from the programme.

Section Five describes the arrangements and actions taken in regard of the projects that have not yet been finalised.

SECTION ONE

1.1   Programme Aim and Objectives

The original aim of the new United Libraries Service programme was to put into place business systems which would enable it to become the source of information for 75% of the UK population. The information provided by the United Library Service was to consist of all published fiction and non fiction books, other publications, government publications, and any available job vacancies publicly known. In order that this aim was met in an economic and efficient manner the following targets were set for the new service:

1. The services must be situated so that they are available within 1 mile of at least 75% of the population.
2. The number of members of each library is to be increased from 1.2K to 4K by extending the services provided to include:
   - Provision of direct access via the Internet and Intranet to UK government departments information and inquiry system's.
   - Relocating local job clubs to the library (they will use the technology provided for the Internet and Intranet service).
   - Increasing the number of publications available for members at each library from 333K to 600K.
3. Reducing the costs of the operation and provision of:
   - The library service. (Planned £11,025K)
   - Government information and inquiries. (Planned £261,000K)
   - The job club service. (Planned £249,080K)
4. Improving the quality of life of the members/general population by:
   - Increasing their average reading age and the number of books read per year. (Planned 30).
   - Reducing the time a job seeker spends looking for employment. (Planned 4 months)
   - Expanding the amount of and access to, government information. (Planned 6,000K)

1.2. PROGRAMME REVIEW

This section is subdivided into an analysis of the benefits achieved by the programme and the effectiveness of the programme management method.

1.2.1 Analysis of the Benefits Achieved

Quantitative Benefits (all figures in £ ,000)

Libraries	
Operational cost	$(0.25-0.17) \times (17-15) \times 2{,}000 \times 1{,}650 = £XXXK$
Cost of procurement of new books	$(7.5-5) \times 450 \times 1{,}650 = £1278K$
Repairs and replacements to books	NIL
Total	£ XXXK *Planned £xxxx*
Government Departments	
Inquiries	$(50-20) \times 5{,}500{,}000 = £ XXXXK$
Minus additional staff	$(300-150) \times 45{,}000$ Minus £K
Total	£ XXXXX K ***Planned £XXXXX***

Job Club	
Reduction in Job Seeker allowance	(1800-1200) x 385,000=£XXXX K
Savings in cost of equipment provided	(300-100) x 385,000=£ XXXX K
Saving in revenue costs	(18.7-10.5) x 385,000=£ XXX K
Total	£ XXXK Planned £XXXX
Grand Total	**£XXXX K Planned XXXX**

Qualitative Benefits

Libraries	
Reading age	+ 0.1 yrs
Availability of service	Nil
Number of books read per year	+ 4
Book loan period	Nil
Government Departments	
Value of Information provided	+ £400
Number of Government Departments on line	+ 45
Job Club	
Time awaiting a job	- 2.5 months
Number of information/job sources	+ 10
Availability of Job Club places	+75 x1,650

1.2.2 Summary of the Achievement of the Programme Blueprint

Aims and Objectives
The programme did not completely achieve its aims and objectives because of the following reasons.

1. The Ministry of Information removed the requirement relating to ensuring that libraries were located with 1 mile. This removed the need for tranche four of the programme and triggered its premature closure.
2. The moving of the responsibility for job clubs did achieve nearly all its objectives (X%). The variation between the planned and actual was due largely to the reduction in level of unemployment that occurred during the programme.
3. The provision of the government information service achieved X% of its targets – the failure to achieve 100% was largely due to the reorganisation in government departments that took place following the XXXX election. The new government's policy remains the same however therefore it is very likely that the full anticipated benefits will be realised during the next four years.
4. The programme was also designed to achieve substantial improvement in the operation of ULS's main business processes. These have largely been achieved.

The variation between the planned and actual benefits was due to the relocation not being carried out and therefore it was not possible to complete the proposed redesign of buildings and shelving and storage systems.

(This resulted in £xxxxx of investment having to be written of in respect of the contracts for the research into the possible sites and design contracts that had been let before the decision was made to abandon tranche 4)

1.2.3 The effectiveness of the Programme Management Method

Overall now major problems were experienced with the programme management method. The particular successes were the communication Strategy and the risk assessment method.

The standard risk checklist has been updated to reflect new risks that were identified during the programme.

1.2.4 Analysis of the Statistics

Planning

(As compared with the versions of the plan included in the final PDS Version 9)

Technical Development: Estimating variance

Resources required	Max +25%	Min 0%	Av +3.2%
Cost incurred	Max +40%	Min - 5%	Av +1.6%
Delays	Max +35%	Min -20%	Av +1.8%

Programme Management:

Resources required	Max +35%	Min -20%	Av +4.2%
Cost incurred	Max +40%	Min - 9%	Av +3.3%
Delays	Max +35%	Min - 0%	Av +3.1%

Quality Management:

Resources required	Max+135%	Min -20%	Av+45.5%
Cost incurred	Max +95%	Min - 9%	Av+36.8%
Delays	Max +97%	Min - 0%	Av+42.1%

Summary data

The planned expenditure was	£XXXX
The actual expenditure was	£XXXX
The planned delivery date was	XXXXX
The actual delivery date was	XXXXX

Programme Issue Reports

During the programme 31 programme issue reports were received.

28 were converted into requests for change and all but three were dealt with during the programme.

Three off specification reports were raised and all were dealt with during the programme. Each of these were investigated and the reason why they occurred was that the reviewers had not applied the quality criteria with sufficient rigour. This had occurred because of their inexperience in the Quality Control Review process which was remedied by some in-house training and assistance from an external consultant with the reviews for the remainder of the project.

The programme issue reports were received as follows

Tranche 1	9	(7-RFC 2-OSR)
Tranche 2	7	(6-RFC 1-OSR)
Tranche 3	15	(15-RFC)

The three outstanding RFCs will be considered at the next meeting of the Board for consideration in future programmes.

Quality Control Reviews

37 quality control reviews were held of which 24 were informal and 13 formal.

The following is an analysis of the faults found

Informal

Total number of faults	385
Serious errors	17
Minor errors	368

Formal	
Total number of faults	174
Serious faults	26
Minor faults	48

Rework required

Max 6 Days   Min 1day   Av 1.5days

SECTION TWO   LESSONS LEARNT THAT ARE PERTINENT TO THIS PROGRAMME ONLY

There are only two Lessons Learnt pertinent to this programme that need to be recorded.

The first of these relate to use of the user liaison group that was established during tranche two – the use of an independent chairman.

The independent chairman although effective during the meetings did not provide the drive that was needed between the meetings to take things forward.

The second issue is the use of the programme and project office. The PPO were not used in the risk identification and assessment process as it was felt that these workshops should be driven by the programme management team. This resulted in the programe team not being consistent in the use of the checklist and failing to ensure that new risks were added to the checklist.

SECTION THREE LESSONS LEARNT THAT ARE PERTINENT TO ALL PROGRAMMES

There are three Lessons Learnt should passed onto future programmes.

The first of these are that the benefits realisation and sustainability plan should used as the basis of a project – The benefits realisation and sustainability project. This would ensure that all the activities need are recorded and planned.

The other two problems involve the delays encountered by the projects in the programme. The major causes of which were an inability to obtain specific staff and problems synchronising the production of major deliverables from the programme and Board meetings (resulting in progress held up whilst awaiting Board approval).

It is recommended that in future programmes that Board responsibility for approving such documents should be delegated to the finance and general purposes sub committee which meets every fortnight.

Secondly that the programme board are given the authority to utilise external resources - up to a limit of £X K per month to meet any shortfall in internal resources that emerges.

SECTION FOUR: THE ARRANGEMENTS TO REALISE AND SUSTAIN THE BENEFITS

The Benefits Realisation Plan has been updated to reflect the arrangements that have already been completed and also to include the latest action plans.

In order that this plan is continues to be monitored and the need for control action identified it has been agreed that Mr XXXX (the programe Director will ensure that the

Board is kept up to date with the further fulfilment of the benefits realisation plan and the operation of the arrangements for sustaining them. (see appendix 1 for the latest Benefits Realisation and Sustainability Plan).

SECTION FIVE: THE ARRANGEMENTS AND ACTIONS FOR THE PROJECTS NOT FINALISED.

There are three projects that were not finalized when the programme was closed:

Project Three   Management of Change
Project Eleven   Library Relocation Designs
Project Twelve   Library Relocations and Up Grades

The following arrangements have been made for these projects

Project Three is to continue until XXX and will be subsumed into the proposed programme on adult literacy

Project Eleven is to continue to the end of its stage three – this is when the draft designs will be completed under the contract – the project will then be closed. Until that point this project will be transferred to the Business As Usual Programme under the Mr XXXX the Programme Manager. Arrangements have been made for this transfer to take place this week together with the transfer of responsibility for the financial aspect of that project.

Project Twelve has been closed – The project has started its Project Initiation Stage. The relevant resource and budget managers have been informed of the closure and the resources and budgets reallocated.

EXAMPLE 26B PROJECT CLOSURE REPORT

To: **The Masterplan Committee**
                 SK Motorised Diggers Plc

From: **The Project Manager and Project Sponsor.**

INTRODUCTION

The stock and sales administration project has now been completed and this report has been prepared for the masterplan committee by the project manager and project sponsor to provide a summary of the lessons learnt during this project which can then be incorporated by the masterplan committee into future projects.

This report is divided into 6 sections:

Section One   Selection and appointment of the project team.

Section Two   The involvement of the project team in planning and controlling the project.

Section Three The operation of the product quality review process.

Section Four   The operation of the project issue report process.

Section Five   Observations on the project management standards and procedures used.

Section Six   Recommendations for consideration for adoption in future projects.

SECTION ONE   **Selection and Appointment of the Project Team.**

This was rather an unusual project in that it was the first major IT project in this company and the use of a structured approach was new to all of the members of SK Motorised Diggers who took roles in this project.

The project sponsor was selected by the members of the masterplan committee. The sponsor and project requester executive and senior user attended an on site 1 day seminar which   was   presented   by   the   external   consultant.

This provided a good basis for their role but the lack of experience showed on two occasions when they accepted a major change to the project by approving requests for changes that took the project outside of the project initiation document. Once this had been pointed out took immediate steps to rectify the situation.

The project team also required training and it was found that they required supplementary help during the project. The role of configuration librarian was split between the project manager and the team leader from IT - this worked well except for a small problem when several pirate copies of a document were made for a cascade briefing and were inadvertently used as the basis of another product. The problem arose because the version used was out of date.

SECTION TWO.   The Involvement of the Project Team in the Planning and Control Process.

The majority of the planning effort came from the development company who did ensure that project team were fully involved in the process of developing and agreeing the deliverable descriptions and in providing input to the weekly and monthly progress reports.

The quality of the involvement and advice given by the project team improved as their experience in grew. The coaching provided for the members of the project team as part of the ongoing consultancy support from the project support office helped this confidence to grow.

The only real problem came from the user department X in Stages 4 and 5 where the volume of work initially overwhelmed the user community until they were allowed to spend additional time on the project.

The estimates provided by the user member of the project team were proved to be extremely accurate this we believe was due to the long experience of the person selected for this role.

SECTION THREE   The Operation of the Product Quality Review Process.

In stage 1 and 2 of the project the project team tended to prefer formal quality reviews. This was caused by their inexperience, the lack of guidance in when to use what form of review. To counter this problem two actions were taken.

The first was to produce a checklist of the considerations that should be made when deciding between formal and informal reviews.

The second was some additional training and coaching in the product quality review process and conduct of the review meeting.

All scheduled product quality reviews were held. The quality of the deliverable descriptions improved during the later stages of the project as the quality criteria became both realistic and useful to the producer of the product. This again was due to the inexperience of the project management team but this time we believe it was due to not having used the XXXX structured project management method previously.

SECTION FOUR   **Involvement of the Project Team in the Project Issue Reporting Process**

There were 31 project issue reports submitted during this project. The majority of these came in the early Stages of the project. The introduction of project information into the regular cascade briefings did reduce the flow of the reports. The only concern that the procedure gave was that twice the scope of the project seemed to be expanding out of control and the freezing of the user requirements did help considerably.

SECTION FIVE.   **Observations on the Project Management Standards and Procedures Used.**

The major success in this project was the use of the planning and control software. This provided all of the planning diagrams and the turnaround document system used for telling team members what is to be done and then for submitting actuals saved a considerable amount of effort. The standard proforma for all of the reports proved to be useful and they were only modified so they could be used in the cascade briefings.

The configuration management system worked effectively and apart from two isolated incidents involving users making pirate copies of documents there were no problems. The allocation of the roles to the individuals was successful although the majority of the appointees had no experience of projects and had not had any training when the job descriptions were agreed.

SECTION SIX.   **Recommendations for Future Projects.**

The recommendations are:

1.   Training in the XXXX project management lifecycle should be undertaken at the outset of the project prior to the discussions about the job descriptions.
2.   When team members are inexperienced then the services of an independent coach/mentor should be employed to help them come to terms with the role and the tasks and activities.
4.   A revised standard for plans should be developed which uses the deliverable flow diagram as the main document rather than the Gantt chart.

EXAMPLE 27A POST PROGRAMME REVIEW

To: The Programme Board
From: The Programme Manager

Post Programme Review Report – United Libraries Service

1.   INTRODUCTION

The purpose of this report is to provide an assessment of the programme and the programme management process and supporting standards so that the experience gained on this programme can be used to improve future programmes.

This report is divided into three sections:

Section One is a review of this programme against its objectives and the effectiveness of the programme management processes and standards. In addition it contains statistics for the following functions:

    Planning and control.
    Exception reports

Section Two contains the observations that are pertinent to this programme only and should not be taken as a global change to the programme management method on future programmes.

Section Three contains the recommendations for change that are pertinent to all future programmes and should be applied as a global change to the programme management method.

SECTION ONE

Programme Aim and Objectives

The original aim of the new United Libraries Service programme was to put into place business systems which would enable it to become the source of information for 75%of the UK population. The information provided by the United Library Service was to consist of all published fiction and non fiction books, other publications, government publications, and any available job vacancies publicly known. In order that this aim was met in an economic and efficient manner the following targets were set for the new service:

1.   The services must be situated so that they are available within 1 mile of at least 75% of the population.
2.   The number of members of each library is to be increased from 1.2K to 4K by extending the services provided to include:
     - Provision of direct access via the Internet and Intranet to UK government departments information and inquiry system's.
     - Relocating local job clubs to the library (they will use the technology provided for the Internet and Intranet service).
     - Increasing the number of publications available for members at each library from 333K to 600K.
3.   Reducing the costs of the operation and provision of:
     - The library service. (Planned £11,025K)
     - Government information and inquiries. (Planned £261,000K)
     - The job club service. (Planned £249,080K)
4.   Improving the quality of life of the members/general population by:
     - Increasing their average reading age and the number of books read per year. (Planned 30).
     - Reducing the time a job seeker spends looking for employment. (Planned 4 months)
     - Expanding the amount of and access to, government information. (Planned 6,000K)

3.   PROGRAMME REVIEW

This section is subdivided into an analysis of the benefits achieved by the programme and the effectiveness of the programme management method.

3.1   Analysis of the Benefits Achieved

Quantitative Benefits (all figures in £ ,000)

Libraries	
Operational cost	(0.25-0.17) x (17-15) x 2,000 x 1,650 = £XXXK
Cost of procurement of new books	(7.5-5) x 450 x 1,650 =£1278K
Repairs and replacements to books	NIL
Total	£ XXXK *Planned £xxxx*
Government Departments	
Inquiries	(50-20) x 5,500,000= £ XXXXK
Minus additional staff	(300-150) x 45,000 Minus £K
Total	£ XXXXX K *Planned £XXXXX*
Job Club	
Reduction in Job Seeker allowance	(1800-1200) x 385,000=£XXXX K
Savings in cost of equipment provided	(300-100) x 385,000=£ XXXX K
Saving in revenue costs	(18.7-10.5) x 385,000=£ XXX K
Total	£ XXXK Planned £XXXX
Grand Total	**£XXXX K *Planned XXXX***

Qualitative Benefits

Libraries	
Reading age	+ 0.1 yrs
Availability of service	Nil
Number of books read per year	+ 4
Book loan period	Nil
Government Departments	
Value of Information provided	+ £400
Number of Government Departments on line	+ 45
Job Club	
Time awaiting a job	- 2.5 months
Number of information/job sources	+ 10
Availability of Job Club places	+75 x1,650

3.2 Summary of the Achievement of the Programme Blueprint

Aims and Objectives

The programme did not completely achieve its aims and objectives because of the following reasons.

1. The Ministry of Information removed the requirement relating to ensuring that libraries were located with 1 mile. This removed the need for tranche four of the programme and triggered its premature closure.
2. The moving of the responsibility for job clubs did achieve nearly all its objectives (X%). The variation between the planned and actual was due largely to the reduction in level of unemployment that occurred during the programme.
3. The provision of the government information service achieved X% of its targets – the failure to achieve 100% was largely due to the reorganisation in government departments that took place following the XXXX election. The new government's policy remains the same however therefore it is very likely that the full anticipated benefits will be realised during the next four years.
4. The programme was also designed to achieve substantial improvement in the operation of ULS's main business processes. These have largely been achieved. The variation between the planned and actual benefits was due to the relocation not being carried out and therefore it was not possible to complete the proposed redesign of buildings and shelving and storage systems.

(This resulted in £xxxxx of investment having to be written of in respect of the contracts for the research into the possible sites and design contracts that had been let before the decision was made to abandon tranche 4)

3.3 The effectiveness of the Programme Management Method

Overall now major problems were experienced with the programme management method. The particular successes were the communication Strategy and the risk assessment method.

The standard risk checklist has been updated to reflect new risks that were identified during the programme.

3.4   Analysis of the Statistics

Planning

(As compared with the versions of the plan included in the final PDS Version 9)

Technical Development: Estimating variance

Resources required	Max +25%	Min 0%	Av +3.2%
Cost incurred	Max +40%	Min - 5%	Av +1.6%
Delays	Max +35%	Min -20%	Av +1.8%

Programme Management:

Resources required	Max +35%	Min -20%	Av +4.2%
Cost incurred	Max +40%	Min - 9%	Av +3.3%
Delays	Max +35%	Min - 0%	Av +3.1%

Quality Management:

Resources required	Max+135%	Min -20%	Av+45.5%
Cost incurred	Max +95%	Min - 9%	Av+36.8%
Delays	Max +97%	Min - 0%	Av+42.1%

Summary data

The planned expenditure was	£XXXX
The actual expenditure was	£XXXX
The planned delivery date was	XXXXX
The actual delivery date was	XXXXX

Programme Issue Reports

During the programme 31 programme issue reports were received.

28 were converted into requests for change and all but three were dealt with during the programme.

Three off specification reports were raised and all were dealt with during the programme. Each of these were investigated and the reason why they occurred was that the reviewers had not applied the quality criteria with sufficient rigour. This had occurred because of their inexperience in the Quality Control Review process which was remedied by some in-house training and assistance from an external consultant with the reviews for the remainder of the project.

The programme issue reports were received as follows

Tranche 1	9	(7-RFC 2-OSR)
Tranche 2	7	(6-RFC 1-OSR)

Tranche 3   15   (15-RFC)

The three outstanding RFCs will be considered at the next meeting of the Board for consideration in future programmes.

Quality Control Reviews

37 quality control reviews were held of which 24 were informal and 13 formal.

The following is an analysis of the faults found

Informal

Total number of faults 385
Serious errors   17
Minor errors   368

Formal
Total number of faults 174
Serious faults   26
Minor faults   48

Rework required

Max 6 Days   Min 1day   Av 1.5days

SECTION TWO   OBSERVATIONS THAT ARE PERTINENT TO THIS PROGRAMME ONLY

The programme review identified only two observations that are pertinent to this programme that need to be recorded.

The first of these relate to use of the user liaison group that was established during tranche two – the use of an independent chairman.

The independent chairman although effective during the meetings did not provide the drive that was needed between the meetings to take things forward.

The second issue is the use of the programme and project office. The PPO were not used in the risk identification and assessment process as it was felt that these workshops should be driven by the programme management team. This resulted in the programe team not being consistent in the use of the checklist and failing to ensure that new risks were added to the checklist.

SECTION THREE OBSERVATIONS THAT ARE PERTINENT TO ALL PROGRAMMES

There are three items that should be considered in all future programmes.

The first of these are that the benefits realisation and sustainability plan should used as the basis of a project – The benefits realisation and sustainability project. This would ensure that all the activities need are recorded and planned.

The other two problems involve the delays encountered by the projects in the programme. The major causes of which were an inability to obtain specific staff and problems synchronising the production of major deliverables from the programme and Board meetings (resulting in progress held up whilst awaiting Board approval).

It is recommended that in future programmes that Board responsibility for approving such documents should be delegated to the finance and general purposes sub committee which meets every fortnight.

Secondly that the programme board are given the authority to utilise external resources - up to a limit of £X K per month to meet any shortfall in internal resources that emerges.

EXAMPLE 27B POST PROJECT REVIEW

To: **The Masterplan Committee**

From: **The Projects Committee**

INTRODUCTION

The post project review of the sales project has been carried out on behalf of the projects committee by Ms A Apple. The report has been prepared in conjunction with the project sponsor; project requester, the original project manager and members of the project team and the following recommendations are made to the masterplan committee for adoption.

THE REVIEW

The review was carried out 6 months from the first complete use of the following functions:

> The mailing list.
> The use of the stocklist.
> The use of the requirements prediction program.
> The use of the average stock level program.

COVERAGE OF THE REVIEW

The deliverable description of the post project review was as follows:

PURPOSE

To evaluate how well the business needs of the organisation have been satisfied by the project.

CONTENT

- The reasons for the project and an assessment of their achievement.

- The objectives of the business system as stated in the business case and an assessment of their achievement.

- An analysis of the costs of developing and running the new systems as stated in the business case and were they achieved.

- An evaluation of actual savings made by the new system as compared to those predicted in the business case.
- An evaluation of the performance of the system as compared to that defined in the project initiation form, project initiation document and the user requirements.

- An evaluation of the performance of the new system as compared to the current business needs.

- An evaluation of the effectiveness of the user and other training that was provided and the applicability of the supporting manuals and guidance provided by the development team.

- An evaluation of the impact of the new system on the organisation and identification of any areas which require further investigation for possible changes to working practice.

- Any other issuers that of a user or technical nature that have been identified since the handover of the project to the organisation by the project manager.

FORMAT & DERIVATION

An A4 report in which conforms to the document standards as defined in the quality manual.

Project initiation form, project initiation documents, project and phase plans, the updated business case, phase end review reports, project closure report.

QUALITY CRITERIA

All figures quoted must be substantiated by relevant documents.

The issues identified must be substantiated by documentary or other evidence.

DISTRIBUTION LIST

The report will be distributed to the following staff:

The masterplan committee
The project sponsor
The project support office.

Action/ Follow up Team
The findings of the report will be actioned by Mr P Tasker (Sales Manager) and Mr O Wilde (Department X Manager).

CONTENTS

1. **The Reasons For The Project And An Assessment Of Their Achievement.**

2. **The Objectives Of The Business System And An Assessment Of Their Achievement.**

3. **An Analysis Of The Costs Of Planned And Actual Costs Of The Project.**

4. **An Evaluation Of Planned And Actual Savings.**

5. An Evaluation Of The Performance Of The System .

6. An Evaluation Of The Performance Of The System As Compared To The Current Business Needs.

7. The Effectiveness Of The User And Other Training And Supporting Manuals Provided.

8. Impact Of The New System On The Organisation And Any Areas Which Require Further Investigation.

9. Any Other Issues That Have Been Identified Since The Handover Of The Project.

EXAMPLE 28 SCALING FACTORS TO BE USED ON A PROJECT MANAGEMENT METHOD

Introduction

This example is an illustration of what advice an organisation could develop to enable it to consistently tailor the project management method to ensure it does not compromise the structural integrity of the method.

This example document should not be used without verifying that it is relevant to the specific organisation.

Project Management Organisation Structure

Factor	Tailoring Advice	Things not to amend
Small project	Consider having the same project board for a number of projects. Consider having the same person perform more than one role. Only hold physical project board meetings when required.	Never have less than two members of a project board. Always have a formal sign off procedure even if the board does not meet.
Large scale or high risk project	Use the most senior members of the management on the project board. Form a project assurance team in addition to the project board. Employ external experts to provide guidance/advice to the project board.	Do not remove responsibility for assurance from the project board.
Organisation or project board members inexperienced in projects/project management method	Add additional role to project board to advise them on the application of project management method. Ensure project manager and their team are very experienced. Commission an independent health check at least once in the project.	Ensure that the job descriptions are discussed with the role holders and ensure that all items are addressed.
Project using techniques or technologies new to the organisation.	Add additional role to project board to advise them on the application of new technique or technologies. Ensure project manager and their team are very experienced. Commission an independent health check at least once in the project.	

Project Planning

Factor	Tailoring Advice	Things not to amend
Small project	Use product flow diagram supplemented by schedule and resource information rather than Gantt charts and separate resource plans. Rather than diagrams convert the information to a table format. Do not have separate stage plans unless required for control purposes Adhere as closely as possible to any template or standard plans and product descriptions that are available.	Always have a plan. Always have product descriptions. Ensure the organisation develops templates for such projects. Develop easy to use estimating systems. Ensure the resources that are to be used are booked.
Large scale or high risk project	Ensure the documents produced as part of the planning process are formally reviewed. Ensure all deviations from the standard project or systems development method are documented in the plans. Convert the plans into a "daily diary" to assist in making the plans easier to use. Include the documentation involved in booking the resources in the plan. Use a Delphi type approach to identifying the risk and the risk management plan. Include risk actions in the plan.	Use all the planning processes.
Organisation or project board members inexperienced in projects/project management method	Provide the plans in a format that they can understand. Give a presentation at the project board meetings about the plans as well as the standard documents. Keep all explanations about the plans simple. Introduce the concept/role of the independent expert witness to explain what the plans mean	Use all the planning process. Ensure plans are subjected to a formal quality control review.
Project using techniques or technologies new to the organisation.	Research the changes needed to the standard project or system development method. Buy in a new project or system development method. Build the new project or system development method using the existing project or system development method. Use an expert to provide assurance.	Use all the planning process. Ensure plans are subjected to a formal quality control review.

Project Controls

Factor	Tailoring Advice	Things not to amend
Small project	Beware – although small in size these types of projects can be high risk which mean that they should not be treated as small. Make extensive use of proforma and template reports. Seek to eliminate as many of the formal meetings as possible. Increase the authority of the project manager to deal with some of the control actions without a project board meeting (telephone approval from a project board member).	Always hold end stage meetings Always develop a project initiation document.
Large scale or high risk project	Increase the frequency of formal review points. Introduce mid stage assessment meetings. Use the project assurance function to assess progress. Include risk actions in the progress reports.	Use all the monitoring and control processes.
Organisation or project board members inexperienced in projects/project management method	Provide the progress reports in a format that they can understand. Give a presentation at the board meetings about the progress reports and control process as well as the standard documents. In all situations give explanations about the reports. Introduce the concept/role of the independent expert witness to explain what the reports mean. Keep It Simple.	Use all the monitoring and control processes.
Project using techniques or technologies new to the organisation.	Increase the number of progress review points. Seek advice from other organisations about which monitoring points to use. Increase control tolerances to deal the learning curve that will be encountered.	Use all the monitoring and control processes.

Project Risk, Issue, Change and Configuration Management

Factor	Tailoring Advice	Things not to amend
Small project	Reduce the amount of bureaucracy to the minimum. Keep all supporting systems as simple as possible. Use the same system to record, assess and manage all these items. Consider increasing the responsibility of the project team in evaluating the impact of changes, issues and risks. Ensure evaluation process is as quick as possible.	Keep the functionality. Ensure configuration management is still carried out.
Large scale or high risk project	Consider the appointment of a project administrator to deal with these aspects of the management of the project. Consider having an integrated database to support all of these functions. Include a configuration status account or audit during each stage.	Ensure all aspects of the processes are carried out.
Organisation or project board members inexperienced in projects/project management method	Provide any reports to the project board in a format that they can understand. Give a presentation at the project board meetings about these functions and the control processes. In all situations give explanations about the functions.	Ensure all aspects of the processes are carried out.
Project using techniques or technologies new to the organisation.	Increase communication about these functions to the project team to ensure they do not get forgotten. Research with other organisations the risks associated with these new techniques and technologies.	Ensure all aspects of the processes are carried out

Product Quality Reviews

Factor	Tailoring Advice	Things not to amend
Small project	Beware – although small in size these types of projects can be high risk which mean that the quality control reviews should not be omitted. Consider more informal reviews. Make extensive use of proforma and template documents. Increase defect protection measures.	The irreducible minimum is A product description Sign off At least one formal QR

Large scale or high risk project	Increase the use of formal reviews. Subject the most important products to external or independent review. Use external experts in the review teams. For critical products ensure the product descriptions are subjected to formal review before the product is developed.	Ensure all aspects of the processes are carried out.
Organisation or project board members inexperienced in projects/project management method	Provide information about the quality review process in a format that they can understand. Give a presentation at the project board meetings about the quality control review process as well as the standard documents. Introduce the concept/role of the independent expert witness to oversee the quality control review process on their behalf.	Ensure all aspects of the processes are carried out.
Project using techniques or technologies new to the organisation.	Increase the number of formal reviews. Perform quality control reviews on all product descriptions. Consider commissioning a quality review on the whole project.	Ensure all aspects of the processes are carried out.

284

EXAMPLE 29 PROJECT INITIATION DOCUMENT

INTRODUCTION

The purpose of this project initiation document is to provide a statement of the environment and products required from the project to support the business goals of the organisation.

The project initiation document has been prepared to ensure that the project board and the project management team have an agreed understanding of the system to be developed. It will be used by the project board to define the initial objectives of the project to develop the stock and sales administration system. It contains the baseline plan which will be used to monitor and control the development of the new system.

CONFIRMED PROJECT BRIEF

Project Background

The Board of Ace Plumbing Supplies Ltd. have agreed that their business goal for this year will be:

> *To ensure continued customer loyalty by providing a service level better than its competitors.*

To help meet this goal three major projects have been identified:

1   To install a new switchboard.
2   To upgrade the decoration of the customer area and the trade counter.
3   To develop a new sales and stock system.

This project brief is concerned with project number three.

The existing sales and stock system is now overstretched to the extent that it is inhibiting the growth of sales to both the trade and the public sectors.

The current system does not identify excess or out of date stocks and also has caused a number of errors when goods were sold when they were not in stock.

The sales manager has identified several new sales campaigns, which require a list of current customers - the present system cannot easily supply this.

Project Aims and Objectives

The aim of the project is:

To provide a new sales and stock system which will support the company's business goals.

The specific objectives are:

1   To ensure the sales section has easy access to details of the existing customers to support new sales initiatives.
2   Ensure out of date or excess stock is easily identified.
3   To reduce existing stock levels by 5%.
4   To eliminate selling of stock that does not exist.

Scope and Constraints

Scope

The project is to concentrate its efforts on the sales and stock sections and its systems. Any links with other sections must be documented and defined.

The new system is to support the sales and stock sections, any other assistance it provides to other sections is not to be regarded as having any priority.

Assumptions that have been identified and agreed

The project is to be developed by an external development team.

The system must be easy to use.

The system must be able to cope with the expected growth of 30% this year and 15% for each successive year for the next five years.

The system must be able to supply word processing facilities for the management team.

The new system must not cost any more than £10,000 to install and have a running cost less than the existing manual systems.

The project is to be completed during this financial year.

Reporting

Ace Plumbing Supplies has given full responsibility for this project to a Project Board consisting of Mr. I Balance, Finance Manager (Executive), Mr. J Yorkshire, Sales Manager (Senior User/*Customer*) and Mr. J Kelly (Senior Specialist Supplier) an external consultant engaged to advise Ace Plumbing Supplies.

The project board has full authority to proceed with this project within the limits of this document. If the project board expects to exceed this Brief then it must report to the full board of Ace Plumbing Supplies within five days of this becoming apparent.

BUSINESS CASE

Project Scope

The scope of the project is the sales and stock section of Ace Plumbing Supplies.

Project Life

The project is a long term investment and as such the project life has been agreed as four years.

Options Examined

1   Improvements to the existing system

    This option will involve improving the existing manual system by updating the records currently held by the sales section and by carrying out a full stock check every week to ensure the stock records are accurate.

2   Installation of a partial computer system

    This option will involve installing a computer system to hold details of the stocks held by Ace Plumbing or details of the sales made to its customers.

3   Installation of an integrated sales and stocks computer system

    This option is to provide an integrated computer system that will hold details of all stocks and sales made by Ace Plumbing with an on-line interrogation facility.

Risk and Sensitivity Analysis

The majority of the benefits from the project come from the computerisation of the stock control system. This area must be closely controlled. The sales information does not provide substantial benefits and if any problems occur with the project development then this aspect could be removed from the project.

The project is not critical for money. However it is important that the benefits are realised. To this end we will extend the development life cycle into benefits realisation and keep the project in place until this Product has been completed.

Recommendations

Proceed with Option 3.

COSTS AND BENEFITS SUMMARY

Option 3	Year 0	Year 1	Year 2	Year 3	Year 4
Costs					
Provision of computer System	5000			5000	
Conversion of records	5000				
	10000			5000	
Benefits					
Reduction in sales errors	8000	8000	8000	8000	8000
Reduction in stocks	2500	250	250	250	250
Additional sales	2000	2000	2000	2000	2000
	12500	10250	10250	10250	10250
Option 3					
Costs	10000			5000	
Benefits	12500	10250	10250	10250	10250
	2500	10250	10250	5250	10250
Discount Factor	1.0	.934	.877	.826	.781
Net Present Value	2500	9573	8989	4336	8005
Cum NPV	2500	12073	21062	25398	33403

DEFINITION OF ORGANISATION AND RESPONSIBILITIES

Project Board

- Mr. I Balance,   Finance Manager   Executive
- Mr. J Yorkshire,   Sales Manager   Senior User/*Customer*
- Mr. J Kelly,   External consultant   Senior Specialist Supplier

Project Manager

Jan McClelland

Project Assurance Function

- Ivor Solder   Business Aspects
- Louise Dargavel   User/*Customer* Aspects
- Trevor Whitlock   Specialist Supplier Aspects

Copies of roles and job descriptions are attached as Annex x.

PROJECT PLAN

This section contains a summary of the information contained in the project plan and the accompanying product breakdown structures, product flow diagrams and product descriptions. These are contained in Annex x.

Stage 1

Work package one: products 1 and 2.

To be completed by 16th March

Budget £1,000

Stage 2

Work package two: products 3, 4, 5, 7 and 8.

To be completed by 24th May

Budget £1,500

Stage 3

Work package three and four: products 6 and 9 to 16.

To be completed by 30th July

Budget £6,000

Stage 4

Work package five and six: products 17,18, 19 and 20.

To be completed by 16th October

Budget £1,500

Total Cost £10,000

Project Tolerance +10 days, +£1,000

QUALITY PLAN

Product descriptions: will be prepared for all the products to be developed. these will be agreed with the members of the project assurance function at the creation of the plan in which the products appear.

Quality reviews: each product will be subjected to either a formal or an informal quality review. The level of review and the review teams will be agreed by the project management team when creating the plan in which the products are created.

Documentation: all reviews will be fully documented. Examples of the documents to be used are attached as Annex x.

Controls and reporting arrangements: checkpoint reports will be produced at the completion of every product. Highlight reports every four weeks and circulated to the project board. Mid-stage assessments will be held if (in the opinion of the project manager) an exception report is raised that requires a meeting of the project board. All other arrangements will be as defined in the PRINCE reporting standards. Example proformas of all the reports are attached as Annex x.

PROJECT PREREQUISITES

All members of Ace Plumbing Supplies who will have a project management team role must receive appropriate PRINCE training.

EXTERNAL DEPENDENCIES

The development is dependent on the issue of a new version of the operating system by Mickey Mousesoft.

PLAN ASSUMPTIONS

Suitable space will be found at Ace Plumbing Supplies to locate the computer.

The current records can be converted to the new system.

Ace Plumbing Staff will be made available in accordance with the agreed stage Plans.

PROJECT RISK ASSESSMENT

A full Risk Assessment has been carried out. The results are held in Annex x. The result of the assessment is that the project risk is low.

CONFIGURATION MANAGEMENT PLAN

Note - in this project the role of configuration librarian will be shared by the project support assistant and specialist supplier team members.

Each product will be uniquely identified by a reference number allocated by the project support assistant. It will contain the Product number, version number and type.

Project support assistant, who will store and issue product copies as required, will exercise configuration control.

All project issue will be logged and controlled by the project manager. The procedures for evaluation and processing of the project issue reports will be in accordance with the PRINCE manual.

ANNEXES

Job Descriptions
   Project Board
   Project Manager
   Team Manager
   Project Assurance Function

Project Plans
   Product Flow Diagram
   Work Package and Product Breakdown Structure
   Project Plan
   Supporting Narrative

Quality Review Proformas
   QR Invitation
   QR Error List
   QR Result Notification
   QR Action List

Reporting Proformas
   Checkpoint Report
   Highlight Report
   ESM Agenda
   Risk Assessment Checklist

Glossary of terms

Activity (pp. 91,109,111,150,153)
The work needed to develop or procure an output, deliverable or product. An activity consists of a number of specific tasks.

Added value (pp. 11,15,67,115-116,139,152, 203)
The achievement of additional benefits or worth from a document or other output which is in addition to its primary purpose. (Similar to synergistic effect).

Added value areas/reports (p. 152)
The areas of activity or reports which are designed to achieve added value.

Amalgam plan
A plan which is derived from a collection and consolidation of the key events in other plans.

Asset register (p. 142)
A list of the assets of an organisation. These registers identify what equipment, buildings, machinery, etc, are held by the organisation and all other details of their purchase and location.

Avoidance strategy
A set of activities that are commissioned in a programme or project which are designed to avoid the identified risk occurring.

Backward pass network analysis
Part of the project network technique that identified which activities have zero float and are therefore on the critical path. *(See also 'second pass network analysis')*.

Baselined (p. 83)
The defined and agreed programme or project plan or costs.

Benchmarks (pp. 137,139,140,142-143,154, 175)
A measure of how much input is used by the organisation to produce a specific output, e.g., cost of producing an invoice.

Benefits framework (p. 22)
The totality of plans and arrangements used to enable the organisation to achieve the defined benefits from a programme or project.

Benefits management plan (pp. 23-24)
The plan which defines the benefits and the way that they will be realised.

Benefits management process
The process used by the organisation to define and manage the achievement of the required benefits.

Benefits profile (pp. 22-23,96)
A representation of when the defined benefits must be realised.

Benefits realisation plan (pp. 83,86,97)

A document used by the programme director, programme manager and business change manager to describe the benefits, how they will be achieved, and the detailed plans for their realisation.

Blueprint (pp. 21-24,30,180,308,319)

A document which defines and describes what a programme is designed to achieve in terms of the business vision (quantitative targets) and operational vision (how the process will be operated when the programme is completed).

BOSCARI (p. 174)

An acronym used to describe the contents of terms of reference. (Background Objectives Scope Constraints Reporting Information)

Break-even period

The time taken to recover the costs of a programme or project through savings or other benefits achieved by the same programme or project.

Budget holder (pp. 76,294)

The accountable member of staff who has been given a defined budget of money or other resources.

Budget variances

The variance between the budget and the expenditure made or incurred.

Budgetary approval

The process used by an organisation to decide on the budgets that will be allocated to each of the budget holders and the approval to spend that sum.

Budgeting committee (p. 76)

The group of executive-level management who decide on the amount of the budget to be allocated to each budget holder.

Budgeting review (p. 72)

The process which the organisation uses to review the bids for budget funds.

Burn rate

A calculation of the amount of resources or deliverables that should be used each day during the programme or project. These are compared to those achieved and what is left to do. (This comparison provides a measure of progress as compared to the plan).

Burn-rate indicators

The calculations of planned, to date, and left to do, burn rates.

Business benchmarks

A measure of the performance of a whole business or a part of that business, e.g., sales and marketing costs are £X per £ of turnover (See also' benchmarks').

Business architectures

The structure of business processes used by an organisation to perform, deliver or provide its products and/or services.

Business areas (pp. 295,317)

A sub-division of an organisation into a recognised and self -contained unit, e.g., sales and marketing.

Business-as-usual (pp. 61,135,143,311)

The non-programme or project activities that

are performed in order to operate or support the business of the organisation.

Business change management
The management of the changes to the organisation needed to achieve the defined benefits of the programme or project.

Business change programmes
Programmes which are primarily designed to change a substantial part of an organisation or the products or services it provides.

Business integrity (p. 308)
Ensuring that the programme or project follows that element of the business case which explains the financial or business reasons for the programme or project.

Business-led initiative (p. 189)
The direction of the programme, project or work package by the management of the relevant business areas.

Business objective (pp. 17,18)
A part of the organisation's business plan or strategy which defines a specific objective.

Business operations (pp.17,18,20,21,22)
The operation of the activities and processes used by the organisation to deliver its products or services.

Business processes (pp. 88,137,138,185,294)
The collection of processes used by an organisation to manage its activities.

Business risks
Those potential events which may occur and,

if they do, affect the operation of the business.

Business strategy level plan
A document which describes how an organisation will deliver the defined and agreed business strategy.

Business strategy process
The process used by an organisation to define or update the business strategy.

Business system project
A project which is designed to provide a new or updated business system or processes.

Capital expenditure
Expenditure made which is not counted as a revenue item in the organisation's accounts. (The expenditure is written off over a number of years.)

Centre of excellence
A term used to describe a department or team which is regarded as the expert in a particular activity or function.

Chairman of a quality review
The senior manager who is appointed by the organisation to ensure that a quality review of an output, deliverable or product is conducted to the agreed process, methods and standards.

Change log (p. 57)
The document used to record details of all the changes requested to the programme or project.

Change management (p. 310)
The management of the receipt, evaluation, decision-making and relevant action relating

to changing an aspect of a programme or project.

Checkpoint report (pp. 110,111)

A report prepared by a member of the programme or project team to notify the programme or project manager that an output, deliverable or product has been completed or procured.

Command-type structures

A strict, hierarchical management structure which has clearly defined roles and responsibilities (similar to a structure found in a military organisation).

Communications plan

A plan developed within a programme or project to ensure that the organisation's requirements or needs for information about the programme or project are defined and that activities are planned and assigned to individuals or groups to meet those needs.

Cone of uncertainty

A diagram used to describe the uncertainty that exists in a programme or project through its life cycle, i.e., at the start of the programme or project the uncertainty is at its greatest and reduces as the programme or project nears completion.

Configuration audit report

A report which summarises the results of a review of the current state of the configuration management process and the configuration records and items.

Configuration item identification and numbering system

The system of numbering used to identify each item in the programme or project – the numbering system should enable the easy identification of the relationship of the configuration items to each other.

Configuration management (pp. 23,29,54, 56,57,98,109,11,137,138,139,140,150,190,195, 203,205,296)

The processes used to ensure that the configuration is managed and controlled effectively.

Configuration management record

The information held about a configuration item. This record may be stored electronically or in a card index.

Configuration status account report

A report which describes the current status of each of the items in the configuration management system.

Conformance audit (pp. 47,48)

An audit of the operation of the programme or project management or other processes to identify if the defined processes are being adhered to.

Constructive audit (pp. 30,47,48,206)

An audit of the operation of the programme, project or other processes to identify if the defined processes are providing the required support or assistance. When they are not, what is being done and should it be adopted as the new standard?

Containment strategy

The strategy which is used by the programme or project manager to contain the impact that an identified risk may have on the programme or project, e.g., if the project is more than x months late then...

Contingency

An allowance made to the programme or project duration or cost to allow for any unplanned activities that may be required.

Contingency plan

A plan which is developed to be deployed if a specified event occurs.

Control actions (pp. 21,149)

The actions commissioned by the programme or project board to rectify a deviation from the agreed plans.

Control documents (pp. 87,109)

The documents which define the baseline of the programme or project which are used by the programme or project board in monitoring the progress made and identifying if any control action is needed.

Cultural change

The change in attitude and beliefs that is needed for the organisation to achieve the objectives of a programme or project (see also attitude change plan)

Data dictionary (pp. 117,118, 120-124,129, 132,150,205)

A document that is used to ensure that each unique data item is identified and defined so that it can be used consistently in each of the information systems that use it.

Data dictionary of tasks/products (pp. 117-118,121)

A document which is used to define and identify uniquely the tasks and products used in the programme and project support infrastructure.

Decision trees

A diagram which describes the logic involved in a decision – often supported by estimates of the probability and potential outcome at those decision points which can enable an expected value to calculated.

Deliverable specification (pp. 92,96,109,111)

A written definition of what deliverable the programme or project team is expected to produce or deliver.

Deliverable/product or task category code

A system of categories and codes which are developed to identify uniquely that particular deliverable, product or task in the form of an abbreviation. These codes should be designed to ensure that they respect or enable 'family' trees of such deliverables, products or tasks.

Deliverable/staff database (pp. 117,125,130, 143)

A database of information which identifies which deliverables or products have been developed by which members of staff. (Used to identify which staff have relevant experience of developing that deliverable or type of deliverable).

Deliverables (pp. 52,64,96,121,153,181,300, 316,318)

An output from a development or procurement process which is recognised as a discrete piece of a programme or project.

Delphi technique

A technique used to assess an unknown situation. The technique consists of asking different teams to asses the situation, collating the reports, identifying those assessments that are at variance with the norm of the others, discussion of the reasons for the variance and a second or more subsequent rounds of such assessment, until a consensus is (or is not) reached.

Dependencies (p. 25)

A relationship that exists between two activities/tasks or deliverables or products, e.g., you cannot do the second until the first has finished.

Design consultant

A member of staff who provides advice or develops the design of a whole (or part of a) business system(s).

Design management plan (p. 23)

The plan developed for the management of the design aspects of a programme or project.

Development approach (p. 38)

The method that will be used to develop the outputs, deliverables or products required from the programme or project.

Development process (pp. 38,103,104,106, 113,121,132,143,188,191)

The sequence of processes used by the programme or project team to develop the outputs, deliverables or products required from the programme or project.

Direct financial benefits

Those financial benefits which are generated as a direct consequence of the programme or project.

Direct review (of quality)

The review of the process or item by its direct examination and assessment.

Discounted cash flow

A method of calculating the effect of 'time preference' on an investment which spans over a number of years. Time preference refers to the preference that money today is worth more than the same money tomorrow – ignoring the effects of interest payments and inflation.

Displaced cost

Costs of operating the current business process that will no longer be needed when the programme or project is completed, e.g., maintenance costs on a piece of equipment that will be eliminated by the programme or project.

Drop-down code

The function available in a software package which is invoked by selecting an icon which reveals a range of codes, which if they are selected, are automatically transferred into the working space in the software package. This working space can be a blank document or a proforma such as a time sheet.

DSDM (p. 104)

Dynamic Systems Development Method. A Rapid Application Development method used on IT projects.

Duration (pp. 123,137,142,186,299,300,305)

A expression used in the planning process to describe the calendar or total time that an activity, output, deliverable, or product will take to complete. This includes pure work effort and any other related non-project work or enforced delay that is needed to complete it .

Earned value (pp. 146,153)

An expression used to describe that part of the planning and the progress monitoring and control processes. A monetary value is assigned to the planned and actual work to enable a calculation to be made which assists in defining the current status of the programme or project.

Economic viability

The results of an assessment of the relationship between the inputs and outputs involved in a programme or project.

Economies of scale (pp. 135,141)

The concept that increasing the volume of output or services of a unit reduces the unit cost of those outputs or services because the fixed costs involved are spread over a greater number of units.

Effort (pp. 154,312)

This term is used in the planning and progress monitoring processes to describe the amount of pure work time needed to complete an activity, output, deliverable or product.

Ego-less development

The concept of the removal of the personalisation of the execution of an activity, output, deliverable or product, e.g., this will be developed by an analyst rather than Mary Smith.

Elapsed (time)

The total time used to complete an activity, output, deliverable or product *(See also duration)*.

End-of-stage report

A report produced by a project manager at the end of a stage which summarises the achievements of that stage, updates the plans for the overall project and provides the basis of the decision of the project board on whether or not the project should continue to the next stage.

End of tranche report

A report produced by a programme manager at the end of a tranche which summarises the achievements of that tranche, updates the plans for the overall programme and provides the basis of the decision of the programme board onwhether or no, the programme should continue to the next tranche.

Error list (p. 314)

A list of the potential errors, or non-conformance to the defined standards, of an output, deliverable or product.

Estimating guidelines (pp. 107,116,117,123, 124,137,139,162,176)

A document which provides advice to the project or programme manager on the pure work effort, or elapsed time and or expenditure, that is required to complete a defined output, deliverable or product.

Estimating system (pp. 107,112,123)

A mechanism used to produce estimates for a variety of situations from the same base data.

e.g., if the situation is x then the estimates are y; if the situation is z then the estimates are y + ...

Euromethod

An initiative started by the EC to have a standard project or system development method for IT projects. This method had defined interfaces to each of the open or standard project or system development methods that were used in each of the members of the EC.

Exceptions report/plan

A report produced by a programme or project manager to notify the programme or project board that a situation has occurred that has caused or will cause the programme or project to exceed its planned costs or delivery dates. This report may be supported with plans for the options available to the programme or project board for actions they could commission to remedy or recover from this situation.

Executive management (p. 30)

The most senior level of management in the organisation.

Executive member

An executive or senior manager who has been appointed as the member of the project board who has the overall responsibility for the project.

Execution options (pp. 22,97)

The various methods or approaches that could be used to execute a programme or project.

First-level decision

A part of the decision making process used to assess such things as issues, changes. The first level relates to the decision being made at the lowest level in the decision-making process.

First-level evaluation

A part of the decision-making process used to evaluate the impact of such things as issues and changes. The first level relates to the evaluation made at the lowest level in the decision-making process.

First-pass network chart

The inclusion on a network diagram for a programme or project of the estimates of cost or duration for each component and the calculation of its total cost or duration (See also 'forward pass network analysis').

Formal review (pp. 69,130)

A system of meetings and documentation of each of the steps in the review or assessment of an output, deliverable or product to ensure that it meets or matches its defined specification.

Forward pass network analysis

See – 'First-pass network chart'.

Gantt chart (pp. 110,311)

Named after its inventor Henry Gantt. A chart used in the planning process which describes what activities, outputs, deliverables or products are to be developed or procured, in what sequence, and their start and finish dates.

Generic resources

A skill group in a plan or report, rather than a specific person.

Granularity (pp. 177,183)

The various levels of detail used in plans or progress reports.

Hard deliverables (p. 64)

Tangible outputs (things), deliverables or products developed or procured as part of a programme or project.

Highlight report (p. 110)

A report produced by the project manager to summarise the progress made over a defined period, usually a month.

Incidental costs

Those costs associated with the programme or project which are not directly caused by it.

Indirect benefits

Benefits that are included in a business case which are not directly caused by, or the primary purpose of the programme or project, e.g., the new ... will enable the organisation to also...

Indirect financial benefits

Financial benefits that are included in a business case which are not directly caused by or the primary purpose of the programme or project, e.g., the new ... will enable the organisation to also...

Indirect review

The review of the item or process by its indirect examination and assessment by using other measures as a guide to its current status, e.g., we have received no requests for changes; therefore the arrangements we have made for the agreement of the requirements are satisfactory.

Informal review

A system of documentation of each of the steps in the review or assessment of an output, deliverable or product to ensure that it meets or matches its defined specification.

Infrastructure projects

Those projects which are designed to provide systems or facilities that will be used by other processes. These projects cannot usually be directly linked to a specific goal or business target.

Integrated framework

A system of processes and information that are integrated, e.g., the same reference number for an output, deliverable or product is used in the template plans, estimating guidelines, deliverable library, etc.

Integrated personal plan

A collation of the extracts of all plans which contains the work to be performed, e.g., by a specific individual or machine.

Interfaces (pp. 41,87,108,109)

The points at which one method, life cycle or process meets, and interacts with, another method, life cycle or process.

Intermediate review points

Those points in a programme or project where a progress review is carried out, usually monthly, or when a defined event occurs, e.g., a major milestone is either achieved or planned to be achieved.

Internal rate of return

A calculation used to assess if a programme or project will produce a defined rate of return (or percentage profit).

ISEB (pp. 45,152,207)

The Information Systems Examination Board – a part of the British Computer Society which sets up and runs examinations and awards certificates in professional IT skills, e.g., programme and project support.

Islands of stability (p. 20)

The points in a programme which mark the end of a tranche. These are where either a significant part of the programme is delivered or a major commitment needs to be made. These are called islands of stability to illustrate that they provide a point at which a gap in the execution process occurs which can be used to reassess the situation.

Issue log

The document used to record details of all the issues raised during the programme or project.

Issue management

The management of: receipt and evaluation of issues raised during a programme or project; decision-making and actions relating to these issues.

IT/IS strategies

The defined strategies for the deployment and use of information technology and information systems in the organisation.

Keeper of the vision

The members of staff who have the responsibility for ensuring that the vision of the programme or project is understood and that only authorised changes in that vision occur.

Knowledge capture

The process of gathering information from existing sources.

Lessons learnt report (p. 138)

A report which documents the lessons learnt during a programme or project that, it is felt, will be of assistance to subsequent programmes or projects.

Levels of plan

The concept of having a structure of interlinking plans for a programme or project. This typical structure has a high-level plan (little detail) for the whole programme or project. This is supported by more detailed plans for each tranche or stage. These in turn are supported by more detailed plans and so on.

Life cycles (pp. 40,50,69,70,74,98,136, 137)

A term used to describe a collection of processes which are used to perform a business process from start to finish.

Logical entity

The operation of a business department predominately or exclusively through processes and functions that require little or no human intervention.

Logical implementation of a PSO

The operation of a PSO predominately or exclusively through processes and functions that require little or no human intervention.

Macro-tuning/tailoring

The significant amendment of a method, process or standard to reflect the specific needs of a programme or project.

Maintainability risks

Those events identified in the risk analysis which may affect the ability of the organisation to maintain the outputs, deliverables or products from a programme or project.

Major decision points

Those points in the execution of either a programme or project where significant decisions need to be made as to its continuation or otherwise.

Major deliverables (pp. 110,111)

Those deliverables which are considered as having a major importance to the successful completion of either a programme or project.

Major interdependencies

The dependencies between the outputs, deliverables or product from one project with another which have a major impact on the delivery of the programme or project.

Making the case (p. 183)

The completion and acceptance of the business case for a recommended course of action.

Masterplan (portfolio) (pp. 71,73-87,137)

The term used in this book to describe the documents and plans which describe all the programmes, projects and other activities that are managed by the masterplan committee.

Masterplan committee (pp. 71,73,75-84,86-87,137)

The term used in this book to describe the committee which is empowered by the organisation to ensure that the programmes, project and activities (the portfolio) which are commissioned will enable the organisation to meet its business strategy and plans. In addition, the committee monitors the execution of the plans, and commissions remedial action if necessary.

Masterplan portfolios

In some organisations the number of programmes or projects may be so large that the masterplan may need to be subdivided into a series of masterplan portfolios.

Maximum cumulative cost

Part of the business case which shows the maximum total cost or expenditure that a programme or project will incur.

Mentor/ing (pp. 47-55,59,139,1670)

An experienced member of staff working with a junior or new member of staff to help them to learn a new skill or improve the performance of their role.

Method of approach (pp. 38,73,109-110,310, 313)

The method, or collection and sequence of processes and outputs, deliverables or products that will be used to execute a programme or project.

METHOD ONE

A project or system development method developed by Andersen Consulting.

Metrics milestones (pp.137,139,143)

An expression used to describe the production of statistics from an existing programme or project that will be used in the management of a future programme or project, e.g., estimating information.

Micro-tuning/tailoring

The detailed amendment of a method, process or standard to reflect the specific needs of a programme or project.

Milestones (pp. 109,111)

Points in a programme or project that mark the significant points in their delivery which are used to measure progress achieved to that planned and to re-assess the remainder of the programme or project.

Minor decision points

Those points in the execution of programme or project where minor decisions may need to be taken as to its direction or method of development (usually identified as such in the project or system development method that is being used).

Monitor/review/control cycle

The collection of processes used to monitor progress made, compare it to that planned, identify and analyse the reasons for any differences, and the identification and commissioning of any necessary control action.

Monitoring and control process (pp.80,299)

The processes used in the monitor/review/ control cycle.

Monte Carlo simulations

The use of a probability-based simulation method – called Monte Carlo because it is based on selecting the potential outcomes that are examined, by random chance.

Multi-level codes

The use of a code system which is hierarchical, e.g., the multi-level code for a business-as-usual activity might use the first part of the code to indicate the department, the second the type of work, the third the task type etc.

Multi-function technology-driven projects

Projects which are driven by the availability and use of a number of technologies.

Net present value (NPV)

The figure calculated in a business case which is the result of applying the discounted cash flow formulae to the costs and/or benefits of a programme or project.

Network diagrams (p. 110)

The construction of a diagram which represents the sequence of activities, outputs, deliverables or products that are to be produced or procured by a programme or project (part of the project network technique).

Nine box matrix (p. 123)

A 3x3 matrix used to contain related information – particularly in estimating guidelines.

Non-productive work (pp. 142-143)

A generic name for sickness, authorised absence, and holidays. (An organisation's total workload consists of programmes or projects, business as usual and non-productive work).

Non-proprietary software tools

Software tools that do not lock the user of the tools into other tools supplied by the same manufacturer – they may be either based on open or standard databases or allow easy transfer of information to and from them.

Off-shore development

The use of a programme or project team which is not based in the same location as the main part of the programme or project – usually where that team is located in another country.

On costs (p. 309)

Additional costs added to the prime or base costs to cover overheads and non-productive cost.

Open or national methods and standards

The methods and standards which have been published and are in the public domain, i.e., they can be used by others. These can usually can be used without charge.

OSINTOT (pp. 177-178,181)

An acronym for Oh Surprise I Never Thought Of That! This describes the reason for using methods and life cycle to provide the programme and project managers with guidance as to what needs to be done to execute the programme and project. This avoids the realisation, later on, that they have forgotten or did not know what was should have been done.

Output (pp. 106,107)

A defined outcome of an activity that is used to execute a programme or project. (Sometimes called a deliverable or product).

Output, deliverable or product quality review process

The process used to conduct a review of an output, deliverable or product to ensure it meets its specification and is therefore fit for purpose.

Output flow diagram

A diagram similar to a network diagram which shows the sequence of production or procurement of the outputs from a programme or project.

Outsourced (p. 192)

The subcontracting or commissioning of a business process, or producing an output or deliverable to an organisation external to the organisation which commissioned it.

Owner of the vision (p. 38)

The member of the management team who has been designated as the prime mover in a programme or project (sometimes known as the champion, requester or sponsor).

Parallel running

The trial running of a new business process or system at the same time as the original. This is to confirm that the new process or system produces the same results, outputs or service level as the existing one before switching over to the new business process or system.

PERT (Project Evaluation or Review Technique)

The name given to a special type of project network technique which, like a decision tree, uses probabilities and a range of possible durations or costs for each of the activities. This is used to produce an overall expected outcome for the whole programme or project.

Physical implementation of a PSO

The operation of a PSO predominately or exclusively through processes and functions that are driven by, and involve, members of the PSO.

Portfolio (pp. 137,152)

A collection of programmes or projects or other activities which the organisation wish to collect together and manage as a set.

Post-programme or post-project review

A review carried out some time after the programme or project has been completed to identify whether the programme or project met its objectives and any lessons that were learnt.

PRINCE (pp. 38,48,91)

PRojects IN Controlled Environments) project management method The latest version which is widely used is PRINCE2.

Probability/impact grids

A matrix which is used to contain a range of information relating to the assessment of the impact of an event on the programme or project and the probability of that event occurring.

Procedures

A set of defined steps that form part of a process.

Process engineering tool

A specialist software tool that enables the organisation to develop a new process and to provide support for the use of that process, in the form of example deliverables, estimates template plans, etc.

Process map

A diagram which describes all the processes in a specific method or life cycle.

Processes (pp. 96,106,137,138,140,145)

A series of steps that are followed to perform a specific activity or achieve a defined output.

Product (p. 150)

An output or deliverable generated from an activity in a programme or project.

Product breakdown structure

A hierarchical chart which describes all the products in the programme or project and their sub-components.

Product descriptions

A document used to define the product given to its developer or procurer, to ensure they provide what is wanted by the programme or project.

Product flow diagram

A chart similar to a network diagram but using products rather than activities.

Programme (pp. 17-26)

A number of projects, work packages and initiatives which need to be managed as a composite set.

Programme (management) documentation

The documents used by the programme manager to manage and control the programme.

Programme or project life cycle (pp. 50, 69-88,89,98,100,135-137)

A series of processes with agreed roles and responsibilities, standards and techniques that are used to decide whether a programme or project should be commissioned, to ensure it is feasible, and that it is executed and completed according to the agreed resources and costs.

Programme and project management methods (pp. 50-53,55,57,58,87,89-102,127, 129,135,138,162,186,187,189,195,204)

A series of processes with agreed roles and responsibilities, standards and techniques that are used to manage a programme or project.

Programme and project team leaders (p. 65)

The members of staff who are responsible to the programme or project manager for the delivery of a part of the programme or project.

Programme and/or project contribution matrix

A document used to record the details of the projects which have been commissioned in order to complete the programme, and the agreed level of contribution that each of the projects makes to the attainment of the programme's aims and objectives.

Programme and/or project management processes

The processes used by the programme and project managers to manage the programme and projects (part of the programme and project management methods).

Programme and/or project management support processes

The supporting processes used to assist the programme and project manager when using the programme or project management method. For example, template documents and reports, and systems that collect or provide information used by the programme and project managers.

Programme and/or project planning software

Specialist software designed to support the programme and project manager in planning and monitoring of the activities and resources needed to execute the programme or project.

Programme and/or project support infrastructure

The collection of supporting processes, standards, information systems and other services provided to support the operation of programme and project management.

Programme benefits realisation

The activities that are performed to enable the programme to realise the benefits. The programme only provides the basic ingredients – the new processes, attitudes and products and services. The benefits are realised by the use or exploitation of these new processes, attitudes and products and services. The realisation process is the arrangements made by the organisation to action the exploitation.

Programme board or executive or sponsoring group

The members of executive-level management

who provide strategic guidance and assistance to the programme director and manager in achieving the programme's aims and objectives.

Programme brief (p. 22)

A small document usually produced as part of the programme-commissioning process to define initially what the programme is to provide, and its budget.

Programme closure and benefits sustainability (p. 96)

The fourth and final phase in a programme where the development activities have been completed, or the programme has been closed by the programme executive or board, and plans agreed for how the planned benefits will be realised and sustained.

Programme closure report (p. 24)

A report produced by the programme manager at the completion of the programme to measure the success of the programme in meeting its aims and objectives and the budgets set for it. It also includes a summary of the lessons learnt during the programme.

Programme definition (pp. 86,97)

A collection of documents including the programme plan and all the other documents which describe the arrangements made to manage the programme. This document is used as the basis of the monitoring and control of the execution of the programme.

Programme definition (process) (pp. 22,86,95-97,109-110)

The second phase in a programme which leads to the production and agreement of the programme definition.

Programme director (pp. 21-23,25,71,81,93)

The member of executive-level management who is responsible for the successful completion of the programme.

Programme execution (pp. 95,97,176)

The third phase in a programme where the projects have been commissioned and are delivering the required outputs, deliverables and products.

Programme identification (pp. 31,95)

The first phase in a programme where the blueprint for the programme is developed and agreed and the attitude change and communication plans are prepared.

Programme initiation

The formal initiation of the programme by the programme executive or board once they are assured that the programme (as defined in the programme definition) will meet the requirements of the organisation.

Programme management (pp. 17-20,25-26, 92-93,95-96,106,174,176)

The processes, standards, outputs and techniques used to manage a programme.

Programme management framework (p. 18)

The framework of processes, organisation structure, techniques and documents which can be deployed by the organisation to manage a programme.

Programme management method (pp. 25, 96,106)

The conversion of the programme management framework into a defined structure of processes, outputs and standards which is used when managing a programme.

Programme management organisation structure (p. 93)

The structure of managers that is implemented to ensure the programme is managed efficiently and effectively.

Programme management process

The processes used to complete the four phases in a programme and to develop the prescribed outputs.

Programme manager (pp. 21,93)

The manager responsible for the day-to-day management of the programme.

Programme or project code (p. 78)

The identification code allocated to a programme or project as part of the commissioning process to ensure that it can be uniquely identified.

Programme or project commissioning process/procedure

The process used in the programme or project life cycle to commission a new programme or project.

Programme or project feasibility study report

The report which summarises the findings of the investigation carried out to determine whether the programme or project is economically or technically feasible, and has a sound business case.

Programme or project idea form

A form containing an overview of the programme or project which is used during the programme and project life cycle to start the process of that programme or project being considered for inclusion in the masterplan.

Programme or project liaison group

A group of relevant experts or interested parties who provide the programme or project management structure with information, advice and other services to assist with the management of the programme or project.

Programme or project monitoring and control (p. 74)

The processes used to monitor the progress made with the programme or project to date and to assess whether control action is required. If control action is needed then these processes should provide sufficient information to the programme executive/board or project board to identify what action is needed.

Programme or project requester

The member of the organisation who has requested the programme or project and will usually complete the programme or project idea form.

Programme or project risks

Events that may occur which will affect (positively or negatively) the programme or project.

Programme or project team costs

The costs of the programme or project team including prime and oncosts.

Programme phases

The four phases that a programme is usually divided into: programme identification; programme definition; programme execution, monitoring and control; and programme closure, benefits realisation and sustainability.

Programme plan (pp. 22,308,310)

A document which contains a description of the activities, resources and timescales need to complete the programme.

Programme progress reports

Reports produced by the programme manager about the progress made to date and an analysis of any variances that have occurred and the projected impact of those variances on the remainder of the programme.

Programme support office/PSO (pp. 25-26)

A department that is established to provide support to the organisation's programmes.

Programme tranche plan

A part of the programme plan which relates to one of the tranches. (This plan is usually in greater detail than that at programme level).

Project (pp. 18,29-30,39)

A temporary structure of activities designed to produce a defined output to meet defined aims and objectives.

Project (management) documents

The documents used by the project manager to manage and control the project.

Project or system development methods documents (p. 53)

The documents used by the project manager to manage and control the project or system development processes.

Project assurance (p. 94)

The provision of assurance to the project board that the project's business integrity (business case) and technical integrity (method of approach) are being maintained.

Project board (pp. 71,94)

The group of senior managers responsible for the strategic direction and successful completion of it.

Project brief

A document developed as part of the project initiation process which provides the basis of the project initiation document.

Project champion

A senior manager who is the driving force behind the project and acts as an ambassador for the project.

Project closure report (pp. 85,86)

A report produced by the project manager at the completion of the project to measure the success of the project in meeting its aims and objectives and the budgets set for it. It also includes a summary of the lessons learnt during the project.

Project filing and document management systems

The system of filing and management of the documents developed during the project. The system must interface with the other processes used by the project such as configuration management, issue and change management.

Project initiation

The formal initiation of the project by the project board once they are satisfied that the project initiation document indicates that the project will meet its defined requirements.

Project initiation document (PID)

The document produced at the end of the project initiation process by the project manager to summarise the arrangements, plans and estimated budgeted resources needed to fulfil the projects aims and objectives.

Project management board (pp. 37-39)

Another name for the *project board*.

Project management framework (pp. 40,176)

The framework of processes, organisation structure, techniques and documents which can be deployed by the organisation to manage a project.

Project management method (pp. 52,89-100)

The conversion of the project management framework into a defined structure of processes, outputs and standards which is used when managing a project.

Project management organisation structure (pp. 94,181)

The structure of managers and their roles and responsibilities that is implemented to ensure the project is managed efficiently and effectively.

Project management process (pp. 48,69,81, 91,96,98,199,203)

The processes used to complete the phases in a project and to develop the prescribed outputs.

Project manager

The manager responsible for the day-to-day management of the project.

Project mandate

The initial terms of reference for the project; in some instances this is the project idea form. This document is used to develop the project brief.

Project network technique (pp. 186,293,304, 305)

A technique defined as a British Standard which is used in the programme and project planning process to identify the sequence that the activities or outputs, deliverables or products should be developed and the resources (timescales, and costs) needed to complete the project. This information is then further refined before being translated into a Gantt chart and resource spreadsheet.

Project or system development methods (pp. 53,101-115,177-178)

A defined set of processes, outputs, standards and techniques which is used as the basis of the project execution.

Project plans (pp.21,26,122,124-125,148-150, 153,175,205)

A document which contains a description of the activities, resources and timescales need to complete the project.

Project progress reports

Reports produced by the project manager about the progress made to date. They include an analysis of any variances that have occurred and the projected impact of those variances on the remainder of the project.

Project status reports

Reports produced by the project manager about the progress made to date. They include an analysis of any variances that have occurred and the projected impact of those variances on the remainder of the project.

Project steering committee (p. 37)

Similar to a project board but with no specific responsibility for the project.

Project Support Office/PSO (pp. 27-32,35,38, 41,73)

A department that is established to provide support to the organisation's projects.

Project team (members) (p. 62)

The members of the organisation and others allocated to the execution of the project.

Project/programme – strategy contribution matrix

A document used to record the details of the projects/programmes which have been commissioned in order to deliver the required business strategy, and the agreed level of contribution that each of the projects/programmes makes to the attainment of the strategy.

Proprietary software tools

Those tools which use proprietary databases or where the information contained in the tools cannot be easily transferred to other tools.

Pseudo project plans

Plans developed for business-as-usual and non-productive work which are used primarily for assessing how much effort is required and when it will be required, and collecting actual expenditure, to ensure that all of the effort expended by the organisation's staff is accounted for.

PSO implementation project (pp. 127,157)

A project commissioned to design and implement a PSO.

PSO programme and project support infrastructure

The infrastructure of processes, standards, information systems and other methods used by the PSO to support its operation.

'Pull then push' time sheets

A time sheet system which sends each member of staff a blank time sheet. Each person completes that time sheet by accessing the relevant programme or project or other plan and transferring those details to the time sheet. The time sheet is then sent to a central point where it is compared to the planned activities for that person; and if any discrepancies are identified, then the time sheet is returned to its author for amendment or confirmation.

'Pull' time sheets

A time sheet system which sends each member of staff a blank time sheet. Each person completes that time sheet which is then sent to a central point where it is compared to the planned activities for that person and if any discrepancies are identified then the time sheet is returned to its author for amendments or confirmation.

Pure work effort (pp. 123,299)
The amount of effort needed to complete an activity, output, deliverable or product.

'Push then pull' time sheets
A time sheet system which sends to each member of staff a time sheet which is pre-loaded with the work allocated to them in the programme, project or other plans.

Qualitative benefits (p. 317)
Benefits defined in the business case which relate to changes or improvement in quality.

Qualitative risk assessment
A method of risk assessment that results in an assessment of the impact of those risks in qualitative terms, such as difficulty of maintenance or enhancement.

Quality control review (pp. 107,314,319)
A review of an output, deliverable or product to ensure that it conforms to its defined and agreed specification and is fit for purpose.

Quality management (pp. 22,29,47,123)
A system of defined and agreed processes and standards used to perform or deliver a defined service or product.

Quality plan (pp. 23,24,97,109,111)
The arrangements made in a programme or project to ensure that it follows the agreed quality management system.

Quality review (pp. 111,151,295,305)
A review of the quality management arrangements deployed in a programme or project to ensure that they are adequate and that they are being adhered to.

Quality review meeting
A meeting to review an output, deliverable or product and to identify any non-conformance to its agreed specification.

Quality standards (pp. 46,71,187)
The standards or criteria that will be used to assess if the output, deliverable or product is fit for purpose.

Quantitative benefits
Benefits identified in a business case which are quantified, e.g., will save £X per year, increase sales to…

Quantitative risk assessment
A method of risk assessment that results in an assessment of the impact of those risks in quantitative terms, such as 'it will be late by x weeks, or will cost £X less'.

RAD (p. 104)
Rapid Application Development method of approach. This refers to the use of techniques which minimise the time needed to complete a programme or project.

Radar charts
A graphical representation of the current status of the programme or project, which looks like a radar screen.

Realisation of business benefits

The process of exploiting the changes provided by the programme or project to provide the organisation with the defined benefits.

Recharge basis

A method of operating a PSO where the programme or project manager is charged for the services provided to them by the PSO.

Recurring costs

Those costs identified in a business case which recur each year – for example, the cost of maintenance of a new item of machinery.

Re-inventing the wheel syndrome

A phrase used to describe rediscovering knowledge that has already been gained, or repeating mistakes.

Repository

A database (either manual or computer based) used to store all relevant information about the organisation's programmes and projects.

Residual value

The written down value of a capital item at the end of the period, used in the business case to assess the financial integrity of the programme or project.

Resource category/code

A system of codes used to identify a resource uniquely.

Resource management system

A 'use booking' system used by a resource or line manager to ensure the effective deployment and allocation of the available resources.

Resource manager (pp. 37,65,73,116,124-125,140,142)

The manager responsible for the resources. (human or machinery or…)

Resource register

A record of all the resources of the organisation. This should interface with other related processes and information systems.

Resource usage

The planned use of resources in a project or programme.

Resources usage spreadsheet

A summary of all the resources required by the programme or project which is displayed in a format similar to that of a spreadsheet.

Resourcing plan (p. 24)

A document which describes the resources required by the programme or project.

'Responsibility flip over'

A description of the situation that the use of a programme or project organisation structure is designed to prevent, in that the senior management are not aware of their responsibilities as a member of the programme or project board and concentrate on tactical matters rather than the strategic direction.

Results management

A phrase used to describe the overall collection of information about all the activities of an organisation in order to assess whether the organisation is deploying its resources effectively.

Review error list

The list of potential errors identified by the reviewers. These are discussed with the producer or developer of the product either at a formal review meeting or an informal review discussion.

Reviewer (quality review)

A defined role in the quality control review process which is responsible for identifying any discrepancies between the output, deliverable or product and its specification.

Risk

An event (positive or negative) that may occur and affect the programme or project.

Risk analysis

The process used to identify the potential risks to the programme or project and their impact.

Risk checklist

A list of the risks identified in previous programmes and projects which is used in the risk analysis process.

Risk identification workshop

The workshop used to identify the risks and assess their impact on the programme or project.

Risk library

A list of both the risks identified in previous programmes and projects and the risk management, containment or assurance measures that were used and their success or failure.

Risk log

A list of the risks identified as relevant to this programme or project and the measures or actions deployed to manage them.

Risk management (pp. 24,141,149)

The generic name given to the risk identification, impact assessment and management, containment, avoidance, or insurance strategy, action plan and review of the effectiveness of the processes.

Risk management history file

A file which provides a complete history of each risk, from their initial identification through to their removal from the risk log.

Risk management monitoring sheet

A document which contains details of all the active risks and the measures in use to manage them.

Risk management plan (p. 24)

A plan which describes the way that the risk management processes will be operated and monitored in a specific programme or project.

Risk management strategy

The strategy applied to each risk, i.e., whether it will be managed, contained, avoided, or insured against.

Risk register

A list of the risks that need to be considered by each programme or project, or the list of risks that were identified for a specific programme or project.

RISKMAN

A risk management method which was

developed by the EC as part of the EUREKA initiative.

'Rule of nine'

This rule refers to the number of discussions needed to arrive at a decision, if the programme or project does not have a defined organisation structure and roles and responsibilities.

'Rule of seven'

This rule refers to the size of the increase in detail or complexity that is needed when a plan is decomposed to a lower level.

'Rule of six' (p. 182)

This rule refers to the number of codes that should be used at each level in a multi-level code system.

Runaway programme or project

An expression used to describe a programme or project in which the programme or project board, and/or the programe or project manager, have lost control and it has taken on a life of its own.

Schedule variance(s) (p. 153)

The difference between the planned or baselined dates for the delivery of the outputs, deliverables and products and that actually achieved. (How late or early the programme or project is.)

Scribe (quality review)

The member of the quality review team who is responsible for ensuring that the decisions made at the review meeting are recorded.

Second-level decision

A part of the decision-making process used to assess such things as issues and changes. The second level relates to the decision being made at the highest level in the decision-making process.

Second-level evaluation

A part of the decision-making process used to evaluate the impact of such things as issues and changes. The second level relates to the evaluation made at the highest level in the decision-making process.

Second pass network chart

The inclusion in a network diagram for a programme or project of the calculation of the float available for each of the activities (and thereby the programme's or project's critical path).

Security risks

Those risks which affect the security of the new business system, or by implication, the security of the other business systems affected by the introduction of the new business system.

Senior management (pp. 62,71,179)

Those managers who are not executive level and not first-line managers.

Senior supplier

A member of a project board who is responsible for providing the resources required to execute the project.

Senior user

A member of the project board who is to represent the end users or customer of the output, deliverables or products from the project.

Sign-off

The acceptance by the customer or user or reviewer that the output, deliverable or product is fit for purpose or use.

Simulation tools

The software and other tools used to simulate the operation of business or other process, so that its effectiveness or efficiency can be assessed.

Single-function projects

Those projects which are commissioned to provide a single, new, business function.

Skeleton project plans

A project plan which has the minimum amount of information, e.g., a list of tasks, dates, estimates and allocated generic resources.

Skills database (pp. 117,124-125)

A database which contains a list of the skills of the members of staff who are available for use in the execution of the programmes and projects.

'So what?' test

This term relates to a method which can be used on intangible or qualitative benefits to identify any partial quantitative measures of the benefits that may apply.

Soft deliverables (p. 64)

Those deliverables which improve the quality of the service and which do not produce easily recognised benefits.

Soft or people-driven projects (p. 30)

Those projects which predominately involve changes in attitude or working practices and which primarily involve the staff of an organisation. 'Soft' here is used to indicate that these projects involve people, not things (hard deliverables).

Soft systems analysis (p.180)

An analysis method which identifies various views of the components of a business or other system.

Sponsor (pp. 21,37,71-72,78,80,83-85,93-94)

The member of executive or senior management who has agreed to act as the ambassador or champion for the programme or project. This person usually has a vested interest in the programe or project.

SSADM (pp. 91,103-104,106)

Structured Systems Analysis and Design Method – the UK Government's standard project or systems development method for IT projects.

Stage plan

A plan which describes only one specific stage of a project.

Strategic and business planning functions

The functions in an organisation which are responsible for the development, updating and review of the strategic and business plans.

Strategic and business risk analysis (p. 29)

The application of the risk analysis process to the strategic and business areas that may affect either a programe or project.

Strategic decision-making process

The process used by the organisation to decide its business strategy.

Strategic guidance (pp. 83,88)

The guidance provided by the programme or project board as to what course of action the programme or project should follow.

Strategic plan (pp. 33-34,59,71,74)

The plan which describes how the business strategy will be delivered.

Supporting software tools (p. 57)

Those software tools which support the operation of the PSO, or a programme or project manager.

Supporting tools

Those other tools which support the operation of the PSO, or a programme or project manager.

Task (pp. 118,121)

A part of an activity – the lowest unit of work in a plan.

Team managers

The manager of the team allocated to execute part of a programme or project.

Team plan

A plan of the work to be performed by a specific team in a programme or project.

Technical assurance (p. 22)

The vetting of the technical matters of the programme or project by an independent expert, to assure the programme or project board that the technical issues are being dealt with appropriately.

Technical design integrity (p. 22)

The assurance that the technical design of the programme or project conforms to relevant independent standards.

Technical design manager

The manager appointed to the programme executive or board to oversee the technical design aspects of the programme and to provide assurance to the organisation of the integrity of the technical design.

Technical development stage

A part of a project or system development method which represents a complete output, deliverable or product. Its completion marks a significant part of that method.

Technical infrastructure (p. 158)

The equipment and machinery installed by the organisation to support its operations, e.g., the computer network.

Technical integrity (p. 310)

The assurance that the technical aspects of the programme or project conform to relevant standards.

Technical viability

The ability of the proposed technical solution to be developed and perform to agreed budgets and requirements.

Techniques (pp. 97,107,182)

Methods used to perform specific tasks, e.g., planning a programme or project.

Technology-driven projects (pp. 30,304)

Those projects which are driven by the availability of a specific technology.

Template deliverables

Those deliverables from previous programmes and projects that have been converted to 'shell' documents (any programme or project specific details have been removed) so that they can be used on subsequent programmes or projects.

Template plans (pp. 121-122,153)

Those plans from previous programmes or projects or plans, which conform to the organisation's standard methods, e.g., project or systems development methods, which are provided to programme and project managers as a start point for the programme or project plan.

Templates

A generic term to describe any template document or plan that is provided.

Terms of reference (p. 174)

A definition of what either the programme or project should provide or what role or function an individual should perform.

The M's (p. 177)

An expression to describe the resources used in a programe or project – Manpower, Money, Minutes (time), Materials, Machinery, Mortar (Bricks and mortar – buildings)

Time sheet system (pp. 143,153,312)

A manual or software driven process which distributes and collects time sheets.

Time sheets (pp. 148,312)

A document used to record details of the activities performed by a member of the organisation and the time taken to do them.

Tolerance (pp. 82,95)

An allowance, made in addition to the agreed budget in respect of time and other resources, to the programme and project manager, within which he or she is allowed to operate before having to notify the programme or project board. This tolerance is given to cover the impact of the inaccuracy of the estimates and unexpected events. (See also *contingency* which is a part of tolerance).

Traffic light reports

A type of progress reports which explains the current status of an aspect of the programe or project in the form of a traffic light colour: red = problems; amber = some concerns; green = no problems.

Tranche (pp. 18,25,82-84,138)

A discrete part of a programme that represents a significant part of the programme, or the delivery of parts of the benefits of the programme.

Transition management (p. 21)

The management plan used to describe how the programme or project will manage the implementation of the changes between the old methods of working and the new ones provided by the programme or project.

Trend analysis

An analysis of the trends that may be occurring, for example, in the patterns of programmes or projects undertaken by the organisation or in the methods of approach used in their execution.

Understood standards

Those standards which are regarded by the members of the organisation as being relevant to a particular situation, but are not documented or formally agreed.

User costs

The cost of the users' involvement in the design, development and implementation of the programe or project.

Vision statement

That part of the programme blueprint or the project documentation that describes the vision of what the programe or project is to provide.

Walkthrough

The process used in a quality control review where the output, deliverable or product is examined systematically, line by line, or demonstrated step by step.

'What if?' analysis (pp. 153-154)

The analysis carried out to examine the hypothetical consequences of a specific action or event.

Work breakdown structure

The decomposition of the activities used to execute a programe or project into its component tasks.

Work flow (p. 190)

The construction of a business process that uses technology to move the document or other piece of work between the various procedures or steps.

Work packages

A collection of products into a discrete group.

Working practices (pp. 42-43)

The methods and rules used to perform a task or activity.

Worksheet

A list of the tasks, activities, outputs, deliverables or products that must be produced, e.g., by an individual or a machine.

Project Manager Today
P U B L I C A T I O N S

Project Manager Today Publications specialises in books and journals related to project management. Titles include:

- *Managing Programmes of Business Change*
- *Managing Risk for Projects and Programmes*
- *Managing Smaller Projects*
- *One Project Too Many*
- *The Programme & Project Support Office Handbook* vol's 1 & 2
- *Using PRINCE2 the project manager's guide*

and the flagship monthly magazine:
- *Project Manager Today*

Publishers of
- *The Cost Engineer*
on behalf of The Association of Cost Engineers

Full details from:
Project Manager Today Publications
Unit 12, Moor Place Farm, Plough Lane, Bramshill, Hook
Hampshire
RG27 0RF

Tel: 0118 932 6665
Fax: 0118 932 6663
Email: info@projectmanagertoday.co.uk
Website: www.pmtoday.co.uk

Project Manager Today also organises topical conferences and seminars.